Self-Initiated Expatriation

Routledge Studies in International Business and the World Economy

For a full list of titles in this series, please visit www.routledge.com.

Self-Initiated Expatriation

Individual, Organizational, and National Perspectives

**Edited by Maike Andresen,
Akram Al Ariss, and Matthias Walther**

Routledge
Taylor & Francis Group

LONDON AND NEW YORK

First published 2013
by Routledge

2 Park Square, Milton Park, Abingdon, Oxon OX14 4RN
711 Third Avenue, New York, NY 10017, USA

*Routledge is an imprint of the Taylor & Francis Group,
an informa business*

First issued in paperback 2016

Library of Congress Cataloging-in-Publication Data
    Self-initiated expatriation : individual, organizational, and national
perspectives / edited by Maike Andresen . . . [et al.]. — 1st ed.
        p. cm. — (Routledge studies in international business and the world
economy ; 54)
    Includes bibliographical references and index.
    1. Emigration and immigration. 2. Exiles. 3. Expatriation.
I. Andresen, Maike, 1971–
    JV2021.S45 2012
    304.8—dc23
    2012012277

ISBN13: 978-0-415-53645-5 (hbk)
ISBN13: 978-1-138-20322-8 (pbk)

Typeset in Sabon
by IBT Global.

Contents

Figures

Tables

Acknowledgments

We would like to gratefully thank Lisa Ullein, Karen Wolff, Christoph Küffner, and Christopher Sabel for their precious help during the creation process of this edited book.

Lisa Ullein, Christoph Küffner, and Christopher Sabel are all student assistants and Karen Wolff is a research assistant at the Chair of Human Resource Management at the University of Bamberg.

Christopher Sabel studies Business Administration at the bachelor's level, Lisa Ullein and Christoph Küffner at the master's level.

Part I
Understanding the Concept

1 Introduction

Self-Initiated Expatriation—Individual, Organizational, and National Perspectives

Maike Andresen, Akram Al Ariss[1], and Matthias Walther

WHY THIS BOOK ON SELF-INITIATED EXPATRIATION?

Globalization and the development of multinational organizations have led to an increase in expatriation (e.g. Richardson & McKenna, 2000; United Nations, 2011). While for a long time, the contemporary expatriate literature has focused on the classical 'Assigned Expatriates' (AEs) sent overseas by their employers (e.g. Thomas, 2002), there is now a growing interest in the potentially larger segment of 'Self-Initiated Expatriates' (SIEs) (Inkson & Myers, 2003; Myers & Pringle, 2005) of whom many thousands are travelling around the global economy (e.g. Howe-Walsh & Schyns, 2010). SIEs decide on their own to live and work abroad (Andresen, Bergdolt, & Margenfeld in this book; Suutari & Brewster, 2000; Thorn, 2009) and cross both national (Crowley-Henry, 2007; Inkson, Arthur, Pringle, & Barry, 1997) as well as organizational frontiers (Banai & Harry, 2004; Carr, Inkson, & Thorn, 2005). Therefore, AEs and SIEs represent two different types of internationally mobile employees, and research results cannot be transferred between these distinct groups.

Inkson et al. (1997) were among the first to address this group of expatriates in their research. Fifteen years have now passed by, and the research interest in this field is increasing steadily. Recently, around 50 papers about SIEs have been published in academic journals. Research on SIEs has addressed a wide variety of professional groups and nationalities. While, for example, Andresen and Biemann (Biemann & Andresen, 2010; Andresen & Biemann, forthcoming) focused on German managers, Suutari and Brewster (2000) investigated Finnish engineers, and Al Ariss (Al Ariss, 2010) put emphasis on highly skilled SIEs from Lebanon. Richardson and colleagues (McKenna & Richardson, 2007; Richardson, 2006; Richardson & Mallon, 2005; Richardson, McBey, & McKenna, 2008; Richardson & McKenna, 2000; 2001; 2006) or Selmer and Lauring (2011) focused their research on academics, whereas Bozionelos (2009) investigated self-initiated expatriated nurses in Saudi-Arabia. Existing studies were, for example, about motives (e.g. Tharenou & Caulfield, 2010; Thorn, 2009), cultural adaptation (Peltokorpi & Froese, 2009), or career-related issues (e.g. Andresen, Biemann, & Pattie, 2012; Biemann & Andresen, 2010; Begley, Collings, & Scullion, 2008; Cerdin & Le Pargneux, 2010) of SIEs. With the growth of interest and research in this field being, beyond doubt, encouraging, many authors have called for further investigations (e.g. Brewster & Suutari, 2005; Jokinen, Brewster, & Suutari, 2008) since this field of research is still only rudimentarily understood. The need for a greater understanding of self-initiated expatriation has also been repeatedly raised in symposiums and other scholarly meetings, such as at the Academy of Management or the European Academy of Management. So far, a holistic picture about the area of self-initiated expatriation is missing as investigations have mostly been conducted from one single perspective. Furthermore, no comprehensive book exists on the dynamics that underlie self-initiated expatriation. Hence, we believe it is time for an edited book studying this type of international mobility from a multi-level perspective. As this is the first book about SIEs, it has a unique and initiative character. Contributors include not only established academics from all over the world who have already made major contributions to highly ranked journals and who are leading experts in the field of self-initiated expatriation but also young researchers at the beginning of their scientific career. This gives this book an exclusive diversity of authors, which should make it all the more interesting.

THE CONTENT OF THE BOOK

This edited collection brings together 13 chapters dealing with self-initiated expatriation written by 21 researchers from eight countries representing four continents. It seeks to extend our understanding of the contribution of and exigencies surrounding self-initiated expatriation from an individual, organizational, and national perspective. The book is divided into three main parts: The first part sets the context of studies on self-initiated expatriation; the second part discusses the process of self-initiated expatriation; and, finally, the third part discusses different groups of individuals who undertake self-initiated expatriation as the population of SIEs was found to be very diverse.

Part I: General Introduction

In Chapter 2, *What Distinguishes Self-Initiated Expatriates from Assigned Expatriates and Migrants? A Literature-Based Definition and Differentiation of Terms*, Andresen, Bergdolt, and Margenfeld examine similarities and differences of using the terms 'assigned expatriate,' 'self-initiated expatriate,' and 'migrant.' By employing qualitative content analysis and a comprehensive review, they show that the criteria for demarcation are not very clear. They suggest that the term 'migration' is an umbrella term for 'self-initiated' and 'assigned expatriation.' In this sense, a SIE is a migrant who embarks on an international career by his/her own means. By contrast, for an AE, the decision of undertaking an international career is rather made by the host country organization.

Chapter 3, *Research on Self-Initiated Expatriation: History and Future Directions*, emerges of key importance because of its visionary nature. Dorsch, Suutari, and Brewster review what research has taught us so far on self-initiated expatriation since the year 2000 and what we still need to know. The authors summarize some key findings by answering the following questions: What differentiates SIEs from AEs? What differentiates expatriates within the self-initiated category? What are the reasons for undertaking self-initiated expatriation? How well do SIEs adjust? What happens when they repatriate? And what is the impact of self-initiated expatriation on careers? In terms of future research, the authors point to several important issues including (1) a need to clarify terminology; (2) a need to explore some of the largely un-researched SIEs, such as those from certain parts of the world that remain a hidden aspect in the literature on self-initiated expatriation (e.g. from South America) or those who work for not-for-profit organizations; (3) a need for research about the different subgroups of SIEs; (4) a need for a better understanding of the impact of gender on self-initiated expatriation; (5) a need to establish a stronger link to migration studies, which could offer a very good basis for collaborative work; (6) a need to undertake studies with larger samples on the topic.

Part II: Understanding the Processes of Self-Initiated Expatriation

In Chapter 4, *Motivation of Self-Initiated Expatriates*, Cerdin explores SIEs' motivation for their international mobility. Understanding their motivations is important for organizations in order to be able to attract talented internationally mobile employees. The author reports results from two studies. The findings show that the first three motivation factors for SIEs are (1) personal challenge, (2) professional development, and (3) importance of the job itself. The first three motivation factors for AEs are (1) professional development, followed by (2) importance of the job itself, and (3) personal challenge. As for some of the push factors, 'desire to escape from personal problems at home' was found to be more frequent for SIEs than for AEs. This same chapter further presents the career anchors of SIEs in order to understand their career orientations.

Chapter 5, *Self-Initiated Expatriation and Talent Flow*, is based on a case study in order to illustrate how expatriation can consist of a flow of moves across different countries. The authors, Thorn and Inkson, point to the importance of considering the relationship of international mobility to work-life events, including partnership and childbirth and to contextualize all mobility over the life course. The meanings of terms such as brain drain, brain gain, brain waste, and talent flow are examined. The authors conclude with a series of questions that are of interest to future studies on SIEs.

Chapter 6, *Differences in Self-Initiated- and Organizational Expatriates' Cross-Cultural Adjustment*, is based on an empirical study of 124 SIEs and 55 organizational expatriates (OEs) in Japan. Peltokorpi and Froese examine how both groups differ in terms of their cross-cultural adjustment. Findings show that they were different in their proficiency of the host country language, overseas experience, job situations, and interaction adjustment. SIEs were more adjusted to interact with host country nationals than OEs due to their better Japanese language proficiency and longer stay in Japan. Some of the practical implications of this study include the fact that organizations need to pay more attention to SIEs in their recruiting efforts. This research also suggests that country-specific training is of great importance in Japan as it helps expatriates improve their adjustment.

In Chapter 7, *Career Concepts of Self-Initiated and Assigned Expatriates: A Theoretical Analysis Based on Coupling and Configuration*, Andresen and Biemann elaborate on links between expatriates' employment settings, career concepts, and career decision making. The authors develop a dynamic model of international careers. They do so by first defining a matrix of career fields based on the degree of coupling and configuration in expatriates' career settings. While coupling refers to the degree to which actors are linked and mutually dependent, configuration describes the rate of change of the social relationships. They locate traditional and boundaryless careers in this matrix and elaborate on a connection with the career concepts of SIEs and AEs. Moreover, the authors discuss a set of interpersonal, organizational, and environmental factors that are suggested to impact the progression toward different career fields for SIEs and AEs. Throughout the chapter, readers are offered a theoretical comparison of career concepts and an explanation of how such concepts can be useful in understanding international careers and their progressions.

In Chapter 8, *Self-Initiated Expatriation: Drivers, Employment Experience, and Career Outcomes*, Doherty and Dickmann explore the employment experience focusing particularly on educational background in relation to motivations to go, the role while abroad, and the perceived impact of the SIE experience on career. Results obtained from a web-based survey suggest that while the experience is perceived as positive by many, some SIEs experienced underemployment. It is found that generating organizational awareness of the motivations of SIEs is fundamental to facilitating capital development and use, both while abroad and on their return to the home country.

Chapter 9, *Tax and Salary Issues in Self-Initiated Expatriation*, deals with tax consequences of self-initiated expatriation on the basis of various scenarios. Egner argues that an employee's liability to pay income tax depends on the individual's residence. The problem seems to be that expatriates often have more than one place of residence. If an individual gives up his residence in his home country and thereby ends his unlimited tax liability in that country, this can additionally trigger one-off tax burdens. It is necessary to analyze the tax conditions in the host country before the expatriation so that when negotiating one's salary, one has a proper idea about the gross income necessary to result in a given target net income.

In Chapter 10, *Self-Initiated Repatriation at the Interplay Between Field, Capital, and Habitus: An Analysis Based on Bourdieu's Theory of Practice*, Andresen and Walther conducted a qualitative study with 22 Self-Initiated Repatriates (SIRs) to Denmark, France, and Germany. Results show that expatriation leads to a modification of the habitus and career capital structure. While economic capital issues were not found to play a major role, the habitus only affected the return into the Danish career field where self-initiated expatriation was valued negatively. Especially institutionalized cultural capital and social capital issues were found pertinent for re-entering the French career field, whereas German returnees, especially, had to be endowed with incorporated cultural capital and, although to some lesser extent, social capital.

Part III: Understanding the Groups Undertaking Self-Initiated Foreign Experiences

In Chapter 11, *Volunteering Abroad—A Career-Related Analysis of International Development Aid Workers*, Andresen and Gustschin investigated 123 development aid workers employed at different German nonprofit organizations that work either with the federal government or with religious organizations. Aid workers participating in their online survey were not only altruistically motivated but also showed self-serving interests and motives. The majority managed their careers independently and were guided by personal values in decisions regarding their professional lives. As continuous learners, they were organizationally mobile and highly adaptable to new working environments.

A main assumption of Chapter 12 *Self-Initiated Expatriation in Academia: A Bounded and Boundaryless Career?* is that most academics are SIEs taking jobs outside of their home countries, on a temporary or permanent basis. Drawing on published work from four different studies (international, Canadian, European, and Italian studies), this chapter explores the career experiences of self-initiate expatriate academics. Richardson examines the way academics' careers reflect six dimensions of the concept of boundaryless career. Results suggest that while there are strong synergies between each of the six dimensions and SIEs' academic careers, there was not always a direct fit.

Chapter 13, *Self-Initiated Career Characteristics of Danish Expatriated Engineers*, written by Andersen and Rasmussen, examines the case of Danish expatriates who work in the engineering profession. Based on surveys carried out by the Danish engineers association during the 2000s, topics such as job positions, pay level and benefits, type of employer, seniority, and finally reasons for deciding to go abroad are discussed. Findings suggest that the old model continues to exist: Status and pay are still high, benefits modest, and expats are locally employed. However, an increasing number stay abroad, indicating that a very large proportion of the Danish engineers develop global careerist behavior.

In Chapter 14, *Ethnic Minority Migrants or Self-initiated Expatriates? Questioning Assumptions in International Management Studies*, Al Ariss critically reviews and questions the terminology used in the literature on international mobility. Three key gaps are shown, and it is demonstrated how this contributes to the exclusion of individuals moving from developing to developed countries. The chapter also puts forward reflexive strategies for expanding the field of research on international mobility.

TARGET AUDIENCE OF THIS BOOK

The primary target group of this book are researchers and practitioners who are interested in understanding self-initiated expatriation as a key form of international mobility. Scholars should primarily be interested in this book due to the scientific pertinence of the research area of self-initiated expatriation. This book covers general areas, e.g. a semantic differentiation (Chapters 2 and 14) or a literature review (Chapter 3), which should be especially interesting for academics who are relatively new in this area. Other chapters are empirical in nature and include quantitative research (Chapters 6 and 11), qualitative research (Chapter 10), or are based on case studies (Chapter 5). Most of the chapters also give future directions on what remains under-researched, which could lead to new ideas for future research projects. For organizations it is essential to understand the dynamics of self-initiated expatriation in order to use the resources of their SIEs properly. SIEs constitute a pool of workforce who gained understanding of local and international markets due to their international mobility and who are likely to be cheaper than AEs. Hence, this book is of special interest for recruiters or talent managers in international companies. For institutions, knowledge about self-initiated expatriation may help preventing talent waste and brain gain by designing and implementing policies that account for the importance of the skills of SIEs. Furthermore, national and international organizations can gain a better understanding how SIEs can be of essential benefit for them as well as the economy of a country. Finally, individuals planning or already undertaking an international mobility might benefit from this book in a way that they can learn from other SIEs' experiences in various international settings. This could also lead to more reasonable expectations in terms of how an international experience can account for their career progress.

Secondary customers of our book are students on a graduate level. The book takes aim on academic courses in human resource management, international management, and strategic management. This book could, among others, be used in classes about International Human Resource Management, Intercultural Management, Strategic Human Resource Management, Diversity Management or Leadership.

We thank all the authors who provided their support in making this book a viable project and hope that readers will enjoy it.

NOTES

1. Université de Toulouse, Toulouse Business School.

REFERENCES

Al Ariss, A. (2010). Modes of engagement: Migration, self-initiated expatriation, and career development. *Career Development International, 15*(4), 338–358.

Andresen, M., & Biemann, T. (forthcoming). A taxonomy of global careers: Identifying different types of internationally mobile managers. *International Journal of Human Resource Management.*Andresen, M., Biemann, T., & Pattie, M. (forthcoming). What makes them move abroad? Reviewing and exploring differences between self-initiated and assigned expatriation. *International Journal of Human Resource Management.*

Banai, M., & Harry, W. (2004). Boundaryless global careers. *International Studies of Management and Organization, 34*(3), 96–120.

Begley, A., Collings, D. G., & Scullion, H. (2008). The cross-cultural adjustment experiences of self-initiated repatriates to the Republic of Ireland labour market. *Employee Relations, 30*(3), 264–282.

Biemann, T., & Andresen, M. (2010). Self-initiated foreign expatriates versus assigned expatriates: Two distinct types of international careers? *Journal of Managerial Psychology, 25*, 430–48.

Bozionelos, N. (2009). Expatriation outside the boundaries of the multinational corporation: A study with expatriate nurses in Saudi Arabia. *Human Resource Management, 48*(1), 111–134.

Brewster, C., & Suutari, V. (2005). Global HRM: Aspects of a research agenda. *Personnel Review, 34*(1), 5–21.

Carr, S. C., Inkson, K., & Thorn, K. (2005). From global careers to talent flow: Reinterpreting "brain drain." *Journal of World Business, 40*(4), 386–398.

Cerdin, J.-L., & Le Pargneux, M. (2010). Career anchors: A comparison between organization assigned and self-initiated expatriates. *Thunderbird International Business Review, 52*(4), 287–299.

Crowley-Henry, M. (2007). The protean career. *International Studies of Management & Organisation, 37*(3), 44–64.

Howe-Walsh, L., & Schyns, B. (2010). Self-initiated expatriation: implications for HRM. *International Journal of Human Resource Management, 21*(2), 260–273.

Inkson, K., Arthur, M. B., Pringle, J., & Barry, S. (1997). Expatriate assignment versus overseas experience: Contrasting models of international human resource development. *Journal of World Business, 32*(4), 351–368.

Inkson, K., & Myers, B. A. (2003). "The big OE": Self-directed travel and career development. *Career Development International, 8*(4), 170–181.

Jokinen, T., Brewster, C., & Suutari, V. (2008). Career capital during international work experiences: Contrasting self-initiated expatriate experiences and assigned expatriation. *International Journal of Human Resource Management, 19*(6), 979–998.

McKenna, S., & Richardson, J. (2007). The increasing complexity of the international mobile professional. Issues for research and practice. *Cross Cultural Management, 14*(4), 307–320.

Myers, B., & Pringle, J. K. (2005). Self-initiated foreign experience as accelerated development: Influences of gender. *Journal of World Business, 40*(4), 421–431.

Peltokorpi, V., & Froese, F. J. (2009). Organizational expatriates and self-initiated expatriates: Who adjusts better to work and life in Japan? *International Journal of Human Resource Management, 20*(5), 1096–1112.

Richardson, J. (2006). Self-directed expatriation: Family matters. *Personnel Review, 35*(4), 469–486.

Richardson, J., & Mallon, M. (2005). Career interrupted? The case of the self-directed expatriate. *Journal of World Business, 40*(4), 409–420.

Richardson, J., McBey, K., & McKenna, S. (2008). Integrating realistic job previews and realistic living conditions previews. Realistic recruitment for internationally mobile workers. *Personnel Review, 37*(5), 490–508.

Richardson, J., & McKenna, S. (2000). Metaphorical "types" and human resource management: Self-selecting expatriates. *Industrial and Commercial Training, 32*(6), 209–218.

Richardson, J., & McKenna, S. (2001). Leaving and experiencing: Why academics expatriate and how they experience expatriation. *Career Development International, 7*(2), 67–78.

Richardson, J., & McKenna, S. (2006). Exploring relationships with home and host countries. A study of self-directed expatriates. *Cross Cultural Management, 13*(1), 6–22.

Selmer, J., & Lauring, J. (2011). Marital status and work outcomes of self-initiated expatriates. Is there a moderating effect of gender? *Cross Cultural Management, 18*(2), 198–213.

Suutari, V., & Brewster, C. (2000). Making their own way: International experience through self-initiated foreign assignments. *Journal of World Business, 35*(4), 417–436.

Tharenou, P., & Caulfield, N. (2010). Will I stay or will I go? Explaining Repatriation by Self-Initiated Expatriates. *Academy of Management Journal, 53*(5), 1009–1028.

Thomas, D. C. (2002). *Essentials of international management: A cross-cultural perspective*. Thousand Oaks: Sage.

Thorn, K. (2009). The relative importance of motives for international self-initiated mobility. *Career Development International, 14*(5), 441–64.

United Nations, Department of Economic and Social Affairs, Population Division (2011). *International Migration Report 2009: A Global Assessment*. United Nations, ST/ESA/SER.A/316.

2 What Distinguishes Self-Initiated Expatriates from Assigned Expatriates and Migrants?

A Literature-Based Definition and Differentiation of Terms

Maike Andresen, Franziska Bergdolt, and Jil Margenfeld

Recent research and literature on international human resource management indicates a growing array of different forms of international work experiences (Briscoe, Schuler, & Claus, 2009; Selmer & Lauring, 2011). So far, the criteria for demarcation of these different forms are often unclear (Baruch, Dickmann, Altman, & Bournois, 2010). In particular, the terms self-initiated expatriation, assigned expatriation, and migration seem to be overlapping, often applied interchangeably in current expatriation research. While several authors agree concerning the difference between the terms 'assigned expatriate' (AE), denominating an employee who is sent abroad by his company, usually receiving a beneficial expatriate contract, and 'self-initiated expatriate' (SIE), meaning an individual who undertakes his international work experience with little or no organizational sponsorship, often with a less favorable local work contract (Biemann & Andresen, 2010; Peltokorpi & Froese, 2009; Suutari & Brewster, 2000), the difference between the terms SIE and migrant seems to be less evident (Al Ariss, 2010). SIEs can be further differentiated in intraorganizational SIEs (Intra-SIEs) not altering the employing organization and interorganizational SIEs (Inter-SIEs) changing their employing organization.

In general, the term migration can be defined as physical movement from one geographic point to another geographic point (Agozino, 2000), crossing national borders (Boyle, Halfacree, & Robinson, 1998). The UN recommendation on the statistics of international migration further specifies a migrant as "any person who changes his or her country of usual residence" (United Nations, 1998, p. 17), with the 'country of usual residence' representing the place where the person has the center of his life (United Nations, 1998).

To date, there are only a few articles in the expatriation literature that demarcate the terms AE, SIE, and migrant (Al Ariss, 2010; Baruch et al.,

2010; Briscoe et al., 2009). However, as becomes evident in the following, the distinction between the terms remains vague. Baruch and colleagues (2010) distinguish different modes of international work experiences along seven dimensions (time spent, intensity of international contacts, breadth of interaction, legal context, international work instigator, extent of cultural gap, and specific position). According to the authors, the time spent abroad is longer for SIEs than for AEs. Further, SIEs in contrast to AEs are not sponsored by an organization and are less likely to gain objective career benefits from their expatriation. Additionally, Baruch et al. (2010) distinguish expatriates from migrants in terms of rights to permanent residency, meaning that an expatriate might become a migrant when gaining citizenship or permanent visa status.

Al Ariss (2010) differentiates the terms SIE and migrant along four main criteria: geographical origin and destination of the international mobility, the forced/chosen nature of the movement, the period of stay abroad, and the positive or negative connotations of the terms. First, the author assumes that migrants, in contrast to SIEs, might often move from less developed countries to developed countries. Second, migrants and not SIEs might be rather forced to leave their home country, e.g. because of unemployment. Third, SIEs might have more temporariness in their movement abroad than migrants, eventually becoming permanent migrant workers, when deciding to stay in the new country. Last, the term migrant might eventually be referred to in more negative terms, e.g. denoting inferiority, than the term SIE (Al Ariss, 2010). In contradistinction to this dissociation of terms, recent literature on migration indicates the existence of migrant subgroups, for instance described as 'qualified migrants' (Zikic et al., 2010) or 'transnational knowledge workers' (TWKs; Colic-Peisker, 2010), neither including individuals that are forced to move nor individuals that are staying permanently in the host country.

Finally, Briscoe, Schuler and Claus (2009) distinguish between 20 different terms of international work experiences, defining SIEs as "individuals who travel abroad (usually as tourists or students) but who seek work as they travel and are hired in the foreign location, often by firms from their home country" (p. 169). Contrarily, migrants are described as employees who are hired to work in a foreign subsidiary or in the parent company and whose citizenship is in another country (Briscoe et al., 2009).

In sum, there is a need to uniquely demarcate the terms AE, SIE, and migrant. The aim of this book chapter is to close this research gap by reviewing existing definitions of an AE, SIE, and migrant in current research literature, by examining regularities and differences in the application of the three above-mentioned terms and by developing a criteria-based definition and differentiation of the terms. The book chapter is organized as follows: First, a description of the methodologies applied to come to a differentiation of the terms AE, SIE, and migrant is given. After that, the final results of the analysis are presented and discussed. Finally, the chapter closes with theoretical as well as practical implications of the results and provides suggestions for further research.

METHODS

Database

The data used for the analysis was taken from journals in order to ensure that the most recent strands of research on the topic of expatriation and migration were covered. Due to the extensive usage of the terms 'expatriate' and 'migrant' in the literature, the analysis for this chapter was narrowed down to 10 peer-reviewed journals. In order to cover the most current discourse on both terms, five business (human resource management [HRM]) and psychological journals (taken as a basis for the definitions of 'expatriate') and five sociological journals (serving as a basis for definitions on the term 'migrant') were selected. The criteria were (1) relevance, i.e. identification of those journals with the highest number of hits in a full-text search using the search terms 'expatriate' and 'migrant' in scientific search engines (EBSCO Host, PsychINFO, Social Sciences Citation Index) in the years 2005 to 2010 and (2) quality, i.e. selection based on the accumulated impact factor for 2005 to 2010 of the respective journals using the ISI-index (see Tables 2.1 and 2.2).

Table 2.1 Impact Factors and Numbers of Hits in the Databases for the Term 'Expatriate'

	Accumulated number of hits for the search term 'expatriate' in the chosen databases (full-text search)	ISI impact factor 2005–2010	Number of relevant articles	Number of relevant definitions
International Journal of HRM	280	1.61	51	
Journal of World Business	64	2.82	10	
Human Resource Management	62	1.83	7	
				74
Career Development International	33	1.31 (not listed in the years 2005–2009)	3	
Journal of Applied Psychology	24	6.73	3	

Table 2.2   Impact Factors and Numbers of Hits in the Databases for the Term 'Migrant'

	Accumulated number of hits for the search term 'migrant' in the chosen databases (full-text search)	ISI impact factor 2005–2010	Number of relevant articles	Number of relevant definitions
Journal of Ethnic and Migration Studies	254	1.42	7	
Ethnic and Racial Studies	173	1.92	16	
Social Science & Medicine	163	3.48	6	84
Global Networks —A Journal of Transnational Affairs	88	2.02	23	
International Migration Review	64	2.15	35	

As a result all publications in the journals *International Journal of Human Resource Management, Journal of World Business, Human Resource Management, Journal of Applied Psychology,* and *Career Development International* from 2005–2010 were screened for any definitions of the term 'expatriate,' and all publications in the journals *Ethnic and Racial Studies, Global Networks, Social Science & Medicine, Journal of Ethnic and Migration Studies,* and *International Migration Review* were screened for any definitions of the term 'migrant.'

Due to the fact that the field of research on SIEs is only emerging, the number of definitions available for the term 'self-initiated expatriate' significantly falls below the number of definitions available for the terms 'expatriate' and 'migrant.' Consequently, all articles on SIEs that have been published in an English-language peer-reviewed journal constituted the basis for analysis. No time limitation has been applied here. The ISI-index of the considered journals can be found in Table 2.3.

Altogether the articles included in the database comprised 74 definitions of the term 'expatriate,' the term 'self-initiated expatriate' was defined 86 times, and the data pool for the term 'migrant' involved 84 definitions. Disjointing them in meaningful clauses, the definitions were coded verbatim using statistical software (SPSS). The clauses were assigned to several criteria, which were deduced from an evaluation of definitions found in standard textbooks on HRM and sociology as well as induced from the data. The criteria will be outlined in the results section.

Table 2.3   Impact Factors for the Papers Relevant for the Definition of the Term 'Self-Initiated Expatriate'

	ISI impact factor 2005–2010 (average)	Number of relevant articles	Number of relevant definitions
International Journal of HRM	1.61	21	
Career Development International	1.31 (not listed in the years 2005–2009)	15	
Cross Cultural Management	not listed	6	
Journal of Managerial Psychology	2.15 (not listed in the years 2005–2007)	6	
Journal of World Business	2.82	5	
Canadian Social Science	not listed	5	
Thunderbird International Business Review	not listed	4	
Employee Relations	not listed	4	
Human Resource Management	1.83	3	86
International Studies of Management & Organization	not listed	3	
Management Review	not listed	2	
Journal of Business Ethics	1.60	2	
Academy of Management Journal	10.78	2	
Ethnic and Racial Studies	1.92	1	
International Journal of Business and Management	not listed	1	
Public Policy and Administration	not listed	1	
University of Auckland Business Review	not listed	1	
Industrial and Commercial Training	not listed	1	

Data Analysis

A qualitative approach has been adopted using the tool of qualitative content analysis (Mayring, 2000) in order to analyze and compare the available definitions on the terms AE, SIE, and migrant. The qualitative content analysis serves to systematically gather and evaluate data and is defined as an empirical analysis of texts within their context (Mayring, 2000). The identified meaning units (= definitions of the three terms in journal papers) have been coded according to primarily developed categories. According to Krippendorf (1980), a category consists of several pieces of content that share a commonality. Using a deductive approach to category application (Mayring, 2000), the categories have been developed before coding the meaning units in statistical software (SPSS). Standard business and sociological text book definitions of the above-mentioned terms have been used to generate the 15 categories. By use of a frequential analysis the categories have been evaluated according to the most frequently emerging characteristics. Using these findings as well as additional current research results on expatriates, SIEs, and migrants sufficient conditions for the differentiation between the three terms were deduced.

RESULTS

The main results of the analysis of the definitions were summarized in morphological boxes (see Table 2.4). The criteria list has been divided into four different aspects: Individual level (criteria concerning the expatriate/migrant himself, e.g. initiative to go abroad), organizational level (criteria concerning the organization, e.g. decision of employment), political level (criteria concerning state or political facilities, e.g. visa status), and finally criteria with respect to mobility in general (e.g. destination country).

Results indicate first that there is no consistency in the literature regarding how each of the three individual terms is defined. Taking the term migrant as an example there are definitions, which indicate that migrants stay permanently in the immigration country (Massey & Bartley, 2006), whereas Wiles (2008), for example, states that the term migrant is rather associated with a temporary dwelling time of the individual in the foreign country.

Secondly, Table 2.4 clearly shows that several criteria for demarcation of the terms AE, SIE, and migrant are available. Whereas the length of stay of SIEs in the host country is considered to be not predetermined (Suutari & Brewster, 2000), AEs are rather expected to stay for a previously predetermined time frame (Peltokorpi & Froese, 2009). This also explains why some authors provide a minimum and maximum duration when defining the term AE (e.g. Collings, Scullion, & Morley, 2007). This does not apply for both other groups. In line with that SIEs are in most cases not expected to repatriate (Crowley-Henry, 2007), while AEs are likely to repatriate to their home country (Huang, Chi, & Lawler, 2005). Regarding the criterion 'initiative' the term SIE is indicative of a more active individual who chooses to leave (Harrison, Shaffer, & Bhaskar-Shrinivas, 2004) and initiates the expatriation himself (Myers & Pringle, 2005), whereas for AEs the transfer is often initiated by the company (Peltokorpi & Froese, 2009). Differences concerning initiative are also reflected by the criterion motives for expatriation. While SIEs seem to expatriate due to personal motives such as self-development, AEs primarily leave in order to accomplish a job- or organizational-related goal (Peltokorpi, 2008). Hence, AEs get support by their organizations (Meyskens, von Glinow, Werther, & Clarke, 2009) such

Table 2.4 Morphological Box 'Self-Initiated Expatriate,' 'Assigned Expatriate,' and 'Migrant' Based on Definitions Found in Academic Journals

Criteria: Individual level		SIE (N = 86)	AE (N = 74)	Migrant (N = 8 4)
		Findings		
Duration	Findings:	Long term (N = 4) [44; 68; 93; 137]	Long term (N = 6) [20; 45; 95; 142; 145; 148]	Long term (N = 3) [80; 99; 127]
		Temporary to permanent (N =4) [3; 14; 137; 152]	Semi-permanent to permanent (N =5) [106; 108; 133; 135; 140]	Permanently (N = 7) [3; 35; 84; 113; 122; 149; 151]
		Temporary (N =3) [3; 10; 72]	Temporary (N =5) [36; 69; 97; 108; 121]	Repeated periods (N = 3) [99; 104; 151]
		Not predetermined (N = 4) [3; 67; 131; 132]	Predetermined (N = 5) [67; 89; 101; 102; 124]	
			Minimum duration: 6 months (N = 3) [67; 101; 102] 1 year (N =2) [95; 133], 2 years (N = 5) [21; 41; 59; 116; 145], 3 years (N = 3) [36; 77; 89]	
			Maximum duration: 1 year (N = 3) [36; 133; 145], 3 years (N = 2) [41; 59], 5 years (N = 8) [21; 36; 67; 77; 89; 101; 102; 116], Several years (N =2) [21; 116]	
	Implication:	**Long term, temporary to permanent, rather not predetermined**	**Long term, temporary to permanent, rather predetermined period**	**Long term, temporary to permanent, repeated periods**
Initiative (psychological decision to move)	Findings:	On the initiative of the expatriate (N = 20) [3; 4; 10; 12; 16; 29; 43; 44; 51; 68; 73; 71; 89; 93; 117; 121; 128; 131; 137; 152]		

Continued

Table 2.4   Continued

Motives	Findings:	Decision of the individual to expatriate (N = 4) [101; 102; 119; 120]	Assigned (N = 6) [20; 81; 108; 116; 129; 148]	
		Choose to leave (N = 4) [44; 68; 109; 132]	Sent (N = 10) [21; 41; 45; 79; 97; 101; 102; 106; 110; 116]	
		Not on the initiative of an organization (N = 4) [12; 16; 43; 117]	Initiative by company (N = 2) [89; 121]	
		Not transferred by organization (N = 7) [101; 102; 110; 119; 120; 131; 132]	Transferred (N = 7) [40; 106; 108; 116; 121; 133; 140]	
		Voluntary (N =3) [16; 68; 70]		
	Implication:	**Individually initiated**	**Organizationally initiated**	
	Findings:	To work/ live (N = 13) [12; 16; 43; 51; 52; 67; 68; 101; 102; 119; 120; 124; 132]	To work/ live (N = 14) [13; 21; 24; 29; 40; 41; 45; 79; 81; 116; 121; 124; 129; 142]	To settle (N = 6) [35; 87; 122; 143; 144; 151]
		Personal reasons (N = 5) [12; 73; 101; 102; 121]	Job or organizational-related goal (N = 4) [97; 101; 102; 146]	To improve economic and social conditions (N = 7) [11; 54; 60; 68; 75; 84; 134]
		Culture, career, and personal motives (N = 3) [44; 93;137]	For the company (N = 1) [133]	Employment (N = 4) [6; 35; 99; 105]
		Self-development and cultural experiences (N = 2) [72; 102]	International mission (N = 1) [116]	Education (N = 1) [38]
	Implication:	**Personal and professional motives with a dominance of personal goals**	**Personal and professional motives with a dominance of organization-related goals**	**Different reasons, rather economic or political**
Repatriation	Findings:	No intention to repatriate before expatriation (N = 3) [3; 16; 68]	No repatriation (N = 1) [21]	No repatriation (N = 2) [3; 58]

Relocation of family	Findings:	Either intention to repatriate or not (N = 1) [137]	Repatriation expected (N = 2) [77; 81]	Expected to repatriate (N = 1) [6]
		Individuals choose whether to return (N =2) [16; 68]	Repatriation planned (N = 4) [59; 69; 89]	Eventual repatriation (N = 1) [103]
				Return only rarely (N = 1) [22]
	Implication:	**Either intention to repatriate or not**	**Rather intention to repatriate, repatriation agreement**	**Either intention to repatriate or not**
	Findings:		Relocation of expatriate and family (N = 4) [36; 41; 49; 59]	
			No relocation of the family (N = 1) [125]	
			Either relocation of family or not (N = 2) [77; 89]	
	Implication:		**Either relocation of family or not**	
Consequences for the individual	Finding:			Multiple social relations across borders (N = 4) [42; 122; 138; 144]
				Assimilation and acculturation (N = 2) [35; 122]
				Influencing daily life (N = 2) [54; 103]
				Termination of ties from

Continued

Table 2.4 Continued

Criteria: Organizational level		Findings		
	Implication:		In tendency social ties in several countries	those left behind (N = 1) 42
Executing work abroad	Findings:	Individual (N = 14) 2; 12; 16; 19; 24; 39; 51; 70; 88; 89; 119; 120; 121; 152	Individuals (N = 4) 24; 41; 121; 146	Individuals (N = 3) 85; 98; 107
		Person (N = 4) 68; 101; 102; 112	Person (N = 3) 45; 89; 142	Person (N = 19) 8; 30; 35; 37; 48; 50; 56; 60; 84; 87; 90; 92; 96; 105; 122; 127; 141; 143; 144
		Professionals, managers (N = 4) 7; 68; 131; 132	Managers (N = 6) 20; 59; 77; 121; 133; 145	Foreigners (N = 2) 84; 104
		Workers (N = 1) 29	Employees (N = 12) 13; 21; 34; 40; 67; 81; 95; 97; 116; 121; 129; 148	Workers (N = 2) 99;103
	Implication:	Employed individuals	Employed individuals	Individuals; occupation not mandatorily necessary
Support	Findings:	Independent job search (N = 5) 74; 111; 112; 118; 119	Funded by company (N = 3) 24; 89; 121	
		No organizational support (N = 9) 4; 12; 43; 88; 94; 117;118; 119; 120	Receive relocation package (N = 2) 101;102	
		Independent (N = 7) 16; 52; 68; 109; 111; 112	Receive training (N = 1) 67	
		Self-funding (N = 5) 51; 101; 102; 128; 130		
	Implication:	No or little support from employer	High support from home and	Depends, all scenarios

			host organization	possible
Career	Findings:	Responsible for own career (N = 6) [7; 16; 118; 119; 120, 121]	Foreign assignment as part of the career (N = 3) [89; 10f; 121]	
		No structured career path (N = 2) [102; 128]		
		International career independent of one single employer (N = 1) [2]		
	Implication:	Self-managed career	Organizational career	
Contract	Findings:	Contractual basis (N = 7) [15; 51; 101; 102; 110; 119; 120]		
		Local contract (N = 3) [16; 39; 68]		
	Implication:	Work contract		
Criteria: Political Approach			Findings	
Citizenship	Findings:		Born in a different country from that in which they reside (N = 9) [27; 50; 61; 84; 85; 90; 92; 98; 136]	
			Non-nationality of the state of residence (N = 2) [18; 98]	
			Entitlement to naturalization (N = 2) [33; 35]	
	Implication:			May be citizen or not
Visa status	Findings:			Legal residency in a foreign

Continued

Table 2.4 Continued

		Findings		
	Implication:			country (N = 4) [35; 58; 84; 99] Violation of visa conditions (N = 4) [48; 84; 99; 141] Temporary visa (N = 1) [105] **Either visa or not**
Criteria: Mobility in general				
Kind of movement	Findings:	Movement in general (N = 13) [3; 10; 16; 29; 39; 44; 68; 73; 101; 102; 117; 131; 137] Movement across organizations (N = 4) [4; 7; 94; 121] Travel (N = 7) [3; 4; 12; 51; 70; 93; 137] Personal odyssey (N = 2) [68; 71]	Movement in general (N = 2) [64; 133] Movement within organizations (N = 4) [24; 36; 121; 124] Crossing boundaries (N = 2) [32; 55]	Movement in general (N = 6) [3; 22; 35; 38; 75; 113] Movement into another country (N = 4) [30; 33; 96; 127] (Geographical) movement across boundaries (N = 8) [11; 37; 54; 56; 90; 122; 144; 151] Movement out of home country/nation state of origin/country of citizenship (N = 3) [68; 144; 151]
	Implication:	**Crossing national and organizational boundaries**	**Crossing national but not organizational boundaries**	**Crossing national boundaries**
Origin	Findings:		Home organization (N = 6) [64; 67; 102; 106; 121; 135] MNC (N = 5) [20; 24; 34; 102; 124]	Country of origin (N = 3) [11; 83; 15f] Developing countries (N = 3) [3; 11; 35]

		Starting from a company	Starting from a (by tendency developing) country
		Business organization (N = 2) [97; 106]	Developed countries (N = 1) [75]
			From beyond the nation state's boundaries (N = 1) [143]
Findings:		Foreign subsidiary (N = 9) [36; 64; 101; 102; 108; 116; 121; 124; 129]	
	Foreign country (N = 8) [10; 16; 39; 44; 67; 68; 93; 137]	Headquarters (N = 3) [106; 108; 133]	
	Abroad (N = 10) [3; 12; 44; 51; 102; 109; 110; 117; 119; 120]	Foreign-acquired company (N = 1) [89]	
	Foreign culture (N = 1) [16]	Foreign country (N = 12) [21; 24; 40; 41; 81; 89; 95; 97; 102; 116; 121; 142]	Different country (N = 2) [3; 54]
		Abroad (N = 10) [13; 20; 45; 69; 102; 110; 116; 121; 133; 146]	Abroad (N = 4) [6; 99; 104; 113]
Destination	Country of choice (N = 3) [3; 131; 132]	Less-advanced economies (N = 1) [89]	Developed countries (N = 4) [3; 11; 35; 134]
Implication:	Going to foreign country	Going to foreign company	Going to different, by tendency developed country

Table 2.5 Final Criteria List for the Demarcation of the Terms Migrant, Assigned Expatriate, and Self-Initiated Expatriate

Criteria	Distinct for demarcation	SIE (N = 86)	AE (N = 74)	Migrant (N = 84)
			Implications	
		Individual level		
Duration	Ambiguous	Long term, temporary to permanent, rather not predetermined	Long term, temporary to permanent, rather predetermined period	Long term, temporary to permanent, repeated periods
Initiative	Distinct	Individually initiated	Organizationally initiated; Added: individually and organizationally initiated [62; 137]	Added: individually initiated [10; 82] or politically initiated [5; 48]
Motives	Ambiguous	Personal and professional motives with a dominance of personal goals	Personal and professional motives with a dominance of organization-related goals	Different reasons, rather economic or political
Repatriation	Ambiguous	Either intention to repatriate or not	Rather intention to repatriate, repatriation agreement	Either intention to repatriate or not
Emotional attachment to home/host country	Ambiguous	Added: home and/or host country [12]	Added: home and/or host country [17]	Added: home and/or host country [11; 58; 122]
Relocation of family	Ambiguous		Either relocation of family or not	

		Organizational level		In tendency social ties in several countries
Consequences for individual	Ambiguous			In tendency social ties in several countries
Executing work abroad	Distinct	Employed individuals	Employed individuals	Individuals; occupation not mandatorily necessary [48; 123; 150]
Mode of employment	Distinct	Added: dependent employment [16; 51]	Added: dependent employment [101]	Added: dependent or independent employment [123]
Decision of employment	Distinct	Added: decision is made by new work contract partner which is either the same (Intra-SIE) or a new organization (Inter-SIE) [16; 39; 128]	Added: decision is made by current work contract partner [114]	Added: not mandatorily necessary, all scenarios possible [150]
Organizational support	Ambiguous	No or little support from employer	High support from home and host organization	Added: depends, all scenarios possible [150]
Career	Ambiguous	Self-managed career	Organizational career	Added: not necessarily career related [39]
Contract		Work contract		
		Political level		
Citizenship	Ambiguous	Added: maybe or not [4]	Added: not aspired, but might change abroad [26; 53]	May be citizen or not
Visa status	Ambiguous	Added: yes, work permit; status	Added: yes, work permit; status	Either visa or not

Continued

Table 2.5 Continued

		depends on immigration policies [4]	depends on immigration policies [100]	
Assessment (taxation)	Ambiguous	Added: rather in host country (local contract) [46]	Added: rather in home country (expatriate contract) [26; 46; 100]	Added: rather in host country (local contract) or no taxes (no contract) [115]
Movement in general				
Kind of movement	Ambiguous	Crossing national and organizational boundaries	Crossing national but not organizational boundaries	Crossing national boundaries
Origin	Ambiguous		Starting from a company	Starting from a, by tendency developing country
Destination	Ambiguous	Going to foreign country	Going to foreign company	Going to foreign country

as training prior to the departure (Howe-Walsh & Schyns, 2010), whereas SIEs are not backed by a company (Carr, Inkson, & Thorn, 2005). A self-initiated expatriation therefore rather implies a movement across different organizations (Inkson, Arthur, Pringle, & Barry, 1997). Contrary to that, AEs move within the boundaries of one organization (Baruch & Altman, 2002). Following this line of thought, definitions of the term AE often refer to employees (Caligiuri, 2000) or managers (Tharenou & Harvey, 2006), whereas SIEs concern individuals who seek employment (e.g. Carr, Inkson, & Thorn, 2005), implying rather independent movement. Consequently, AEs regard their foreign assignment as part of their organizational career (Siljanen & Lämsä, 2009) unlike SIEs who rather follow an individualized career path (Carr et al., 2005).

For migrants in contrast to AEs and SIEs, the movement across geographical borders (Milewski & Hamel, 2010) is of primary focus rather than organizational ones. Main motives for migration are settlement in the new country (Waldinger, 2008) and improvement of individual economic conditions (Tharmaseelan, Inkson, & Carr, 2010). The literature on migrants also acknowledges that there are several consequences for the individual that result from the geographical relocation, such as relationships that span across borders (Glick-Schiller, 2003). This circumstance it not considered in the definitions of expatriates. Furthermore, migrants are characterized by political characteristics such as country of birth (Massey & Bartley, 2006) and country of residence (Parreñas, 2010) as well as visa status (Preibisch, 2010). Strikingly, organization-related criteria emerging in the expatriate literature, for instance, organizational support, do not appear in the migration literature.

Hence, the concept of expatriation is tailored rather to the organizational context of crossing borders, whereas the concept of migration is tailored to the general context of crossing geographical borders.

Summing up, the criteria resulting from the content analysis of current business, psychological and sociological definitions of the terms AE, SIE, and migrant were not sufficient to clearly differentiate the three subgroups. Consequently, the present database was screened concerning research results, indicating either similarities or differences between AEs, SIEs, and migrants. Not yet considered information, either new criteria or new characteristics, were added to the original criteria list (see Table 2.5). For some criteria (e.g. assessment), the present database did not include research results for all subgroups. In this case, the database was broadened to further peer-reviewed journal articles. All criteria were assessed if they are distinct for demarcation of the terms AE, SIE, and migrant.

The main finding of this second step of our analysis is that there are four relevant criteria that plainly demarcate the terms AE, SIE, and migrant. To start with, we found two sufficient criteria distinguishing between the terms expatriate (including AEs and SIEs) and migrant. The first criterion is 'executing work abroad' (see Table 2.5). First, a person can only be named AE or SIE if the person executes his work abroad. Therefore, individuals who move to a foreign country without taking up employment cannot be categorized as expatriates. The second criterion to demarcate between migrant and expatriate is 'mode of employment' (see Table 2.5). To be considered as an expatriate, a person must have an employment contract. Consequently, individuals working illegally in a foreign country and self-initiated entrepreneurs starting a venture abroad are excluded from the expatriate category. Current research on AE and SIE supports these claims, revealing that expatriates are always associated with a dependent work context, having the work contract either with the home or the host organization (Biemann & Andresen, 2010; Doherty, Dickmann, & Mills, 2011; Suutari & Brewster, 2000).

Two other criteria, 'decision of employment' and 'initiative' sufficiently differentiate between the terms AE and SIE (see Table 2.5). While the decision to assign the expatriate to a position abroad is always made by the current work contract partner, usually in the home country, the decision to employ the SIE is always made by a new work contract partner, usually in the host country, either the same organization (Intra-SIE), e.g. in a foreign subsidiary, or a new organization (Inter-SIE). With respect to initiation, expatriate assignments can be individually and organizationally initiated (cf. Harris & Brewster, 1999; Thorn, 2009). Harris and Brewster (1999) describe a process they call "coffee machine system" (p. 497), grounding on

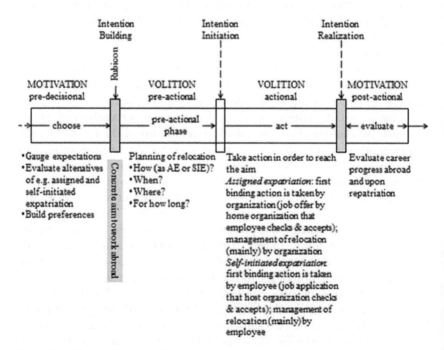

Figure 2.1   Rubicon model of action phases.

the practical observation that expatriates might initiate their own assignment during an informal discourse with their superior who in the following offers an expatriation opportunity if in interest for the organization. Self-initiated expatriates, by contrast, initiate their foreign movement individually. The difference between AEs and SIEs concerning the criteria, initiative' can be best explained by the rubicon model of action phases (see Figure 2.1; Heckhausen & Gollwitzer, 1987; Heckhausen & Heckhausen, 2010).

The model starts with the pre-decisional phase, where alternatives are evaluated, preferences are built and motivation is formed (e.g. the diffuse idea to work abroad and evaluation of options such as assigned or self-initiated expatriation). The next step is the intention building, i.e. the concrete decision or goal setting process (e.g. the concrete aim to work abroad in the next year). Since both, AEs and SIEs, decide for themselves to work in a foreign country, they do not differ at this point of the model.

The post-decisional phase can be subdivided into a pre-actional, an actional and a post-actional phase. In the pre-actional or planning phase a concrete action plan is formed, e.g. how (as AE or SIE), when and for how long to work abroad. After the intention initiation the action phase follows, i.e. (1) in case of an assigned expatriation, an employee receives a formalized job offer for a position in a foreign subsidiary by their current work contract partner that the employee needs to check and accept (i.e. first formalized action is taken by the organization, i.e. the current work contract partner). (2) In case of a self-initiated expatriation, an employee applies for a foreign job directly at the foreign subsidiary on his own (i.e. first formalized action is taken by the individual), and the new work contract partner abroad checks the offer and accepts it. Both alternatives lead to a realization of the intention, i.e. the conclusion of a contract, followed by the management and implementation of the concrete assignment (mainly) by the current work contract partner in case of an assignment or a self-organization of the relocation by the employee in case of a self-initiated expatriation. SIEs might face more obstacles in the action phase than AEs (e.g. financial challenges, resulting in negative emotions like fear or uncertainty), thus, need a more strong volition, e.g. self-regulation strategies and discipline, to reach their goal (i.e. work in a foreign country for a certain period of time). According to Heckhausen & Gollwitzer (1987), volition is a crucial factor in the goal achievement process, deciding whether an action goal (e.g. completion of expatriate assignment) is achieved or not.

Finally, in the post-actional phase, when action is implemented, action results (e.g. career progress abroad and after repatriation in the home country) are evaluated. Success or failure judgments are often accompanied by emotions, with positive emotions (e.g. pride), reinforcing similar action in the future (e.g. working abroad on an expatriate contract) and negative emotions (e.g. anger), hampering similar action in the future (e.g. not initiating expatriation on their own again; Weiner, 1985).

DISCUSSION

The goal of this study was to find relevant demarcation criteria that plainly differentiate between the terms AE, SIE, and migrant. Based on a qualitative content analysis of 244 definitions from sociological, psychological, and business journals, we finally arrived at four main demarcation criteria that can be applied to define and differentiate the above-mentioned terms. In order to visualize the definition process, Figure 2.2 shows a decision tree.

To start with, a person is considered as migrant, if he (1) moves from one geographical point to another geographical point (Agozino, 2000) crossing national borders (Boyle et al., 1998) and (2) changes his dominant place of residence, which is the center of a person's life (United Nations, 1998). According to the OECD Model Tax Convention (Art. 4(2)), the dominant place of residence can be defined in a four-step process, called 'tie-breaker rule' (Stuart, 2010; see chapter by Egner in this volume). If the first criterion does not result in a plain demarcation of the person's dominant place of residence, the next criterion has to be considered. If the second criterion neither leads to a clear result, the third criterion should be answered, and so forth. First, an individual's center of life is usually (1) where the person's

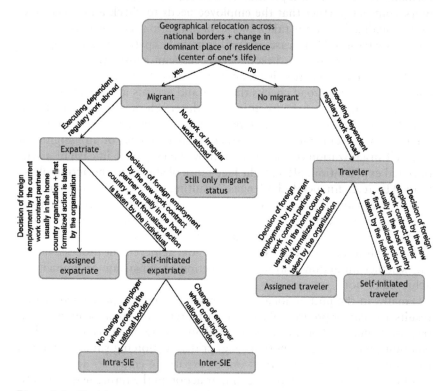

Figure 2.2   Decision tree.

family (domestic partner or spouse, and children) live. If this does not lead to a clear result, (2) the person's economic interests should be considered (e.g. administration of property). Then, (3) the person's habitual abode is of interest, which is usually assumed to be where the person spends more than 183 days of the year. The last criterion is (4) the person's nationality (e.g. as indicated in the identity card; Stuart, 2010).

If a person is considered to have migrant status, the next decision step includes the criterion 'executing dependent work abroad.' A person is called expatriate if he moves to another geographical point crossing national borders and changes his dominant place of residence and executes dependent work in a foreign country. At this point, the decision tree splits into the two branches AEs and SIEs. If the initiative, representing the first formalized action taken by the organization (offering an expatriation contract), and the legal decision to employ the expatriate abroad is made by the current work contract partner the person is categorized as AE. In contrast to that SIEs take the first formalized action themselves (applying for a job abroad) and the legal employment decision is made by the new work contract partner. SIEs can be subdivided into two groups: Intra-SIE, if the legal decision of employment is made by the new work contract partner in the same organization, e.g. foreign subsidiary. Inter-SIE, if the person takes up employment in a new organization and the new work contract partner finally makes the legal decision to hire that person.

To sum up, all expatriate subgroups, which are located on the left side of the decision tree, simultaneously belong to the umbrella category migrant.

Moving on to the right side of the tree: A person that moves to another geographical point crossing borders without changing his dominant place of residence (i.e. center of his life) is not considered to be a migrant. For instance, 'International Business Travelers' (IBT) can be excluded from the migrant category as IBTs frequently move between different countries without changing their dominant place of residence, e.g. the family or partner remains in the home country (Collings et al., 2007; Welch, Welch, & Worm, 2007). As the decision of employment is made by the current work contract partner and the first formalized action (offering an IBT agreement) is taken by the organization, i. e. the current work contract partner, an IBT belongs to the category of assigned travelers. Cross-border commuters regularly move between different geographical points crossing national borders in order to get to their place of employment without changing their place of dominant residence (Knowles & Matthiesen, 2009). The decision of employment is made by the new work contract partner and the first formalized action (applying for a job abroad) is undertaken by the individual. Hence, cross-border commuter can be categorized as self-initiated travelers. Summing up, all international workers, which are located on the right side of the decision tree, do not belong to the umbrella category migrant or expatriate. Thus, they are called 'travelers.'

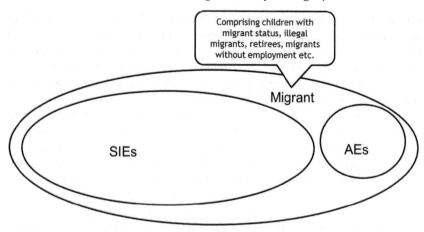

Figure 2.3   Illustration of the interrelation between the terms.

Figure 2.3 clarifies the above explained relation between the terms AE, SIE, and migrant. It becomes obvious that migrant is an umbrella term, including all kinds of AEs and SIEs. Previous research claimed that migrants and expatriates are two exclusive groups (Al Ariss, 2010; Baruch et al., 2010).

From the findings above, the following definitions for the terms AE and SIE have been deduced.

> An expatriate is an individual who moves to another country while changing the dominant place of residence and executes dependent work abroad. As such, the expatriate has migrant status. In case of SIEs, the first formalized action to move internationally is solely made by the individual who initiates the expatriation, whereas the legal decision of employment is made by the new work contract partner, which is either a different subsidiary of the organization where they are currently employed (Intra-SIEs) or a new organization (Inter-SIEs). In case of AEs, the first formalized action to expatriate is taken by the organization, i. e. current work contract partner, and the legal decision of employment is made by the current work contract partner.

Implications of the Findings

Our findings have crucial implications for future expatriation research, as they contradict currently available models on the demarcation of the terms SIE, AE, and migrant (Baruch et al., 2010). Suutari and Brewster (2000) were one of the first who recognized that SIEs are not a homogeneous group" (p. 430). Based on our results, researchers are able to clearly define if their sample consists of AEs, SIEs (Intra-SIEs or Inter-SIEs) or migrants, which could serve to explain existing heterogeneous results on expatriates and to facilitate interpretation of future research results.

Our research identified that only four demarcation criteria (executing work abroad, mode of employment, initiative, and legal decision of employment) are sufficient for plain differentiation between the terms AE, SIE, and migrant, while the other discussed criteria do not provide a satisfactory distinction (e.g. organizational support).

Limitations of the Study

Notwithstanding some limitations restrict the validity of our research results. First, the database for AEs and migrants was constrained to 10 sociological, business, and psychological journals, considering all publications in the period from 2005 to 2010. Especially the term migrant has a long tradition in the sociological field of research (Millar & Salt, 2007). Conceivably our database does not include older definitions of the term migrant and other forms of scientific publications such as monographs. However, the primary goal of the present study was to outline the current state of research concerning the definition of the terms AE, SIE, and migrant. A second limitation is caused by the fact that many definitions did not contain all of the defined demarcation criteria, resulting in a high level of missing values and low frequencies of characteristics. Still, this might also be some kind of result, eventually revealing that a special criterion (e.g. visa status) is not important to define the term (e.g. SIE or AE).

Implications for Further Research

Future research should provide empirical proof for our demarcation model and test whether the different subgroups can be plainly distinguished by the identified sufficient criteria. Besides, future research could build on our study trying to find further differences between AEs and SIEs. For instance, further research on the criterion motives for going abroad is necessary as most of the studies do not reveal major differences so far (e.g. Cerdin chapter in this volume; Doherty et al., 2011). An important area of research that could further serve to sufficiently demarcate the above mentioned terms is the field of tax law, particularly whether the assessment takes place in the home or host country (Endres, Spengel, Elschner, & Schmidt, 2005). So far no sufficient research has been conducted on this issue (see Enger chapter in this volume). Currently, many nations define the term migrant differently. Due to this inconsistency, a person might have migrant status in one country but not in another (e.g. the German definition of immigrants is based on nationality, whereas in the Netherlands immigrant status depends on the country of birth of the individual and its parents; Euwals, Dagevos, Gijsberts, & Roodenburg, 2010). The criteria presented here could serve as a basis for a classification of the different samples found in research studies in order to determine what kind of subgroups of international movers were included in the migrant category and to better understand and interpret the results found.

REFERENCES

1   Agozino, B. (2000). *Theoretical and methodological issues in migration research: Interdisciplinary, intergenerational and international perspectives.* Aldershot Hants: Ashgate.
2   Agullo, B., & Egawa, M. (2009). International careers of Indian workers in Tokyo: Examination and future directions. *Career Development International, 14*(2), 148–168.
3   Al Ariss, A. (2010). Modes of engagement: Migration, self-initiated expatriation and career development. *Career Development International, 15*(4), 338–358.
4   Al Ariss, A., & Özbilgin, M. (2010). Understanding self-initiated expatriates: Career experiences of Lebanese self-initiated expatriates. *Thunderbird International Business Review, 54*(4), 275–285.
5   Allen, R. (2009). Benefit or burden? Social capital, gender, and the economic adaptation of refugees. *International Migration Review, 43*(2), 332–365.
6   Arguillas, M. J. B., & Williams, L. (2010). The impact of parents' overseas employment on educational outcomes of Filipino children. *International Migration Review, 44*(2), 300–319.
7   Banai, M., & Harry, W. (2004). Boundaryless global careers. *International Studies of Management & Organization, 34*(3), 96–120.
8   Barrett, A., & Duffy, D. (2008). Are Ireland's immigrants integrating into its labor market? *International Migration Review, 42*(3), 597–619.
9   Baruch, Y., & Altman, Y. (2002). Expatriation and repatriation in MNCs: A taxonomy. *Human Resource Management, 41*(2), 239–259.
10 Baruch, Y., Dickmann, M., Altman, Y., & Bournois, F. (2010, June). *Exploring international work: Types and dimensions of global careers.* Paper presented at the International Human Resource Management Conference, Birmingham UK.
11 Beck-Gernsheim, E. (2007). Transnational lives, transnational marriages: A review of the evidence from migrant communities in Europe. *Global Networks, 7*(3), 271–288.
12 Begley, A., Collings, D. G., & Scullion, H. (2008). The cross-cultural adjustment experiences of self-initiated repatriates to the Republic of Ireland labour market. *Employee Relations, 30*(3), 264–282.
13 Benson, G. S., & Pattie, M. (2008). Is expatriation good for my career? The impact of expatriate assignments on perceived and actual career outcomes. *International Journal of Human Resource Management, 19*(9), 1636–1653.
14 Bhuian, S. N., & Al-Jabri, I. M. (1996). Expatriate turnover tendencies in Saudi-Arabia: An empirical examination. *The International Journal of Organizational Analysis, 4*(4), 393–407.
15 Bhuian, S. N., Al-Shammari, E. S., & Jefri, O. A. (2001). Work-related attitudes and job characteristics of expatriates in Saudi Arabia. *Thunderbird International Business Review, 43*(1), 21–31.
16 Biemann, T., & Andresen, M. (2010). Self-initiated foreign expatriates versus assigned expatriates: Two distinct types of international careers? *Journal of Managerial Psychology, 25*(4), 430–448.
17 Black, J. S., Gregersen, H. B., & Mendenhall, M. E. (1992). Toward a theoretical framework of repatriation adjustment. *Journal of International Business Studies, 23*(4), 737–760.

18 Böhning, R. (2009). Getting a handle on the migration rights-development nexus. *International Migration Review, 43*(3), 652–670.
19 Bonache, J., Brewster, C., & Suutari, V. (2007). Preface, knowledge, international mobility and careers. *International Studies of Management and Organization, 37*(3), 3–15.
20 Bonache, J., & Zárraga-Oberty, C. (2008). Determinants of the success of international assignees as knowledge transferors: A theoretical framework. *International Journal of Human Resource Management, 19*(1), 1–18.
21 Bossard, A., & Peterson, R. (2005). The repatriate experience as seen by American expatriates. *Journal of World Business, 40*(1), 9–28.
22 Boswell, C., & Ciobanu, O. (2009). Culture, utility or social systems? Explaining the cross-national ties of emigrants from Borşa, Romania. *Ethnic and Racial Studies, 32*(8), 1346–1364.
23 Boyle, P., Halfacree, K., & Robinson, V. (1998). *Exploring contemporary migration.* Harlow: Addison Wesley Longman.
24 Bozionelos, N. (2009). Expatriation outside the boundaries of the multinational corporation: A study with expatriate nurses in Saudi Arabia. *Human Resource Management, 48*(1), 111–134.
25 Briscoe, D., Schuler, R. S., & Claus, L. (2009). *International human resource management,* 3rd ed. London: Routledge.
26 Brody, E. S., & Binder, J. K. (2010). IRS Guidance adds body to the heart act's new tax regime for expatriates. *Canadian Tax Journal, 58*(2), 447–458.
27 Buzdugan, R., & Halli, S. S. (2009). Labor market experiences of Canadian immigrants with focus on foreign education and experience. *International Migration Review, 43*(2), 366–386.
28 Caligiuri, P. M. (2000). Selecting expatriates for personality characteristics: A moderating effect of personality on the relationship between host national contact and cr oss-cultural adjustment. *Management International Review, 40*(1), 61–80.
29 Cappellen, T., & Janssens, M. (2008). Global managers' career competencies. *Career Development International, 13*(6), 514–537.
30 Carling, J. (2008). Toward a demography of immigrant communities and their transnational potential. *International Migration Review, 42*(2), 449–475.
31 Carr, S., Inkson, K., & Thorn, K. (2005). From global careers to talent flow: Reinterpreting "brain drain." *Journal of World Business, 40*(4), 386–398.
32 Cerdin, J.-L., & Pargneux, M. L. (2009). Career and international assignment fit: Toward an integrative model of success. *Human Resource Management, 48*(1), 5–25.
33 Chew, K., Leach, M., & Liu, J. M. (2009). The revolving door to Gold Mountain: How Chinese immigrants got around U.S. exclusion and replenished the Chinese American labor pool, 1900–1910. *International Migration Review, 43*(2), 410–430.
34 Colakoglu, S., Tarique, I., & Caligiuri, P. (2009). Towards a conceptual framework for the relationship between subsidiary staffing strategy and subsidiary performance. *International Journal of Human Resource Management, 20*(6), 1291–1308.
35 Colic-Peisker, V. (2010). Free floating in the cosmopolis? Exploring the identity-belonging of transnational knowledge workers. *Global Networks, 10*(4), 467–488.
36 Collings, D., Scullion, H, & Morley, M. (2007). Changing patterns of global staffing in the multinational enterprise: Challenges to the conventional expatriate assignment and emerging alternatives. *Journal of World Business, 42*(2), 198–213.

37 Collins, F. L. (2008). Bridges to learning: International student mobilities, educa-tion agencies and inter-personal networks. *Global Networks, 8*(4), 398–417.
38 Conway, D., Potter, R. B., & Bernard, G. (2008). Dual citizenship or dual identity? Does "transnationalism" supplant "nationalism" among return-ing Trinidadians? *Global Networks, 8*(4), 373–397.
39 Crowley-Henry, M. (2007). The protean career: Exemplified by first world foreign residents in Western Europe? *International Studies of Management and Organization, 37*(3), 44–64.
40 De Cieri, H., Fenwick, M., & Hutchings, K. (2005). The challenge of interna-tional human resource management: Balancing the duality of strategy and practice. *International Journal of Human Resource Management, 16*(4), 584–598.
41 Dickmann, M., & Harris, H. (2005). Developing career capital for global careers: The role of international assignments. *Journal of World Business, 40*(4), 399–408.
42 Diehl, C., Koenig, M., & Ruckdeschel, K. (2009). Religiosity and gender equality: Comparing natives and Muslim migrants in Germany. *Ethnic and Racial Studies, 32*(2), 278–301.
43 Doherty, N., Dickmann, M., & Mills, T. (2011). Exploring the motives of company-backed and self-initiated expatriates. *International Journal of Human Resource Management, 22*(3), 595–611.
44 Ellis, D. R. (2012). Exploring cultural dimensions as predictors of perfor-mance management preferences: The case of self-initiating expatriate New Zealanders in Belgium. *International Journal of Human Resource Management,23(10)*, 2087–2107.
45 Emmerik, I. H. V., & Euwema, M. C. (2009). The international assignments of peacekeepers: What drives them to seek future expatriation? *Human Resource Management, 48*(1), 135–151.
46 Endres, D., Spengel, C., Elschner, C., & Schmidt, O. (2005). The tax burden of international assignments. *Intertax, 33*, 409–502.
47 Euwals, R., Dagevos, J., Gijsberts, M., & Roodenburg, H. (2010). Citizenship and labor market position: Turkish immigrants in Germany and the Neth-erlands. *International Migration Review, 44*(3), 513–538.
48 Fargues, P. (2009). Work, refuge, transit: An emerging pattern of irregular immigration South and East of the Mediterranean. *International Migra-tion Review, 43*(3), 544–577.
49 Farndale, E., Scullion, H., & Sparrow, P. (2010). The role of the corporate HR function in global talent management. *Journal of World Business, 45*(2), 161–168.
50 Feld, S. (2005). Labor force trends and immigration in Europe. *International Migration Review, 39*(3), 637–662.
51 Fitzgerald, C., & Howe-Walsh, L. (2008). Self-initiated expatriates: An inter-pretative phenomenological analysis of professional female expatriates. *International Journal of Business and Management, 3*(10), 156–175.
52 Forstenlechner, I. (2010). Brain drain in developed countries: Can govern-ments do anything to bring expatriates back? *Public Policy and Adminis-tration, 25*(2), 156–174.
53 Freeman, G. P., & Ögelman, N. (1998). Homeland citizenship policies and the status of third country nationals in the European Union. *Journal of Ethnic and Migration Studies, 24*(4), 769–788.
54 Furman, R., Negi, N., Schatz, M. C. S., & Jones, S. (2008). Transnational social work: Using a wraparound model. *Global Networks, 8*(4), 496–503.
55 Gabel, R. S., Dolan, S. L., & Cerdin, J.-L. (2005). Emotional intelligence as predictor of cultural adjustment for success in global assignments. *Career Development International, 10*(5), 375–395.

56 Gardner, K. (2006). The transnational work of kinship and caring: Bengali-British marriages in historical perspective. *Global Networks*, 6(4), 373–387.

57 Glick-Schiller, N. (2003). The centrality of ethnography in the study of transnational migration: Seeing the wetlands instead of the swamp. In E. N. Foner (Ed.), *American Arrivals* (pp. 99–128). Santa Fe: School of American Research Press.

58 Gustafson, P. (2008). Transnationalism in retirement migration: The case of North European retirees in Spain. *Ethnic and Racial Studies*, 31(3), 451–475.

59 Guzzo, R. A., Noonan, K. A., & Elron, E. (1994). Expatriate managers and the psychological contract. *Journal of Applied Psychology*, 79(4), 617–626.

60 Haller, W., & Landolt, P. (2005). The transnational dimensions of identity formation: Adult children of immigrants in Miami. *Ethnic and Racial Studies*, 28(6), 1182–1214.

61 Hao, L., & Kim, J. J. H. (2009). Immigration and the American obesity epidemic. *International Migration Review*, 43(2), 237–262.

62 Harris, H., & Brewster, C. (1999). The coffee-machine system: How international selection really works. *International Journal of Human Resource Management*, 10(3), 488–500.

63 Harrison, D. A., Shaffer, M. A., & Bhaskar-Shrinivas, P. (2004). Going places: Roads more and less traveled in research on expatriate experiences. *Research in Personnel and Human Resources Management*, 23(4), 199–247.

64 Haslberger, A., & Brewster, C. (2009). Capital gains: Expatriate adjustment and the psychological contract in international careers. *Human Resource Management*, 48(3), 379–397.

65 Heckhausen, H., & Gollwitzer, P. M. (1987). Thought contents and cognitive functioning in motivational versus volitional states of mind. *Motivation and Emotion*, 1(2), 101–120.

66 Heckhausen, J., & Heckhausen, H. (2010). *Motivation and action*. Cambridge: Cambridge University Press.

67 Howe-Walsh, L., & Schyns, B. (2010). Self-initiated expatriation: Implications for HRM. *International Journal of Human Resource Management*, 21(2), 260–273.

68 Hu, M., & Xia, J.-M. (2010). A preliminary research on self-initiated expatriation as compared to assigned expatriation. *Canadian Social Science*, 6(5), 169–177.

69 Huang, T.-J., Chi, S.-C., & Lawler, J. (2005).The relationship between expatriates' personality traits and their adjustment to international assignments. *International Journal of Human Resource Management*, 16(9), 1656–1670.

70 Hudson, S., & Inkson, K. (2006). Volunteer overseas development workers: The hero's adventure and personal transformation. *Career Development International*, 11(4), 304–320.

71 Inkson, K., Arthur, M. B., Pringle, J., & Barry, S. (1997). Expatriate assignment versus overseas experience: Contrasting models of international human resource development. *Journal of World Business*, 32(4), 351–368.

72 Inkson, K., Carr, S., Edwards, M., Hooks, J., Johnson, D., Thorn, K., & Allfree, N. (2004). From brain drain to talent flow: Views of Kiwi expatriates. *University of Auckland Business Review*, 6(2), 29–39.

73 Inkson, K., & Myers, B. A. (2003). "The big OE": Self-directed travel and career development. *Career Development International*, 8(4), 170–181.

74 Jokinen, T., Brewster, C., & Suutari, V. (2008). Career capital during international work experiences: Contrasting self-initiated expatriate experiences

38   *Maike Andresen, Franziska Bergdolt, and Jil Margenfeld*

75   and assigned expatriation. *International Journal of Human Resource Management, 19*(6), 979–998.
76   Knowles, C. (2006). Seeing race through the lens. *Ethnic and Racial Studies, 29*(3), 512–529.
77   Knowles, R. D., & Matthiesen, C. W. (2009). Barrier effects of international borders on fixed link traffic generation: The case of Īresundsbron. *Journal of Transport Geography, 17*(3), 155–165.
78   Konopaske, R., Robie, C., & Ivancevich, J. (2005). A preliminary model of spouse influence on managerial global assignment willingness. *International Journal of Human Resource Management, 16*(3), 405–426.
79   Krippendorff, K. (1980). *Content analysis. An introduction to its methodology.* London: Sage Publications.
80   Lauring, J., & Selmer, J. (2009). Expatriate compound living: An ethnographic field study. *International Journal of Human Resource Management, 20*(7), 1451–1467.
81   Levels, M., & Dronkers, J. (2008). Educational performance of native and immigrant children from various countries of origin. *Ethnic and Racial Studies, 31*(8), 1404–1425.
82   Lii, S.-Y., & Wong, S.-Y. (2008). The antecedents of overseas adjustment and commitment of expatriates. *International Journal of Human Resource Management, 19*(2), 296–313.
83   Lu, M. (1999). Do people move when they say they will? Inconsistencies in individual migration behavior. *Population and Environment: A Journal of Interdisciplinary Studies, 20*(5), 467–488.
84   Martiniello, M., & Lafleur, J.-M. (2008). Towards a transatlantic dialogue in the study of immigrant political transnationalism. *Ethnic and Racial Studies, 31*(4), 645–663.
85   Massey, D. S., & Bartley, K. (2006). The changing legal status distribution of immigrants: A caution. *International Migration Review, 39*(2), 469–484.
86   Maxwell, R. (2010). Evaluating migrant integration: Political attitudes across generations in Europe. *International Migration Review, 44*(1), 25–52.
87   Mayring, P. (2000). *Qualitative Inhaltsanalyse. Grundlagen und Techniken,* 7th ed. Weinheim: DeutscherStudienVerlag.
88   Mazzucato, V., & Kabki, M. (2009). Small is beautiful: The micro-politics of transnational relationships between Ghanaian hometown associations and communities back home. *Global Networks, 9*(2), 227–251.
89   McKenna, S., & Richardson, J. (2007). The increasing complexity of the internationally mobile professional: Issues for research and practice. *Cross Cultural Management, 14*(4), 307–320.
90   Meyskens, M., Von Glinow, M. A., Werther, W. B., & Clarke, L. (2009). The paradox of international talent: Alternative forms of international assignments. *International Journal of Human Resource Management, 20*(6), 1439–1450.
91   Milewski, N., & Hamel, C. (2010). Union formation and partner choice in a transnational context: The case of descendants of turkish immigrants in France. *International Migration Review, 44*(3), 615–658.
92   Millar, J., & Salt, J. (2007). Portfolios of mobility: The movement of expertise in transnational corporations in two sectors—Aerospace and extractive industries. *Global Networks, 8*(1), 25–50.
93   Moldenhawer, B. (2005). Transnational migrant communities and education strategies among Pakistani youngsters in Denmark. *Journal of Ethnic and Migration Studies, 31*(1), 51–78.
94   Myers, B., & Pringle, J. (2005). Self-initiated foreign experience as accelerated development: Influences of gender. *Journal of World Business, 40*(4), 421–431.

95 Näsholm, M. (2009). An identity construction perspective on careers of Swedish international itinerants. *Management Revue, 20*(1), 53–69.

96 O'Sullivan, A., & O'Sullivan, S. L. (2008). The performance challenges of expatriate supplier teams: A multi-firm case study. *International Journal of Human Resource Management, 19*(6), 999–1017.

97 Oda, E. (2010). Ethnic migration and memory: Disputes over the ethnic origins of Japanese Brazilians in Japan. *Ethnic and Racial Studies, 33*(3), 515–532.

98 Olsen, J. E., & Martins, L. L. (2009). The effects of expatriate demographic characteristics on adjustment: A social identity approach. *Human Resource Management, 48*(2), 311–328.

99 Painter, G., & Yu, Z. (2010). Immigrants and housing markets in mid-size metropolitan areas. *International Migration Review, 44*(2), 442–476.

100 Parreñas, R. S. (2010). Homeward bound: The circular migration of entertainers between Japan and the Philippines. *Global Networks, 10*(3), 301–323.

101 Paull, B., & Chu, W. (2003). Expatriate assignments—Tax and non-tax considerations. *International Tax Review,Special Issue: China Country Guide,* 63–75.

102 Peltokorpi, V. (2008). Cross-cultural adjustment of expatriates in Japan. *International Journal of Human Resource Management, 19*(9), 1588–1606.

103 Peltokorpi, V., & Froese, F. J. (2009). Organizational expatriates and self-initiated expatriates: Who adjusts better to work and life in Japan? *International Journal of Human Resource Management, 20*(5), 1096–1112.

104 Portes, A. (2009). Migration and development: Reconciling opposite views. *Ethnic and Racial Studies, 32*(1), 5–22.

105 Portes, A., Escobar, C., & Radford, A. W. (2007). Immigrant transnational organizations and development: A comparative study. *International Migration Review, 41*(1), 242–281.

106 Preibisch, K. (2010). Pick-your-own labor: Migrant workers and flexibility in Canadian agriculture. *International Migration Review, 44*(2), 404–441.

107 Pruthi, S., Wright, M., & Meyer, K. E. (2009). Staffing venture capital firms' international operations. *International Journal of Human Resource Management, 20*(1), 186–205.

108 Redstone Akresh, I. (2006). Occupational mobility among legal immigrants to the United States. *International Migration Review, 40*(4), 854–884.

109 Reiche, B. S. (2006). The inpatriate experience in multinational corporations: An exploratory case study in Germany. *International Journal of Human Resource Management, 17*(9), 1572–1590.

110 Richardson, J. (2006). Self-directed expatriation: Family matters. *Personnel Review, 35*(4), 469–486.

111 Richardson, J., & Mallon, M. (2005). Career interrupted? The case of the self-directed expatriate. *Journal of World Business, 40*(4), 409–420.

112 Richardson, J., & McKenna, S. (2000). Metaphorical "types" and human resource management: Self-selecting expatriates. *Industrial & Commercial Training, 32*(6), 209–218.

113 Richardson, J., & McKenna, S. (2006). Exploring relationships with home and host countries: A study of self-directed expatriates. *International Journal of Cross Cultural Management, 13*(1), 6–22.

114 Richardson, J., & Zikic, J. (2007). The darker side of an international academic career. *Career Development International, 12*(2), 164–186.

115 Rosen, P. B., Ekelman, F. B., & Lubbe, E. J. (2000). Managing expatriate employees: Employment law issues and answers. *Journal of Employment Discrimination Law, 2*(1), 110–123.

40   Maike Andresen, Franziska Bergdolt, and Jil Margenfeld

116 Rowthorn, R. (2008). The fiscal impact of immigration on the advanced economies. *Oxford Review of Economic Policy, 24*(3), 560–580.
117 Sánchez Vidal, M. E., Sanz Valle, R., & Aragón, M. I. B. (2008). International workers' satisfaction with the repatriation process. *International Journal of Human Resource Management, 19*(9), 1683–1702.
118 Scullion, H., Collings, D. G., & Gunnigle, P. (2007). International human resource management in the 21st century: Emerging themes and contemporary debates. *Human Resource Management Journal, 17*(4), 309–319.
119 Selmer, J., & Lauring, J. (2010). Self-initiated academic expatriates: Inherent demographics and reasons to expatriate. *European Management Review, 7*(3), 169–179.
120 Selmer, J., & Lauring, J. (2011a). Marital status and work outcomes of self-initiated expatriates: Is there a moderating effect of gender? *Cross Cultural Management: An International Journal, 18*(2), 198–213.
121 Selmer, J., & Lauring, J. (2011b). Acquired demographics and reasons to relocate among self-initiated expatriates. *International Journal of Human Resource Management, 22*(10), 2055–2070.
122 Siljanen, T., & Lämsä, A.-M. (2009). The changing nature of expatriation: Exploring cross-cultural adaptation through narrativity. *International Journal of Human Resource Management, 20*(7), 1468–1486.
123 Snel, E., Engbersen, G., & Leerkes, A. (2006). Transnational involvement and social integration. *Global Networks, 6*(3), 285–308.
124 Soehl, T., & Waldinger, R. (2010). Making the connection: Latino immigrants and their cross-border ties. *Ethnic and Racial Studies, 33*(9), 1489–1510.
125 Sparrow, P. R. (2007). Globalization of HR at function level: Four UK-based case studies of the international recruitment and selection process. *International Journal of Human Resource Management, 18*(5), 845–867.
126 Starr, T. L., & Currie, G. (2009). "Out of sight but still in the picture": Short-term international assignments and the influential role of family. *International Journal of Human Resource Management, 20*(6), 1421–1438.
127 Stuart, E. (2010). Art. 4 (2) of the OECD Model Convention: Practice and case law. In G. Maisto (Ed.), *Residence of Individuals under Tax Treaties and EC Law* (pp. 181–194). Amsterdam: IBFD Publications BV.
128 Surak, K. (2008). Convergence in foreigners' rights and citizenship policies? A look at Japan. *International Migration Review, 42*(3), 550–575.
129 Suutari, V., & Brewster, C. (2000). Making their own way: International experience through self-initiated foreign assignments. *Journal of World Business, 35*(4), 417–436.
130 Tams, S., & Arthur, M. B. (2007). Studying careers across cultures: Distinguishing international, cross-cultural, and globalization perspectives. *Career Development International, 12*(1), 86–98.
131 Tharenou, P. (2009). Self-initiated international careers: Gender differences and career outcomes. In S. G. Baugh and S. E. Sullivan (Eds.), *Maintaining Focus, Energy and Options over the Career* (pp. 197–226). Charlotte: Information Age Publishing.
132 Tharenou, P. (2010). Women's self-initiated expatriation as a career option and its ethical issues. *Journal of Business Ethics, 95*(1), 73–88.
133 Tharenou, P., & Caulfield, N. (2010). Will I stay or will I go? Explaining repatriation by self-initiated expatriates. *Academy of Management Journal, 53*(5), 1009–1028.
134 Tharenou, P., & Harvey, M. (2006). Examining the overseas staffing options utilized by Australian headquartered multinational corporations. *International Journal of Human Resource Management, 17*(6), 1095–1114.

135 Tharmaseelan, N., Inkson, K., & Carr, S. C. (2010). Migration and career success: Testing a time-sequenced model. *Career Development International, 15*(3), 218–238.

136 Thite, M., Srinivasan, V., Harvey, M., & Valk, R. (2009). Expatriates of host-country origin: "coming home to test the waters." *International Journal of Human Resource Management, 20*(2), 269–285.

137 Thomas, K. J. A. (2007). Child mortality and socioeconomic status: An examination of differentials by migration status in South Africa. *International Migration Review, 41*(1), 40–74.

138 Thorn, K. (2009). The relative importance of motives for international self-initiated mobility. *Career Development International, 14*(5), 441–464.

139 Trotz, D. A. (2006). Rethinking Caribbean transnational connections: Conceptual itineraries. *Global Networks, 6*(1), 41–59.

140 United Nations (1998). *Recommendations on statistics of international migration.* Statistical Papers Series M, No. 58, Rev. 1. New York: United Nations.

141 van der Heijden, J. A. V., van Engen, M. L., & Paauwe, J. (2009). Expatriate career support: Predicting expatriate turnover and performance. *International Journal of Human Resource Management, 20*(4), 831–845.

142 van Meeteren, M., Engbersen, G., & van San, M. (2009). Striving for a better position: Aspirations and the role of cultural, economic, and social capital for irregular migrants in Belgium. *International Migration Review, 43*(4), 881–907.

143 Vance, C. (2005). The personal quest for building global competence: A taxonomy of self-initiating career path strategies for gaining business experience abroad. *Journal of World Business, 40*(4), 374–385.

144 Waldinger, R. (2007). Did manufacturing matter? The experience of yesterday's second generation: A reassessment. *International Migration Review, 41*(1), 3–39.

145 Waldinger, R. (2008). Between "here" and "there": Immigrant cross-border activities and loyalties. *International Migration Review, 42*(1), 3–29.

146 Walsh, J., & Zhu, Y. (2007). Local complexities and global uncertainties: A study of foreign ownership and human resource management in China. *International Journal of Human Resource Management, 18*(2), 249–267.

147 Wang, M., & Takeuchi, R. (2007). The role of goal orientation during expatriation: A cross-sectional and longitudinal investigation. *Journal of Applied Psychology, 92*(5), 1437–1445.

148 Weiner, B. (1985). An attributional theory of achievement motivation and emotion. *Psychological Review, 92*(4), 548–573.

149 Welch, D. E., Welch, L. S., & Worm, V. (2007). The international business traveller: A neglected but strategic human resource. *International Journal of Human Resource Management, 18*(2), 173–183.

150 Wiles, J. (2008). Sense of home in a transnational social space: New Zealanders in London. *Global Networks, 8*(1), 116–137.

151 Williams, A. M. (2007). International labour migration and tacit knowledge transactions: A multi-level perspective. *Global Networks, 7*(1), 29–50.

152 Yamanaka, K. (2005). Changing family structures of Nepalese transmigrants in Japan: Split-households and dual-wage earners. *Global Networks, 5*(4), 337–358.

153 Zikic, J., Bonache, J., & Cerdin, J.-L. (2010). Crossing national boundaries: A typology of qualified immigrants' career orientations. *Journal of Organizational Behavior, 31*(5), 667–686.

3 Research on Self-Initiated Expatriation

History and Future Directions

Michael Dorsch, Vesa Suutari, and Chris Brewster

It is now well over a decade ago that our article "Making their own way: International experience through self-initiated foreign assignments" (Suutari & Brewster, 2000) introduced the concept of the Self-Initiated Expatriate (SIE). This is perhaps a good time to review what subsequent research has taught us and what we still need to know—a research agenda.

Of course, this is another case of academia identifying something that has existed for a long time. SIEs are not new; they have been around in employment for many years, though it is only recently that academics have realized they are there and begun to study them. Equally, as in all serious academic research, the field builds on the work of previous researchers: in this case a seminal piece of work by Inkson, Arthur, Pringle, and Barry from 1997, which looked at young people from the Antipodes (to use the British term) who were taking advantage of lighter visa restrictions to travel for a short period to the other side of the world (their antipodes) to get the "Big O"—overseas experience.

What distinguished SIEs from the "assigned expatriates" (AEs), as we called them, that had been the sole focus of study up to that time, was the fact that they had made their own way to a country other than their own and were now working there. Hence, we tried to distinguish them from (1) AEs sent by their organization on expatriate terms and conditions of employment, (2) students attending programs or parts of programs in other countries and retired people moving to (usually) warmer climates—each of these groups, while they might occasionally take a job, were not in the country for that purpose, and (3) immigrants who had made a commitment to a new country and intended, at least when they arrived, to stay there for the rest of their lives. As always with social science, these categories are clearer on paper than in reality, but the central distinctions were, we believed and still believe, clear.

This chapter examines the research that has been done on this group since 2000. This is not an easy task as more texts appeared even as we wrote this piece, and our summary does not include, for example, the work published in this book. Nevertheless, we attempt to summarize what we know from the work that has been done, using the mechanism of a series of questions and then, at the end of the chapter, identifying some things that we do not know so that we can suggest the outline of a research agenda.

WHY HAVE SIES ONLY RECENTLY BEEN NOTICED?

SIEs have only recently come to our attention: There are conceptual and empirical reasons for this. Conceptually, the study of SIEs fell between the disciplines of international human resource management (IHRM) and migration studies (see, for example, Dustmann, 1999; Millar & Salt, 2008; Navas, Garcia, Sánchez, Rojas, Pumares, & Fernández, 2005; Navas, Rojas, García, & Pumares, 2007; Salt, 2009; William & Balaz, 2005). The former were mostly interested in multinational company (MNC) strategies: This meant little attention to not-for-profit organizations, where SIEs were much more common, and little attention to issues that were not included in company strategies—and SIEs rarely were. Even when organizations employed significant numbers of them, SIEs were included in either the "expatriate" or, more usually since these were categories linked to their terms and conditions of employment, the "locally employed" categories. The approaches and views of the expatriates themselves only figured as issues for the company to deal with; the issues for expatriates and their families were seen as lying in the field of psychology. Migration studies were usually much more interested either in the effects of the geographical move on the economies losing the migrants or the economies they were joining or in the social, rather than the work, situation. Methodologically, most research into expatriates was carried out through MNCs. As they didn't generally categorize SIEs as a separate group, they did not show up in the research.

Things changed on both fronts. Conceptually, there has been some questioning of the IHRM literature's focus on the standard two/five-year expatriate assignment and increasing attention being paid to differing forms of expatriation (see e.g. Collings, Scullion, & Morley, 2007; Suutari & Brewster, 2009), and this is leading to a breaking down of the "expatriate or not expatriate" distinction and raising awareness of other options. Partly under pressure from politics, where governments have tried to square the circle of society's need for immigrants with the unpopularity of immigration in some quarters by focusing on high-level immigration, the line between the latter and expatriation is beginning to blur. It is clear that some immigrants return home quickly, and some expatriates stay on in their new country. Some authors (e.g. Haslberger & Brewster, 2008; 2009) are using the literature from one field to re-invigorate the other. In addition, there is more research now examining the issue from the point of view of the expatriate rather than their company, sometimes using narrative (e.g. Al Ariss, 2010; Inkson et al., 1997; Richardson, 2006; Vance, 2005) and sometimes using surveys (e.g. Biemann & Andresen, 2010; Cerdin & Le

Pargneux, 2010; Doherty, Dickmann, & Mills, 2011; Jokinen, Brewster, & Suutari, 2008) and in both cases realizing that there are a lot more foreigners working for companies than the expatriation literature allows for. There has also been increasing awareness of the impact of SIEs as a significant element of both company HRM strategy and an individual's career (e.g. Howe-Walsh & Schyns, 2010; Tharenou, 2010). Methodologically, partly as MNCs became increasingly unwilling to allow surveys, researchers looked for other sources: trade unions (Suutari & Brewster, 2000) or websites (Doherty et al., 2011), the public sector international organizations (Toomey & Brewster, 2008), or not-for-profits (Brewster & Lee, 2006; Hudson & Inkson, 2006). Inevitably these were not restricted to those that the MNCs categorized as expatriates, and so the phenomenon of SIE research began.

SO, WHAT DO WE KNOW ABOUT SIES?

What has the literature to date taught us about SIEs? To check this out, we examined articles that included the key words 'self-initiated,' 'global careers,' 'migrant workers,' 'labor mobility,' or 'self-development' in *Journal of World Business, International Journal of Human Resource Management, Career Development International, Thunderbird International Business Review,* and other journals from the years 2000 to 2010. Given the space constraints here, we summarize some of the main findings in response to six questions: What differentiates SIEs from AEs? What differentiates expatriates within the self-initiated category? What are the reasons for undertaking self-initiated expatriation? How well do SIEs adjust? What happens when they repatriate? And, what is the impact of self-initiated expatriation on careers?

WHAT DIFFERENTIATES SELF-INITIATED EXPATRIATES FROM ASSIGNED EXPATRIATES?

The fundamental difference that distinguishes AEs and SIEs revolves around the initiator of the decision to work outside the home country. SIEs decide on their own to go abroad to find work, without being sent by an organization from their home country, and they decide when to repatriate. In contrast, the initiative for a traditional expatriate assignment comes from an internationally operating company (Inkson et al., 1997) that sends employees abroad to perform in specified roles—even when the employees has asked for a foreign assignment, the decision to accede belongs with the organization. These two types of expatriates can often also be contrasted in terms of career type (see also Chapter 7). AEs are usually following an organizational career, whereas it is argued that SIEs pursue a boundaryless career (Biemann & Andresen, 2010; Inkson et al., 1997; Jokinen et al., 2008) in which they move between companies and countries. It is worth a small diversion here: SIEs and boundaryless careers are different concepts. They will in many cases overlap, but it is important to point out that there should be no assumption that they do—some SIEs will move to another country, speak the language of that country (Vance, 2005), have a partner from that country (Thorn, 2009), take a job, and remain in that country and job for the rest of their working lives.

Jokinen et al. (2008) found that Finnish AEs and SIEs differ significantly in terms of age, assignment tenure, number of previous work experiences, total length of previous foreign work experience, organizational position, promotion, as well as their concentration in public vs. private sector organizations. Furthermore, SIEs are on average slightly younger than AEs and are more often single (Suutari & Brewster, 2000). This group also contains a higher percentage of females. On the other hand, SIEs are less likely to be married or living with a partner and much less likely to have children with them (Cerdin & Le Pargneux, 2010). There appears to be no major difference between AEs and SIEs when it comes to the level of academic achievement—most hold at least a graduate degree. Most expatriates belong to the "middle or senior management" category, but SIEs are less likely to work for big international companies than AEs, and they tend to work at lower organizational positions (Jokinen et al., 2008).

Additionally, SIEs are more likely to accept further foreign assignments (Suutari & Brewster, 2000), have a higher organizational mobility in their careers, and have more intentions to change organizations (Biemann & Andresen, 2010). However, both types of expatriates report similar outcomes of their international assignments. Both groups perceive that working abroad had developed their competencies and career capital (Jokinen et al., 2008).

WHAT DIFFERENTIATES EXPATRIATES WITHIN THE SELF-INITIATED CATEGORY?

Researchers have divided expatriates up in a number of different ways since Suutari and Brewster (2000) suggested their categorization: (1) *Young opportunists* including the young people heading abroad for a prolonged period of travel, work, and tourism, as described by Inkson et al. (1997). In the 2000 study 15% of the self-initiated group were below 30 years old; (2) *job seekers* who had not gotten jobs or were unsatisfied with their jobs or careers at home (around a quarter); (3) *officials* typically working within international organizations such as the European Union and the United Nations, sometimes higher paid than the AEs (12% of the respondents); (4) *localized professionals* who went abroad as AEs but decided to stay there rather than return home at the end of their assignment (7% of the sample); (5) *international professionals*—the global careerists, "mercenaries," or international

46   *Michael Dorsch, Vesa Suutari, and Chris Brewster*

itinerants (Banai & Harry, 2004; Cappellen & Janssens, 2005; Jokinen, 2010; Mäkelä & Suutari, 2009; Suutari & Brewster, 2009; Suutari & Taka, 2004), who may have long experience of working in international operations, often for a wide range of companies and often among the high earners (another quarter of the SIEs); (6) *dual career couples* where one partner had followed the other to a foreign country and found themselves a job when they got there (38% of the dual couples in our sample).

Some researchers have divided the group by function: selecting out, for example, academics (Fu, Shaffer, & Harrison, 2004; Richardson, 2006; 2009; Richardson & Mallon, 2005; Richardson & McKenna, 2006) or students (Baruch, Budhwar, & Khatri, 2007; Fitzgerald & Howe-Walsh, 2008; Lee, 2005). There have been studies of SIE managers (Biemann & Andresen, 2010; Myers & Pringle, 2005; Suutari & Brewster, 2000) and non-managers (Al Rajhi, Poultry, Altman, Meltcalfe, & Roussel, 2006; Bozionelos, 2009; Fu et al., 2004).

SIEs have been studied from and in various geographies: with an extensive stream of studies from Australasia (De Cieri, Sheehan, Costa, Fenwick, & Cooper, 2009; Hudson & Inkson, 2006; Inkson et al., 1997; Inkson & Myers, 2003; Myers & Pringle, 2005; Tharenou, 2003; Tharenou & Caulfield, 2010; Thorn, 2009) and from Western Europe (Begley, Collings, & Scullion, 2008; Biemann & Andresen, 2010; Cerdin & Le Pargneux, 2010; Doherty et al., 2011; Jokinen et al., 2008; Peltokorpi & Froese, 2009; Suutari & Brewster, 2000). There have been interestingly few studies from the US (though see Vance, 2005). This may reflect the fact that little of this stream of literature has been in USA journals—itself probably a reflection of the relative youth of this research area—and that most research in the USA is done through companies and so tends to fail to identify SIEs. There has been, by contrast, a lot of research on self-initiated expatriation from the developing countries (Al Ariss, 2010; Al Ariss & Özbilgin, 2010; Dustmann, 1999; Felker, 2011; Tung & Lazarova, 2006; William & Balaz, 2005).

Others have picked up the Suutari and Brewster (2000) approach and explored particular types of SIEs. Thus, Banai and Harry, (2004) both of whom are expatriates and one of whom is an international itinerant himself have outlined the world of the peripatetic "footloose" SIE. McKenna and Richardson (2007) look at a similar group but using the terminology of the "internationally mobile professional."

WHAT ARE THE REASONS FOR UNDERTAKING SELF-INITIATED EXPATRIATION?

SIEs and company-AEs tend to have broadly similar motivations for their international experience, though the weight of particular motivations does seem to vary. Lifestyle is the dominant career anchor for both (Cerdin &

Le Pargneux, 2010; Doherty et al., 2011) but is more important for SIEs. Although, as might be expected, both have lifestyle and internationalism as significant motivators, perhaps slightly surprisingly internationalism is a more potent motivator for company-AEs (Cerdin & Le Pargneux, 2010). This might indicate that while the AE/ SIE distinction is important in ensuring that SIEs are not overlooked and are perhaps more significant for company HRM policies than had been understood, the distinction may not be so precise at the individual level: Some internationalism-anchored individuals will become SIEs; others may be inclined to use an organization as a means of facilitating their expatriation. Going abroad within the frames and with the support of a structured organization can be perceived as less risky and complicated than engaging in self-expatriation. Cerdin and Le Pargneux (2010) draw on Arthur and Rousseau's (1996) boundary-less career concept and its concerns with work-life balance, which lies at the heart of the lifestyle career anchor. The internationalism career anchor entails by definition the crossing of physical boundaries such as organizational and geographic ones. This is consistent with the boundaryless career, which encompasses crossing various kinds of boundaries, not only organizational ones (Arnold & Cohen, 2008; Inkson, 2006). That these two anchors are equally prevalent for both AEs and SEs indicates that both types of expatriates can be engaged in a boundaryless career.

Motivation can be examined through different lenses than career anchors. Doherty et al. (2011) show that while, for example, career factors were seen as important by both AEs and SIEs—more by the former—for SIEs location and the host country reputation were particularly important. Where SIEs are focused on career, the prestige of posts in the host country is an important factor.

The motivations of different types of SIEs have been studied by a number of authors (and see also Chapter 3). They have examined particularly the motivations of students, graduates, and academics: presumably because they were a more available sample rather than through self-obsession. Thus, we find that being educated or taking a course in another country is likely to lead to a significant percentage of students looking for work there; some intending to stay for a long time (Baruch et al., 2007; Vance, 2005). Ties with family members in the country make staying more likely; strong ties with family members at home reduce the likelihood. Students from India were more likely to want to stay in the UK than students from China, Taiwan, and Thailand (Baruch et al., 2007).

Young graduates were studied by Tharenou (2003), who found that the major reasons for taking international jobs were cross-cultural experiences, growth, career prospects, excitement, and meeting new and different people. Like Baruch et al. (2007) and Jokinen et al. (2008), she found that labor markets—or perceptions of labor markets—at home and abroad influenced the decision. Other factors were working in organizations with an increasing international focus and having low family influence and no partner.

Academic SIEs have been studied by Fu et al. (2004), Richardson (2009), Selmer and Lauring (2010; 2011), and Richardson and Mallon (2005). Richardson and Mallon (2005) found that in most cases the opportunity to expatriate came by chance: A meeting at a conference or 'coming across' an advertisement rather than deliberately setting out to seek a foreign position. The chance having arisen, these academics were then driven by three dominant motivations: adventure/travel, life change, and family (though financial reasons were significant in a number of cases). For the academics in their sample, it seemed that demographic factors were of little significance. All of their respondents expected the international experience to be positive for their career prospects, based on perceptions of the "internationalization" of higher education. The research also suggests that family plays a key role—the academic SIEs argued that the desire to broaden their children's experiences was an important incentive.

Although there have been few empirical studies of the motivations of SIEs in the not-for-profit arena, there is some evidence in the work that has been done to indicate that SIEs are more likely to have motivations that include drivers such as being values based (Doherty et al., 2011) or having dedication to a cause (Cerdin & Le Pargneux, 2010) that fit well with such a motivation. Hudson and Inkson (2006) examined volunteer overseas development workers: Their article having the great sub-title of "the hero's adventure and personal transformation," reflecting some attempts in the standard expatriation literature to draw parallels between expatriation and Parsifal's journey. Volunteers from richer countries working in underdeveloped states understood their assignments as opportunities for challenges, related to physical difficulties, to cultural attitudes and to a psychological questioning of themselves, their own motivations, and the assignment. They acquired personal and technical skills, awareness and discovery of self, cross-cultural adjustment skills, and, significantly for us here, developed a much clearer and more profound understanding of their personal values (see also Chapter 10).

HOW WELL DO SIES ADJUST?

Once the SIEs have made the decision to move internationally, their adjustment becomes a key issue. Adjustment is perhaps not well conceptualized at present (see Haslberger, Brewster, & Hippler, 2012) and Al Ariss (2010) has offered a framework for understanding different "modes of engagement" through which ethnic minority SIEs approach and work their way through the various national and work structures and barriers that they have to cope with. These are maintenance, transformation, entrepreneurship, and opt out. Maintenance implies recognizing career barriers and working with them in order to obtain a desired career outcome; transformation denotes identifying barriers to career advancement and trying to alter them; entrepreneurship means taking an additional risk by opening a new business to avoid discrimination and legal constraints; and opt out occurs when SIEs are confronted with obstacles which push them to operate outside existing structures and entails an individual sense of objective and subjective failure to develop a desirable career outcome.

The existing research tells us that as far as adjustment—and perhaps performance?—are concerned, mentoring and supportive relationships with peers are far more beneficial than cultural training for SIEs (Bozionelos, 2009). It seems, though, that SIEs tend to be rather good at adjusting to host country nationals (Peltokorpi & Froese, 2009). Indeed, Richardson and McKenna (2006) conducted a careful examination of SIEs relationships with their host and home country; also finding, as might have been anticipated, that the host country relationships took an important place for SIEs and suggesting that the composite and dynamic dimension of those relationships might be used to inform more effective management practices. Fu et al. (2004) examined the adjustment of SIE English teachers in Hong Kong and found relationships between socialization tactics and organizational fit, social fit, and cultural fit. They noted that SIEs tend to adopt proactive socialization tactics on these issues and are sometimes helped in that by their organizations. Not surprisingly, it seems that language skills assist the process of adjustment (Dustmann, 1999).

It has also been argued that HRM for SIEs should consider expanding support into non-work areas, such as supporting partner relocation or helping to find accommodation (Howe-Walsh & Schyns, 2010).

Like Al Ariss (2010) and Begley et al. (2008), among others, Lee (2005) reminds us that not all SIEs adjust easily or successfully and that there is a dark side to this aspect of IHRM as there is, perhaps, to others.

WHAT HAPPENS WHEN SIES REPATRIATE?

Many SIEs never return home. They adopt the lifestyle of their new country, and for them it becomes home. However, others do return home, and there have been a number of studies of their desire to repatriate (and see also Chapter 8). As would be expected, the more embedded in work and the community the SIE is, the less likely they are to want to return to their country of origin. Pressures from home were the counter to that as were "shocks" (loss of work, family separation, etc.) that tended to trigger thoughts of return. SIEs who had experienced these declared that they would be considering repatriation within the year (Tharenou & Caulfield, 2010). Career issues tended to figure rarely in such decisions, but lifestyle issues were important.

De Cieri et al. (2009) found, unsurprisingly, that AEs are more likely to repatriate than SIEs and that the longer one is abroad the more likely one is to stay there. More interestingly, they found that demographic factors had little impact on a decision as to whether or not to repatriate but, similar to Tharenou and Caulfield (2010), they found that lifestyle was important—though in this case in the opposite direction. For their sample of Australian SIEs, a strong national identity, often linked to their feeling that quality of life is higher in Australia than in their host country, was positively associated with an intention to repatriate. Cultural similarity between the home country and the host country seems to play a part in the decision as to whether to stay abroad or return home—at least for nurses in Saudi Arabia (Bozionelos, 2009). Other evidence indicates that family plays an important role too (Richardson, 2006): Relationships and interaction with family back home may lead to greater likelihood of repatriation, especially at particular points in life (sick parents, etc.), while having more extended family members in the new country may encourage intention to stay.

There have also been studies of repatriates and what they feel about returning to their country of origin. Tung and Lazarova (2006) examined repatriation to central and Eastern Europe of people who had lived abroad for an extensive period of time. They found that in most cases they readjusted very quickly after return. This may have been because they found work relatively easily upon return, and their language and cultural competencies, their technical skills, and international experience held them in good stead. Repatriates from higher developed countries found it more difficult than repatriates from poorer countries. By contrast, Begley et al. (2008), reporting on Ireland using data collected before the economic crisis that began in that year and was more severe in that country than in most others, found that even then SIEs had real problems finding work. Having difficulties in finding a job leads to feelings of frustration, disappointment, and dissatisfaction with life back home.

As we have seen, most studies of SIEs are studies of highly qualified employees. This may reflect the reality or it may reflect the research tools and databases that the researchers are using. Studies from the migration world (William & Balaz, 2005) show that as far as Slovakians returning from the UK are concerned, most of whom had travelled under government, European Union, or British Council exchanges, it is clear that the financial gains to professional and managerial migrants are, comparatively, slightly better than those for unskilled SIEs.

WHAT IS THE IMPACT OF SELF-INITIATED EXPATRIATION ON CAREERS?

The final issue that we have space to address here concerns the longer-term consequences of self-initiated expatriation on employment careers (see also Chapter 7). Again, the few studies that there are tend to be concerned with the top end of the employment market (see, for example, Al Ariss & Özbilgin, 2010; Felker, 2011). It is clear that SIEs, as much as AEs, are looking for successful careers and that they define success in similar ways (Cerdin & Le Pargneux, 2010). Furthermore, there seems some evidence that the experience of being a SIE tends to be good for careers (Richardson & McKenna, 2006). Al Ariss and Özbilgin (2010), on the other hand, explored the international work experiences of Lebanese SIEs living in and around Paris and found that they faced significant problems in utilizing their skills. Felker (2011) similarly studied the experiences of young, well-educated Eastern Europeans who have moved to Western Europe in search of opportunities for professional development, largely because of the lack of such opportunities in their home countries. It seems that although this opportunity push out of their own countries is the motivation for the move, few of them seriously research the career and employment options in the host country prior to moving and hence, like the Lebanese in Paris, often find that their skills are underutilized. From a human resource management point of view, it means that organizations are often failing to get the maximum, or even an optimum, value from the SIEs.

WHAT DO WE NOT KNOW? WHAT ARE THE DIRECTIONS FOR FUTURE RESEARCH?

The reality of course is that research into self-initiated expatriation is in its infancy. This book may be seen as a kind of milestone or rite of passage— getting a book published on an area is an indication that it is beginning to grow beyond the baby stage toward adulthood. As we indicate, none of the questions that we raised above has anything approaching a definitive answer and even with the addition of the contributions to this text, there is still much to research. The following paragraphs indicate some of the areas in which further contributions are needed.

We need to clarify our terminology. Without explicit definition, little progress can be made. What are the boundaries to be drawn between, for example, high level immigrants who may or may not stay in a country for a lengthy period, company-AEs, and highly skilled SIEs? When we discuss SIEs are we talking about highly skilled and qualified individuals, poorly qualified individuals, or both? It seems unlikely that similar findings will apply in all cases. Are we talking about all those working in the country who have not been sent by a company or are there significant differences between SIEs from different parts of the world (developed countries versus developing countries, for example, or different cultural groupings)?

Connected to the terminological issues, we need to explore some of the largely unresearched SIEs—those from certain parts of the world (South America, for instance), those who have applied through competitive examination to join the United Nations or the World Bank, those who work for not-for-profit organizations such as governments, charities, and religious bodies, and those who are in effect "trailing" others who have made the move more deliberately.

Since the group of SIEs is so diverse, the differences between the different subgroups of SIEs need to be explored more seriously in the future. It may be that the differences between different subgroups of SIEs (e.g. global careerists within global companies vs. international academics) are from some perspectives (e.g. career or compensation perspectives) even larger than the differences between some groups of SIEs and AEs (e.g.at the higher levels of global organizations). There is therefore a need to do more comparative research among these different types of SIEs in order to really take the diversity into account.

Despite the encouraging number of studies contrasting SIEs and AEs (eg. Biemann & Andresen, 2010; Cerdin & Le Pargneux, 2010; Doherty et al., 2011; Jokinen et al., 2008; Peltokorpi, 2008; Peltokorpi & Froese, 2009; Suutari & Brewster, 2000), clearly more research is still needed in order to validate the different findings appearing from very different samples. Without that, we will be unable to identify the extent to which these two categories really are different.

We need to be clearer about the theoretical base that underpins our research. Until very recently at least, most of the work on SIEs has been largely a (much needed) data collection exercise. Theories will follow focus and different aspects of the topic may base themselves on different theoretical foundations, but resource dependency theory and theories of resource-based value might be appropriate in some cases. There are increasingly strong theoretical developments underlying career theory and the development of social capital.

Theoretically too, we need more studies of the impact of gender on self-initiated expatriation. The studies by Fitzgerald and Howe-Walsh (2008) and Tharenou (2003) indicate that there are differences. The study by Myers and Pringle (2005), which found that women may get more career benefits than men, contrasts with some other studies (see e.g. Jokinen et al., 2008; Selmer & Lauring, 2011), which found little impact from gender and others (Al Ariss & Özbilgin, 2010) that found significant gender-related disadvantages. The focus of studies and the contextual environment may account for some of these differences, but there must be a call for more research in this area.

The link to migration studies also offers a rich basis for collaborative work. The IHRM and the migration literatures have tended to run along parallel tracks—going in the same direction but rarely crossing over. We need more points at which the learning from one can reinforce the other. As Al Ariss and Özbilgin (2010) remind us, the migration literature has hardly ever explored the management of skilled migrants, but equally the SIE literature has failed to learn much from the migration theories.

There is scope for development on the empirical side too. It will be important to spread the research to more countries. In this respect, the SIE literature is perhaps less guilty of focusing on the developed countries than many other of the IHRM literatures and the claim that we made in previous work, that developing countries are an "almost hidden aspect of the international labor market" (Jokinen et al., 2008, p. 979) may be becoming less true. This is a positive trend. The problems that SIEs can face, partly perhaps as a result of ethnic discrimination (Al Ariss & Özbilgin, 2010), need further study.

Also empirically, much of the research that we have cited above has been dependent on small samples. This may explain some of the varying findings between researchers that have been achieved up to now—though we are tempted to think that contextual factors may also be important in those explanations. However, the need for more soundly based research is apparent. We do not argue that quantitative research is the only way forward—some of the more recent narrative research has been richly informative—but we would argue that SIE research has by now gone past the stage where statistically dubious findings and assumptions were, even so, a step forward in our understanding. There is a need for the more serious research that can only be done with larger samples and the more sophisticated statistics that such samples provide. One consequence is that very little of this research has been published in the prestigious journals. It is time that this was changed.

REFERENCES

Al Ariss, A. (2010). Modes of engagement: Migration, self-initiated expatriation, and career development. *Career Development International, 15*(4), 338–358.

Al Ariss, A., & Özbilgin, M. (2010). Understanding self-initiated expatriates: Career experiences of Lebanese self-initiated expatriates in France. *Thunderbird International Business Review, 52*(4), 275–285.

Al Rajhi, I., Poultry, A.-W., Altman, Y., Meltcalfe, B., & Roussel, J. (2006). Managing impatriate adjustment as a core human resource challenge. *Human Resource Planning, 29*(4), 15–23.

Arnold, J., & Cohen, L. (2008). The psychology of careers in industrial and organizational settings: A critical but appreciative analysis. In G. P. Hodgkinson and J. K. Ford (Eds.), *International Review of Industrial and Organizational Psychology 2008, Vol. 23* (pp. 1–44). Chichester, UK: Wiley.

Arthur, M. B., & Rousseau, D. M. (1996). *The boundaryless career: A new employment principle for a new organizational era*. New York: Oxford University Press.

Banai, M., & Harry, W. (2004). Boundaryless global careers. The international itinerants. *International Studies of Management and Organization, 34*(3), 96–120.

Baruch, Y., Budhwar, P. S., & Khatri, N. (2007). Brain drain: Inclination to stay abroad after studies. *Journal of World Business, 42*(1), 99–112.

Begley, A., Collings, D. G., & Scullion, H. (2008). The cross-cultural adjustment of self-initiated repatriates to the Republic of Ireland labour market. *Employee Relations, 30*(3), 264–282.

Biemann, T., & Andresen, M. (2010). Self-initiated foreign expatriates versus assigned expatriates. Two distinct types of international careers? *Journal of Managerial Psychology, 25*(2), 430–448.

Bozionelos, N. (2009). Expatriation outside the boundaries of the multinational corporation: A study with expatriate nurses in Saudi Arabia. *Human Resource Management, 48*(1), 111–134.

Brewster, C., & Lee, S. (2006). HRM in not-for-profit international organizations: Different, but also alike. In H. H. Larsen and W. Mayrhofer (Eds.), *European Human Resource Management* (pp. 131–148). London: Routledge.

Cappellen, T., & Janssens, M. (2005). Career paths of global managers: Towards future research. *Journal of World Business, 40*(4), 348–360.

Cerdin, J.-L., & Le Pargneux, M. (2010). Career anchors: A comparison between organization-assigned and self-initiated expatriates. *Thunderbird International Business Review, 52*(4), 287–299.

Collings, D. G., Scullion, H., & Morley, M. J. (2007). Changing patterns of global staffing in the multinational enterprise: Challenges to the conventional expatriate assignment and emerging alternatives. *Journal of World Business, 42*(2), 198–213.

De Cieri, H., Sheehan, C., Costa, C., Fenwick, M., & Cooper, B. K. (2009). International talent flow and intention to repatriate: An identity perspective. *Human Resource Development International, 12*(3), 243–261.

Doherty, N., Dickmann, M., & Mills, T. (2011). Exploring the motives of company-backed and self-initiated expatriates. *International Journal of Human Resource Management, 22*(3), 595–611.

Dustmann, C. (1999). Temporary migration, human capital, and language fluency of migrants. *Scandinavian Journal of Economics, 101*(2), 297–314.

Felker, J. A. (2011). Professional development through self-directed expatriation: Intentions and outcomes for young, educated Eastern Europeans. *International Journal of Training and Development, 15*(1), 76–86.

Fitzgerald, C., & Howe-Walsh, L. (2008). Self-initiated expatriates: An interpretative phenomenological analysis of professional female expatriates. *International Journal of Business and Management, 3*(10), 156–175.

Fu, C. K., Shaffer, M. A., & Harrison, D. A. (2004, December). *Adaptation of self-initiated foreign employees: The influence of organizational and proactive socialization tactics.* Paper presented at the Asian Academy of Management, Shanghai, China.

Haslberger, A., & Brewster, C. (2008). The expatriate family—An international perspective. *Journal of Managerial Psychology, 23*(3), 324–346.

Haslberger, A., & Brewster, C. (2009). Capital gains: Expatriate adjustment and the psychological contract in international careers. *Human Resource Management, 48*(3), 379–397.

Haslberger, A., Brewster, C., & Hippler, T. (2012). *Expatriate adjustment: A new model for understanding and managing performance.* London: Routledge.

Howe-Walsh, L., & Schyns, B. (2010). Self-initiated expatriation: Implications for HRM. *International Journal of Human Resource Management, 21*(2), 260–273.

Hudson, S., & Inkson, K. (2006). Volunteer overseas development workers: The hero's adventure and personal transformation. *Career Development International, 11*(4), 304–320.

Inkson, K. (2006). Protean and boundaryless careers as metaphors. *Journal of Vocational Behaviour, 69*(1), 48–63.

Inkson, K., Arthur, M. B., Pringle, J., & Barry, S. (1997). Expatriate assignment versus overseas experience: Contrasting models of international human resource development. *Journal of World Business, 32*(4), 351–368.

Inkson, K., & Myers, B. A. (2003). "The big OE": Self-directed travel and career development. *Career Development International, 8*(4), 170–181.

Jokinen, T. (2010). Development of career capital through international assignments and its transferability to new contexts. *Thunderbird International Business Review, 52*(4), 325–336.

Jokinen, T., Brewster, C., & Suutari, V. (2008). Career capital during international work experiences: Contrasting self-initiated expatriate experiences and assigned expatriation. *International Journal of Human Resource Management, 19*(6), 979–998.

Lee, C. H. (2005). A study of underemployment among self-initiated expatriates. *Journal of World Business, 40*(2), 172–187.

Mäkelä, K., & Suutari, V. (2009). Global careers: A social capital paradox. *International Journal of Human Resource Management, 20*(5), 992–1008.

McKenna, S., & Richardson, J. (2007). The increasing complexity of the internationally mobile professional. Issues for research and practice. *Cross Cultural Management, 14*(4), 307–320.

Millar, J., & Salt, J. (2008). Portfolios of mobility: the movement of expertise in transnational corporations in two sectors—Aerospace and extractive industries. *Global Networks, 8*(1), 25–50.

Myers, B., & Pringle, J. K. (2005). Self-initiated experience as accelerated development: Influence of gender. *Journal of World Business, 40*(4), 421–431.

Navas, M., Garcia, M. C., Sánchez, J., Rojas, A. J., Pumares, P., & Fernández, J. S. (2005). Relative Acculturation Extended Model (RAEM): New contributions with regard to the study of acculturation. *International Journal of Intercultural Relations, 29*, 21–37.

Navas, M., Rojas, A. J., García, M., & Pumares, P. (2007). Acculturation strategies and attitudes according to the Relative Acculturation Extended Model (RAEM): The perspectives of natives versus immigrants. *International Journal of Intercultural Relations, 31*(1), 67–86.

Peltokorpi, V. (2008). Cross-cultural adjustment of expatriates in Japan. *International Journal of Human Resource Management, 19*(9), 1588–1606.

Peltokorpi, V., & Froese, F. (2009). Organizational expatriates and self-initiated expatriates: Who adjusts better to work and life in Japan? *International Journal of Human Resource Management, 20*(5), 1096–1112.

Richardson, J. (2006). Self-directed expatriation: Family matters. *Personnel Review, 35*(4), 469–486.

Richardson, J. (2009). Geographic flexibility in academia: A cautionary note. *British Journal of Management, 20*, 160–170.

Richardson, J., & Mallon, M. (2005). Career interrupted? The case of the self-directed expatriate. *Journal of World Business, 40*(4), 409–420.

Richardson, J., & McKenna, S. (2006). Exploring relationships with home and host countries. A study of self-directed expatriates. *Cross Cultural Management: An International Journal, 13*(1), 6–22.

Salt, J. (2009). New forms of mobility in Europe: Global corporate labour markets and the international movement of expertise. In M. Duszczyka and M. Lesinskiez (Eds.), *Wspolczesne Migracje: Dylematy Europy I Polski* (pp. 15–25). Warsaw: University of Warsaw Press.

Selmer, J., & Lauring, J. (2010). Self-initiated academic expatriates: Inherent demographics and reasons to expatriate. *European Management Review, 7*(3), 169–179.

Selmer, J., & Lauring, J. (2011). Marital status and work outcomes of self-initiated expatriates: Is there a moderating effect of gender? *Cross Cultural Management: An International Journal, 18*(2), 198–213.

Suutari, V., & Brewster, C. (2000). Making their own way: International experience through self-initiated foreign assignments. *Journal of World Business, 35*(4), 417–436.

Suutari, V., & Brewster, C. (2009). Beyond expatriation: Different forms of international employment. In P. Sparrow (Ed.), *Handbook of International Human Resource Management: Integrating People, Process and Context* (pp. 131–150). Chichester, UK: Wiley.

Suutari, V., & Taka, M. (2004). Career anchors of managers with global careers. *Journal of Management Development, 23*(9), 833–847.

Tharenou, P. (2003). The initial development of receptivity to working abroad: Self-initiated international work opportunities in young graduate employees. *Journal of Occupational and Organizational Psychology, 76*(4), 489–515.

Tharenou, P. (2010). Women's self-initiated expatriation as a career option and its ethical issues. *Journal of Business Ethics, 95*(1), 73–88.

Tharenou, P., & Caulfield, N. (2010). Will I stay or will I go? Explaining repatriation by self-initiated expatriates. *Academy of Management Journal, 53*(5), 1009–1028.

Thorn, K. (2009). The relative importance of motives for international self-initiated mobility. *Career Development International, 14*(5), 441–464.

Toomey, E., & Brewster, C. (2008). International HRM in International Organizations. In C. Brewster, P. Sparrow and M. Dickmann (Eds.), *International Human Resource Management: Contemporary Issues in Europe*, 2nd ed. (pp. 289–306) London: Routledge.

Tung, R. L., & Lazarova, M. (2006). Brain drain versus brain gain: An exploratory study of ex-host country nationals in Central and Eastern Europe. *International Journal of Human Resource Management, 17*(11), 1853–1872.

Vance, C. (2005). The personal quest for building global competence: A taxonomy of self-initiating career path strategies for gaining business experience abroad. *Journal of World Business, 40*(4), 374–385.

William, A. M., & Balaz, V. (2005). What human capital, which migrants? Returned skilled migration to Slovakia from the UK. *International Migration Review, 39*(2), 439–468.

Part II

Understanding the Processes of Self-Initiated Expatriation

4 Motivation of Self-Initiated Expatriates

Jean-Luc Cerdin

This chapter examines Self-Initiated Expatriates' (SIE) motivation to go abroad. Although SIEs tend to be extensively used by organizations (Jokinen, Brewster, & Suutari, 2008), their drivers to go abroad remain largely unknown. Only very recently, researchers have focused on the specific drivers of SIEs (e.g. Cerdin & Le Pargneux, 2008 ; Dickmann, Doherty, & Mills, 2008). As the labor market becomes more and more global, the number of SIEs is likely to increase. Therefore, organizations should improve their knowledge of individuals' motivations to go abroad, so that they can attract them. The motivation behind expatriation constitutes a very relevant piece of information for HR practices (Howe-Walsh & Schyns, 2010). As SIEs represent an increasing source of talents which organizations can harness, this type of information is invaluable for organizations seeking to improve their talent management.

Research on motivation factors of expatriates essentially concerns assigned expatriates (AEs), henceforth AEs (e.g. Dickmann, Doherty, Mills, & Brewster, 2008; Stahl & Cerdin, 2004; Stahl, Miller, & Tung, 2002). As international experience encompasses more and more diverse types of mobility (e.g. Collings, Scullion, & Morley, 2007), studies on motivation to go abroad should reach beyond traditional expatriates. More empirical studies are needed to understand the motivation of SIEs to go abroad and what differentiates this particular kind of expatriates from the more traditional AEs.

SIEs are individuals who choose to go abroad on their own to find work there, or after having found a job prior to departure, without having been sent by an organization from their home country. They may not have a definite time frame in mind at the moment of leaving (e.g. Suutari & Brewster, 2000). However, the label "SIE" implies to some extent the wish of returning to the home country (e.g. Tharenou & Caulfied, 2010). Although migrants too are SIEs, the time frame for their international experience is usually longer than for expatriates. Cerdin, Abdeljalil Diné, and Brewster (2011) underscore that a defining feature of qualified immigrants (QIs) is an international move undertaken with a very long-term perspective. Thus, all QIs can be considered as SIEs to the extent that they initiate their move, but all SIEs are not migrants. Only SIEs who stay abroad definitively become permanent immigrants (Al Ariss & Özbilgin, 2010). This long-term time frame leads to consider immigrants' motivation as idiosyncratic among SIEs (Cerdin & Abdeljalil, 2007). In any case, a self-initiated expatriation is a personal odyssey (Inkson, Arthur, Pringle, & Barry, 1997) whose motivations are not sufficiently known.

Comparing SIEs and AEs is useful in understanding factors, which motivate SIEs. Traditional expatriates, labeled here as AEs, are usually defined as employees who temporarily leave their home country organization for an assignment lasting from two to five years in a foreign subsidiary with the intention of returning to their home country once the assignment is completed (Guzzo, 1997).

Based on the theory of fit, Cerdin and Le Pargneux (2009) suggest that variables of career decision, such as motivation to go abroad, and individual career characteristics, such as career anchors, influence international assignment (IA) success. Cerdin and Le Pargneux (2010), in exploring the career orientations of SIEs and AEs in terms of career anchors, went beyond expatriates' motivation factors. This chapter will attempt to show that studying career anchors helps to explain the motivation of SIEs to go abroad, as do the variables of protean and boundaryless career attitude (Briscoe, Hall, & DeMuth, 2006).

The first section of this chapter addresses pull and push factors in order to explain the drivers to go abroad for SIEs. It relies on two studies, one conducted on a sample of professional SIEs and the other on a sample of QIs. Then, the second section presents the career anchors of SIEs in order to understand their career orientation. The third section focuses on protean and boundaryless career attitudes. For each of these sections, this chapter contrasts the results obtained for SIEs with those for AEs. The last section discusses the results and presents an agenda for future research on SIEs as well as some practical implications.

PULL AND PUSH FACTORS

Recent research focuses on expatriate motivation through 12 factors, namely, (1) monetary considerations, (2) family considerations (non-job related), (3) normal career advancement pattern, (4) professional development, (5) personal challenge, (6) importance of the job itself, (7) future opportunities for advancement, (8) encouragement from colleagues and superiors, (9) encouragement from spouse or partner, (10) geographic location of the assignment, (11) desire to escape from a social or economic environment related to the home country, and (12) desire to escape from personal problems at home. Cerdin and Le Pargneux (2008) measure motivation using these 12 items. They have taken the 10 first items from Stahl et al. (2002) and Stahl and Cerdin (2004). These factors correspond to positive or pull factors. The last two factors come from Borg (1988) and Torbiörn (1976). They represent negative motivation, otherwise known as push factors.

PULL FACTORS

Some studies on AEs have found that "personal challenge" and "professional development" are the most important drivers of going abroad (Stahl & Cerdin, 2004; Stahl et al., 2002). These results are notably explained by the fact that individuals today are engaged in new careers, characterized by diminished job security. Additionally, the relationships between employers and employees also have changed and taken on a more transactional nature. In this context, they place the acquisition of skills and capacities first to preserve their employability in the long-term (Arthur & Rousseau, 1996; Eby, Butts, & Lockwood, 2003). In this context, individuals are deeply concerned by their own development, both personal and professional. In particular, they seek psychologically meaningful work in an effort to improve their employability (Sullivan, 1999). An expatriation can be perceived as "on-the-job training" through the development of skills highly rewarded on both the internal and external job markets. Drivers related to career development and advancement, such as "future opportunities for advancement" and "normal career advancement pattern," should rank high for SIEs because they reflect a concern for employability, which SIEs especially should seek to maintain. However, as they are to some extent left "on their own" for an international mobility, their international experience is likely to be more of a "personal challenge" than it is for AEs.

SIES AND AES SAMPLE

Results reported in this chapter stem from a sample of 138 SIEs. The comparison sample is made of 165 AEs. Theses expatriates come from a large variety of sectors such as information, major consumer outlets, automobile, food industry, banking, IT, hotel management, and metallurgy. Of all the expatriates, men make up 71.6% of the sample, and women account for the remaining 28.4%. Among the SIEs, 58.7% are men and 41.3% women. One striking difference between SIEs and AEs is the highest percentage of women among SIEs.

Cerdin and Le Pargneux (2008) asked SIEs and AEs the following question using a 5-point Likert-type scale ranging from 1 = not at all to 5 = very highly: "To what extent would you say the following items were motivational drivers for your decision to go abroad?" Figure 4.1 sums up expatriates' responses on the 12 motivation factors based on Borg (1988), Stahl et al. (2002), Stahl and Cerdin (2004), and Torbiörn (1976).

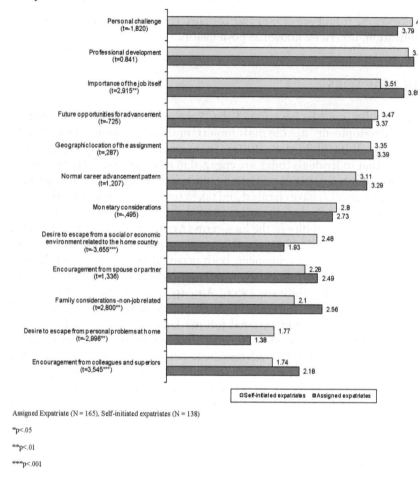

Assigned Expatriate (N = 165), Self-initiated expatriates (N = 138)

*p<.05

**p<.01

***p<.001

Figure 4.1   Motivations to be SIEs or AEs (mean scores and significance).

The results in Figure 4.1 indicate that for SIEs and AEs motives such as professional development, the importance of the job itself, and personal challenge played a major role in the decision to embark on an international mobility. The three first motivation factors for SIEs are, in order of importance, (1) personal challenge, (2) professional development, and (3) importance of the job itself. The three first motivation factors for AEs are (1) professional development, followed by (2) importance of the job itself, and (3) personal challenge.

Cerdin and Le Pargneux (2008) anticipated that professional development and career advancement were likely to be among the most important motivation factors for both SIEs and AEs. The mean of the motivation factor "professional development" for SIEs is 3.96, and the mean for AEs is 4.05. This mean difference was not statistically significant. The mean difference between SIEs and AEs for the motivation factor "future opportunities for advancement" was not statistically significant either (mean for SIEs was 3.47, mean for AEs was 3.37). Nor was the mean difference between SIEs and AEs for the motivation factor "normal career advancement pattern" (mean for SIEs was 3.11; mean for AEs was 3.29).

For both types of expatriates, the five factors mentioned above rank among the top six motivation factors out of 12. "Professional development" ranks second for SIEs, closely following "personal challenge" and is the first motivation factor for AEs. Personal challenge, as expected, is the first motivation factor for SIEs, while it ranks second for AEs. Indeed, the mean of the motivation factor "personal challenge" is higher for SIEs (4.02) than for AEs (3.79), but the mean difference does not turn out to be statistically significant.

The boundaryless career model may apply more self-evidently to SIEs. However, even if AEs are sent abroad by their organization, Cerdin and Le Pargneux (2010) have shown that they too can be included in this model. Indeed, the sole fact of their being assigned by an organization does not mean that they are going to spend their entire career within this organization, even though their link to it is, by definition, stronger than for SIEs.

SIEs are likely to be less strongly motivated by the job related to the expatriation than AEs, since they decide to go abroad on their own, outside the framework of an organization and the certainty it provides. Indeed, AEs are in a better position to get information on their future job abroad than SIEs are. Nevertheless, the importance of the job itself also should rank high with SIEs who pursue an international mobility for professional reasons. The motivation factor "Importance of the job itself" ranks third for SEs and second for AEs. The mean of the motivation factor "importance of the job itself" for SEs is 3.51, and the mean for AEs is 3.89. This mean difference was statistically significant ($t = 2.915$, $p < .01$). The "Importance of the job itself" is a weaker motivation factor for SIE than for AE. However, the importance of the job itself is quite high for SIEs as it is among the first three motivation factors.

Encouragement from colleagues should be less important for SIEs than for AEs, the former being less influenced by the organizational environment than the latter. However, based on past research (Stahl & Cerdin, 2004; Stahl et al., 2002), this motivation factor should rank low for both SIEs and AEs. Indeed, in the context of boundaryless career, expatriates are internally motivated and individually responsible for their career management, which is why encouragement from colleagues and superiors is likely to weigh less. The motivation factor "Encouragement from colleagues and superiors" ranks 12th for SIEs and AEs. The mean of this motivation factor for SIEs is 1.74 and 2.18 for AEs. The mean difference was statistically significant ($t = 3.545$, $p < .01$).

Whereas pay, promotion, and status appear to be central in the traditional model of career, it is less true for new, boundaryless careers. Considering that both SIEs and AEs are likely to be engaged in such new careers, the motivation factor related to monetary considerations should rank lower than career development and advancement, for both SIEs and AEs. Figure 4.1 shows that the motivation factor "monetary considerations" ranks seventh out of 14 motivation factors for both SIEs and AEs. The mean of the motivation factor "monetary considerations" for SIEs is 2.8 and for AEs 2.73. The mean difference is not statistically significant.

Comparative studies on SIEs and AEs suggest that the former are on average younger than the latter (Inkson et al., 1997; Myers & Pringle, 2005) and therefore, less likely to have a family with children. Consequently, when making their decision to go abroad, motivation factors such as "family considerations" and "encouragement from spouse or partner" are likely to matter less for SIEs than for AEs. Figure 4.1 indicates that these two motivation factors, related to family, are higher for AEs. The mean of the motivation factor "family considerations" is 2.1 for SIEs and 2.56 for AEs. The difference is statistically significant for family considerations ($t = 2.800$, $p < .01$). The mean of the motivation factor "encouragement from spouse or partner" is 2.28 for SIEs and 2.49 for AEs. However, the difference is not statistically significant.

Studies on the willingness to relocate, both nationally (e.g. Noe & Barber, 1993) and internationally (e.g. Brett & Stroh, 1995) suggest that location matters. Therefore, the motivational factor "geographic location of the assignment" should rank high for both SIEs and AEs. The mean difference between SIEs and AEs for the motivation factor "geographic location of the assignment" was not statistically significant (mean for SIEs was 3.35, mean for AEs was 3.39).

PUSH FACTORS

Motives to work abroad are not always positive (Borg, 1988; Torbiörn, 1976). Indeed, in addition to positive motives, or pull factors, that arise from individuals' willingness to gain new personal and/or professional experiences, negative motives, also known as push factors, arise from individuals' dissatisfaction with prevailing conditions at home or personal issues. Even though it can be expected that the negative reasons would be rare for SIEs (Cerdin & Le Pargneux, 2008), they should nevertheless play a bigger role in the decision to leave than they do for AEs. In particular, the negative motive arising from a desire to escape a social or economic environment related to the home country should appear more frequently for SIEs than for AEs.

Figure 4.1 indicates that the "desire to escape from a social or economic environment related to the home country" ($t = 3.655$, $p < .001$) and "desire to escape from personal problems at home" ($t = 2.996$, $p < .01$) vary significantly from SIEs to AEs. The mean of the motivation factor "desire to escape from social or economic environment related to the home country" for SIEs is 2.48, and the mean for AEs is 1.93. The mean of the motivation factor "desire to escape from personal problems at home" for SIEs is 1.77, and the mean for AEs is 1.38. These results show that push factors are more frequent for SIEs than for AEs. However, it is important to note that the push factors are probably much more frequent than expatriates' responses to survey may suggest (Cerdin & Dubouloy, 2004).

PULL AND PUSH FACTORS FOR QIS

Both SIEs and AEs embark on an international mobility with the intention to one day return to their home country. Therefore, they both have a short-term perspective in mind during their international mobility. It is interesting to contrast this perspective with that of QIs, who place themselves in a long-term perspective of living and working abroad.

QIs' motivation to migrate is likely to have an impact on their motivation to adjust to their host country and their success (Cerdin & Abdeljalil, 2007; Cerdin et al., 2011).

QIs SAMPLE

Results reported in this chapter stem from a sample of 53 QIs that migrated to France. This sample is made up of immigrants of various nationalities, who have arrived in France at different times, with different levels of education, professions, and ages. It includes immigrants of both genders.

The literature on IA and the migration of QIs (Carr, Inkson, & Thorn, 2005) identifies five main reasons to move abroad, namely, political factors and insecurity, economic factors, cultural factors, family factors, and career factors. While push and pull factors are intertwined, Cerdin and Abdeljalil (2007) divide these factors into push and pull factors from their interviews of QIs. The QIs present political and insecurity factors and economic factors as having pushed them away from their home country. They present family factors, cultural factors, and career factors as having pulled them to the host country.

CAREER ANCHORS

Individuals are guided in their decisions regarding career by so-called career anchors. A career anchor is "that one element in a person's self-concept, which he or she will not give up, even in the face of difficult choices" (Schein, 1990, p. 18). For SIEs, the decision to go abroad can be one of those "difficult choices." The type of international career they will lead can depend on their career anchors (Cerdin & Bird, 2008). A career anchor has three components: (1) self-perceived talent and abilities, (2) self-perceived motives and needs, and (3) self-perceived concept attitudes and values (Schein, 1990). The theory of career anchors concentrates on the individual's internal career (Suutari & Taka, 2004). It proposes that individuals have a long-term preference regarding their work and work environment (Schein, 1996).

Cerdin and Le Pargneux (2010) anticipated that SIEs and AEs would differ in terms of their career anchors. Schein (1978, 1990) identified eight career anchors. More recently, Suutari and Taka (2004) proposed a new career anchor called the internationalism anchor. Schein's eight anchors include (1) technical/functional competence, (2) managerial competence, (3) security and stability, (4) entrepreneurial creativity, (5) autonomy and independence, (6) dedication to a cause, (7) pure challenge, and (8) lifestyle. Cerdin and Le Pargneux (2009), in their integrative model of IA success, assert that some career anchors would be more congruent with the characteristics of an IA than others. The measures used and reported in Cerdin and Le Pargneux (2010) are the same as Schein's (1990) for the eight career anchors he introduced, with the exception of the technical/functional competence anchor, which had to be omitted in their analysis of French-speaking expatriates. The measure of the internationalism career anchor was developed by Cerdin (2007).

Figure 4.2 indicates that the three dominant career anchors for SIEs are, in order of importance, lifestyle, pure challenge, and internationalism. The three most common career anchors are identical for AEs, though the order is slightly different, with lifestyle followed by internationalism and pure challenge. The mean difference between SIEs and AEs for the career anchor "pure challenge" was not statistically significant. However, this anchor ranked second for SIEs and third for AEs, which can be explained. Indeed, a self-initiated expatriation may represent even more of a personal challenge than an assigned expatriation. The pure challenge anchor characterizes individuals who like to solve nearly unsolvable problems and who perceive their career in terms of daily struggle or competition, where winning is everything (Schein, 1990). This career anchor plays an important role in the career orientation of SIEs.

Cerdin and Le Pargneux (2010) found that the managerial competence anchor was less widespread among SIEs than AEs. A self-initiated expatriation is a personal endeavor, which is not guided by the traditional purposes associated with an IA. Even though AEs are guided by personal goals when embarking upon an IA, their expatriation fits into a set of objectives set by their organization. These are (1) filling a position, (2) developing the organization, and (3) developing managers (Edström & Galbraith, 1977).

The security and stability anchor ranks low for SIEs. Cerdin and Le Pargneux (2010) found the mean difference between AEs and SIEs for the career anchor "security and stability" to be statistically significant. However, unexpectedly, it was the mean for SIEs, which was higher (at 3.00) than that of AEs (2.53).

The autonomy career anchor ranks fifth out of eight anchors for SIEs (Figure 4.2). Though the ranking differs slightly between SIEs and AEs, the mean

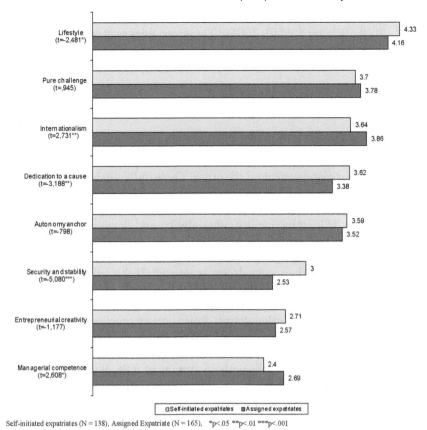

Self-initiated expatriates (N = 138), Assigned Expatriate (N = 165), *p<.05 **p<.01 ***p<.001

Figure 4.2   Career anchors of SIEs and AEs (mean scores and significance).

differences between the two types of expatriates were not statistically significant. Cerdin and Le Pargneux (2010) expected that this anchor would guide SIEs much more than AEs, since initiating one's own expatriation may be seen as part of a quest for autonomy. However, this hypothesis was not confirmed, with the autonomy anchor ranking slightly higher for AEs than for SIEs.

The dedication to a cause anchor ranks fourth for SIEs (Figure 4.2). Individuals anchored by dedication to a cause wish to improve the world in some way, particularly by helping others (Schein, 1990). Therefore, they are likely to be drawn to self-initiated expatriation, as a way of reaching people in need. The dedication to a cause anchor is more common among SIEs than among AEs.

PROTEAN AND BOUNDARYLESS CAREER ATTITUDE

In addition to motivation factors and career anchors, Cerdin and Le Pargneux (2009) include in their integrative model of IA success other career variables such as protean and boundaryless career attitude (Briscoe et al., 2006; Briscoe & Hall, 2006;). These variables may contribute to better understanding the drivers of SIEs to go abroad. The comparison with AEs will also help to point out the specific nature of SIEs' motivations.

PROTEAN CAREER ATTITUDE

Protean career attitude characterizes those who base their career decisions on personal values on the one hand and who display an attitude of self-directed career management on the other. These individuals have a capacity of adaptation in terms of performance and learning requirements (Briscoe et al., 2006; Briscoe & Hall, 2006). Characteristics of a protean career attitude, such as learning facility, adaptability, and flexibility, are valuable assets in an IA (Lazarova & Cerdin, 2007; Lazarova & Tarique, 2005).

Briscoe et al. (2006) proposed two scales to measure protean career attitude, namely (1) the values-driven scale and (2) the self-directed career management scale. Based on the SIEs and AEs sample used in this chapter, the value-driven dimension of protean career is high for SIEs (average of 3.80). The mean of the value driven dimension of protean career for AEs is 3.56, which is lower than for SIEs. This mean difference was statistically significant (t = –3.371, p < .01). The self-directed career management dimension is also high for SIEs with an average of 3.96. It is lower for AEs, with an average of 3.75. This mean difference was also statistically significant (t = –3.067, p < .01). As a conclusion, SIEs are much more likely to have a protean career attitude than AEs.

BOUNDARYLESS CAREER ATTITUDE

Boundaryless career attitude implies that individuals are stimulated by new experiences and new situations they are confronted with. A boundaryless career is made up of two components, namely (1) the boundaryless mindset and (2) a preference for organizational mobility (Briscoe et al., 2006). In the perspective of boundaryless mindset, individuals enjoy new experiences and enjoy working in an open environment, outside of an organizational framework. As for the preference for organizational mobility, it implies individuals wish to work in multiple organizations within the course of their career.

Briscoe et al. (2006) proposed two scales to measure boundaryless career attitude, namely (1) the boundaryless mindset scale and (2) the organizational mobility preference scale. Based on the SIEs and AEs sample used in this chapter, the boundaryless mindset dimension is high for SIEs (average of 3.93). The mean of this dimension is even higher for AEs with 3.97. However, this mean difference was not statistically significant. The mean of the dimension "organizational mobility preference" is high for SIEs with a score of 4.11 on a scale of 5 points. It is a bit lower for AEs with a score of 3.99. However, the mean difference for "organizational mobility preference" is not statistically significant.

DISCUSSION

Both Personal and Professional Factors Matter

The objective of this chapter was to examine the motivation of SIEs to go abroad. The study of SIEs in itself brings new insights into the pull and push factors of this specific type of expatriates. Additionally, the comparison between SIEs and AEs brings to light the idiosyncrasies of SIEs in relation to more traditional (and more thoroughly studied) expatriates. This chapter proposes and shows that SIEs pursue a boundaryless career, seeking fulfillment at work as well as pursuing their personal goals. Indeed, personal challenge and professional development are the first two motivation factors for SIEs.

SIEs and AEs share the first three pull factors (personal challenge, professional development, and importance of the job itself), even though they are ranked in a different order. For QIs, who are a particular subset of SIEs, pull and push factors are more balanced than for SIEs in general.

This chapter goes beyond merely studying a list of SIEs' motivation factors. The analysis of SIE's career anchors allows a more in-depth analysis of the drivers to go and work abroad to be carried out. Again, the comparison between SIEs and AEs turns out to be beneficial in this endeavor.

The lifestyle career anchor is the most common one among SIEs, ranking just before pure challenge and internationalism. According to Schein's career anchor theory, this anchor is not favorable to geographic mobility. Yet, Cerdin and Le Pargneux's (2010) results show the exact opposite. Other research also found the lifestyle career anchor to be important for expatriates (Suutari & Taka, 2004). Even though this anchor ranks first for both types of expatriates, it scores significantly higher for SIEs (Figure 4.2). The lifestyle anchor captures an attachment to achieving balance between work and personal/family life. The dominant position of the lifestyle anchor for SIEs indicates that a self-initiated expatriation may also serve as a means to achieve this balance.

Surprisingly, the internationalism anchor ranks only third for SIEs studied by Cerdin and Le Pargneux (2010). As this career anchor ranks higher for traditional expatriates, the authors suggest that internationalism-anchored individuals may be inclined to use an organization as a means of facilitating their expatriation. It may be easier to get a job in an organization and let oneself be expatriated by it rather than go alone, without any organizational support. For SIEs, however, expatriation itself is not a goal but rather a result of their pursuing other objectives.

Even though the security anchor ranks low for SIEs, it is more important than for AEs. Cerdin and Le Pargneux (2010) point out that here too, expatriation for SIEs may be a means to attain a level of security and stability that individuals cannot find in their home country.

SIEs are likely to display a protean career attitude, more so than AEs. As initiators of their own expatriation, SIEs tend to base their career decisions on personal values and display a greater attitude of self-directed career management than AEs do. However, even though SIEs are highly stimulated by new experiences and new situations they are confronted with, they are no different than AEs in terms of their boundaryless career attitude. This result is not surprising as any kind of expatriaton presents similar opportunities for new experiences.

All the drivers studied in this chapter—push and pull factors, career anchors, and protean and boundaryless career attitude—concur to give a nuanced understanding of the motivations of SIEs as to this particular international mobility. The results show that self-management and personal odysseys are particularly important for SIEs and that push factors may not be insignificant, particularly in comparison with AEs.

RESEARCH AGENDA

Research focusing on expatriate motivation presents the expatriates with a list of factors to be ranked (e.g. Dickmann et al., 2008; Stahl & Cerdin, 2004; Stahl et al., 2002). This list of factors, such as those presented in this chapter, is determined a priori, based on previous research. However, more qualitative studies on SIEs could widen the scope of motivators beyond those measured in quantitative studies. Most studies, including those reported in this chapter, ask expatriates who are already abroad to report on their motivation. Past research has suggested that people may re-interpret their past motivations, making interpretative retrospective probing problematic. However, researchers have also found that when asked about important and meaningful experiences in their past (like going abroad to work and live there for a certain number of years), subjects are quite reliable in recalling "personal historical facts" (Lazarova & Cerdin, 2007). Consequently, capturing these motivators before the expatriation would discard any doubts on potential reinterpretation. Unfortunately, it is more difficult to identify SIEs than AEs before their expatriation.

International business experience can be obtained through numerous strategies (Vance, 2005), which require closer examination. SIEs include all types of individuals, from students going abroad for an internship, to professionals working outside their country of origin for a limited period of time, to individuals who migrate. Research on SIEs motivation should explore this diversity of strategies in going abroad, instead of treating SIEs as one homogenous group. The very definition of SIEs is still controversial, and criteria to distinguish SIEs from other types of expatriates and to distinguish SIEs between their different types are crucially needed.

Career anchors offer a way to deepen our understanding of the drivers to go abroad. Even though they address mainly the issue of career orientation, they also take into account individuals' personal aspirations and values. The internationalism career anchor seems very promising in terms of understanding the motivations of SIEs to go abroad. Even though this career anchor is less common among SIEs than AEs, it appears in the dominant ones. Overall, career anchors deserve more attention in the study of career and all types of expatriation.

The motivation to go abroad for SIEs, as for any other types of expatriates, may rely on profound and very personal drivers. Some authors suggest adopting a psychoanalytical approach to shed light on the expatriate experience, from the decision to go abroad to the success of the expatriation (e.g. Cerdin & Dubouloy, 2004; Schneider & Asakawa, 1995). This would enable capturing the unconscious forces at play, in addition to the conscious aspects of the decisions to go abroad. As Cerdin and Dubouloy (2004) underscore, the reasons expatriates cite as justifying their expatriation may be very different from the real motives that drive them abroad. "Life story-" type approaches could offer a way of capturing the genuine drivers of a self-initiated expatriation.

PRACTICAL IMPLICATIONS

As self-initiated expatriation seems a phenomenon on the rise, and organizations resort to SIEs more and more (Jokinen et al., 2008), the knowledge of SIEs motivations to go abroad turns out to be invaluable in helping organizations to better attract and keep these particular expatriates.

Employers should be aware that if they have hired an SIE in a certain country, the individual might not wish to be re-expatriated to another, since it was the result of his or her own personal decision to be in that country. Therefore, organizations should expect talent management of SIEs to be a more delicate affair than for AEs. To ensure that SIEs will remain with their organization in the long run, employers should take into account individuals' personal drivers.

Motivation factors related to career play an important role for SIEs as our results show. Thus, organizations must offer them opportunities for professional development. However, organizations should also put a lot of emphasis on the personal drivers that may guide SIEs in their decision to go abroad. Employers need to address personal challenge, since it ranks high among SIEs motivation factors. The need for such emphasis is reinforced by the importance of the lifestyle career anchor for this particular type of expatriates. Thus, employers should promote work and family life balance for the SIEs that they recruit.

CONCLUSION

In summary, this chapter sheds light on the drivers of SIEs to go abroad, through the study of motivation factors, career anchors, and protean and boundaryless career attitudes. SIEs display some unique characteristics in terms of what drives them to go abroad, making the study of SIEs themselves useful in comparison with traditional expatriates. Personal issues are of particular importance for SIEs even though career drivers also matter.

SIEs encompass a whole range of individuals embarking on some kind of international mobility. This chapter shows that unlike QIs, in general, SIEs base their decision to go abroad on pull factors rather than push factors. Future research should further examine the diversity of SIEs. Addressing this diversity requires resorting to a range of methodologies, including qualitative studies such as life story. Identifying SIEs drivers to go abroad can help improve the management of this type of expatriates, who are on the rise and fuel organizations' global talent flow.

ACKNOWLEDGMENTS

Some of the studies presented in this chapter were conducted with Marie LePargneux. The author gratefully acknowledges her contribution, as well as the helpful comments of the editors on an earlier version of this chapter.

REFERENCES

Al Ariss, A., & Özbilgin, M. (2010). Understanding self-initiated expatriates: Career experiences of Lebanese self-initiated expatriates. *Thunderbird International Business Review, 52*(4), 275–285.
Arthur, M. B., & Rousseau, D. M. (1996). *The boundaryless career: A new employment principle for a new organizational era.* New York: Oxford University Press.
Borg, M. (1988). *International transfers of managers in multinational corporations.* Studia Oeconomiae Negotorium, 27. Uppsala: Acta Universitatis Upsaliensis.
Brett, J. M., & Stroh, L. K. (1995). Willingness to relocate internationally. *Human Resource Management, 34*(3), 405–424.
Briscoe, J. P., & Hall, D. T. (2006). The interplay of boundaryless and protean careers: Combinations and implications. *Journal of Vocational Behavior, 69*(1), 4–18.
Briscoe, J. P., Hall, D. T., & DeMuth, R. F. (2006). Protean and boundaryless careers: An empirical exploration. *Journal of Vocational Behavior, 69*(1), 30–47.
Carr, S. C., Inkson, K., & Thorn, K. (2005). From global careers to talent flow: Reinterpreting "Brain Drain." *Journal of World Business, 40,* 368–398.
Cerdin, J.-L. (2007). *S'expatrier en toute connaissance de cause.* Paris: Eyrolles.
Cerdin, J.-L., & Abdeljalil, M. (2007, August). *The success of highly qualified foreigners in France.* Paper presented at the Academy of Management, Philadelphia.

Cerdin, J.-L., Abdeljalil Diné, M., & Brewster, C. (2011, June). *Qualified immigrants' success: exploring the motivation to migrate and to adjust.* Paper presented at the EURAM Conference, Tallinn, Estonia.
Cerdin, J.-L., & Bird, A. (2008). Careers in a global context. In M. Harris (Ed.), *Handbook of Research in International Human Resource Management* (pp. 207–227). New York: Erlbaum Associates.
Cerdin, J.-L., & Dubouloy, M. (2004). Expatriation as a maturation opportunity: A psychoanalytical approach based on "copy and paste." *Human Relations, 57*(8), 957–981.
Cerdin, J.-L., & Le Pargneux, M. (2008, October). *Career anchors and motivation: A comparison between self-initiated expatriates and organization assigned expatriates.* Paper presented at the EIASM Workshop on Expatriation, Las Palmas de Gran Canaria, Spain.
Cerdin, J.-L., & Le Pargneux, M. (2009). Career and international assignment fit: Toward an integrative model of success. *Human Resource Management, 48*(1), 5–25.
Cerdin, J.-L., & Le Pargneux, M. (2010). Career anchors: A comparison between organization assigned and self-initiated expatriates. *Thunderbird International Business Review, 52*(4), 287–299.
Collings, D. G., Scullion, H., & Morley, M. J. (2007). Changing patterns of global staffing in the multinational enterprise: Challenges to the conventional expatriate assignment and emerging alternatives. *Journal of World Business, 42,* 198–213.
Dickmann, M., Doherty, N., & Mills, T. (2008, August). Exploring differences in drivers of self-initiated and company-sent expatriates. Paper presented at the Academy of Management, Anaheim, CA.
Dickmann, M., Doherty, N., Mills, T., & Brewster, C. (2008). Why do they go? Individual and corporate perspectives on the factors influencing the decision to accept an international assignment. *International Journal of Human Resource Management, 19*(4), 731–751.
Eby, L. T., Butts, M., & Lockwood, A. (2003). Predictors of success in the era of the boundaryless career. *Journal of Organizational Behavior, 24*(6), 689–709.
Edström, A., & Galbraith, J. R. (1977). Transfer of managers as a control and coordination strategy in multinational organizations. *Administrative Science Quarterly, 22,* 11–22.
Guzzo, R. A. (1997). The expatriate employee. *Trends in Organizational Behavior, 4,* 123–137.
Howe-Walsh, L., & Schyns, B. (2010). Self-initiated expatriation: Implications for HRM. *International Journal of Human Resource Management, 21*(2), 260–273.
Inkson, K., Arthur, M. B., Pringle, J., & Barry, S. (1997). Expatriate assignment versus overseas experience: Contrasting models of international human resource development. *Journal of World Business, 32*(4), 351–368.
Jokinen, T., Brewster, C., & Suutari, V. (2008). Career capital during international work experiences: Contrasting self-initiated expatriate experiences and assigned expatriation. *International Journal of Human Resource Management, 19*(6), 979–998.
Lazarova, M., & Cerdin, J.-L. (2007). Revisiting repatriation concerns: Organizational support vs. career and contextual influences. *Journal of International Business Studies, 38,* 404–429.
Lazarova, M., & Tarique, I. (2005). Knowledge transfer upon repatriation. *Journal of World Business, 40*(4), 361–373.
Myers, B., & Pringle, J. K. (2005). Self-initiated foreign experience as accelerated development: Influences of gender. *Journal of World Business, 40,* 421–431.

Noe, R. A., & Barber, A. E. (1993). Willingness to accept mobility opportunities: Destination makes a difference. *Journal of Organizational Behavior, 14*(2), 159–175.

Schein, E. H. (1978). *Career dynamics: Matching individual and organizational needs.* Reading, MA: Addison-Wesley.

Schein, E. H. (1990). *Career anchors: Discovering your real values.* San Diego: Pfeiffer & Company.

Schein, E. H. (1996). Career anchors revisited: Implications for career development in the 21st century. *Academy of Management Executive, 10*(4), 80–88.

Schneider, S. C., & Asakawa, K. (1995). American and Japanese expatriate adjustment: A psychoanalytic perspective. *Human Relations, 48*(10), 1109–1127.

Stahl, G. K., & Cerdin, J.-L. (2004). Global careers in French and German multinational corporations. *Journal of Management Development, 23*(9), 885–902.

Stahl, G. K., Miller, E. L., & Tung, R. L. (2002). Toward the boundaryless career: A closer look at expatriate career concept and the perceived implications of an international assignment. *Journal of World Business, 37*(3), 216–227.

Sullivan, S. E. (1999). The changing nature of careers: A review and research agenda. *Journal of Management, 25*(3), 457–484.

Suutari, V., & Brewster, C. (2000). Making their own way: International experience through self-initiated foreign assignment. *Journal of World Business, 35*(4), 417–436.

Suutari, V., & Taka, M. (2004). Career anchors of managers with global careers. *Journal of Management Development, 23*(9), 833–847.

Tharenou, P., & Caulfield, N. (2010). Will I stay or will I go? Explaining repatriation by self-initiated expatriates. *Academy of Management Journal, 53*(5), 1009–1028.

Torbiörn, I. (1976). *Att leva utomlands—En studie av utlandssvenskars anpassning, trivsel och levnadsvanor (Living abroad—A study of the adjustment of Swedish overseas personnel).* Stockholm: SNS.

Vance, C. M. (2005). The personal quest for building global competence: A taxonomy of self-initiating career path strategies for gaining business experience abroad. *Journal of World Business, 40*, 374–385.

5 Self-Initiated Expatriation and Talent Flow

Kaye Thorn and Kerr Inkson

GLOBAL NOMADS: A CASE STUDY

Kate, a lawyer with a specialization in environmental law, and her husband Paul, an information technology worker, left New Zealand, their home country, when they were in their mid-20s, and went to live in Melbourne, a city they had long wanted to experience. They had no pre-arranged jobs to go to but had a self-confident belief in themselves, in the portability of their qualifications, and their ability to improvise. They both got jobs, Kate in a small law firm and Paul in a banking software company. Their intention had been to spend a few years enjoying Melbourne and then to return to New Zealand.

Then, out of the blue, Paul's company offered him a huge promotion to the job of managing its Thailand subsidiary. It was too good an offer to pass up, so Kate and Paul moved to Thailand, eventually spending seven years there. Environmental law had few opportunities as a practice in Thailand, so Kate adapted by working as a corporate lawyer, providing advice to foreign companies who wanted to establish in Thailand. Like Paul, she was successful, starting as a senior associate but moving up to partner.

However, the birth of their two children changed their focus. As their son approached school age, Kate and Paul began looking for the next move. Paul was headhunted by a different software company and offered two new positions—Moscow or Tokyo. They decided they had had enough of Asia for a while, so Russia became their next destination. Visa requirements meant Kate was unable to work in Moscow, so she spent that time with the children. When the financial crisis of 1987 hit, prices climbed dramatically overnight, and the risks of living in the city also increased. For safety reasons, the family was moved to Latvia where they stayed for three years, with Paul commuting to work in Moscow, while Kate worked for Deloitte Touche in Latvia.

After three years, a restructuring of Paul's company resulted in a shift to London for a year, followed by a transfer to Singapore, a move partially based on the children's schooling and the environment in which they would be living. Kate's experience as an international corporate lawyer has enabled her to work in both London and Singapore. Kate and Paul are anticipating their next move, although they are unsure where that will be.

CAREER ANALYSIS AND 'TALENT FLOW'

Kate and Paul have become 'global nomads,' people who "cross physical and cultural barriers with apparent ease in the search for difference and differentiation" (Richards & Wilson, 2004, p. 5). They tend to consider themselves part of a unified world, moving from one part of the world to another, rather than crossing national boundaries. But within their complex careers, their apparently endless and effortless series of expatriations, there are variations in terms of initiation, motivation, adaptation, learning, and chance. Yet, if we look beyond Kate and Paul's individual actions, we find they are also elements in much larger patterns of global mobility. How does this work? Let us consider the five types of variation noted above.

- In terms of *initiation,* who took the initiative for each of Kate and Paul's moves? Kate and Paul or their employers? The move to Melbourne, without jobs to go to, was purely self-initiated. The moves to Moscow and Singapore were also self-initiated, but with the lure of a job offer for Paul. The moves to Thailand, Latvia, and London were corporate expatriations: the organization asked Paul to relocate, but Kate and Paul were happy to do so. One of the features of expatriation is that it is always, to some extent, self-initiated, or at least self-agreed. No company can force its employees to go overseas.
- In terms of *motivation,* expatriation can be based on any of a wide variety of motives, and Kate and Paul's motivations for moving changed over the years reflecting a change in their priorities. The initial move to Melbourne seems to have been in pursuit of a broad wish to travel and to live in a cosmopolitan center and the move to Thailand by a desire to boost Paul's career possibilities. Paul's career again figured in the Moscow decision, as did an apparent restlessness and concerns about family, while the move to Latvia was occasioned by safety concerns. When the couple moved to London and Singapore, concerns about their children's education were again important. The changing cycles of motivation reflect the life cycle (Super, 1990) and family cycle (Parasuraman & Greenhaus, 1997); issues that are familiar in career theory.
- In terms of *adaptation,* Kate and Paul constantly have to adapt to new national, cultural, organizational, and job-related settings as well as changing family circumstances, but Kate, in addition, also has to adapt her career to Paul's and, more than Paul does, to the raising of a family. Each move after the first has been determined mainly on the basis of Paul's career, and Kate finds herself in the familiar position of 'trailing spouse'(Harvey, 1998), whose career takes second place to that of her partner. Kate, however, shows good adaptability and is able to find work wherever she goes, apart from Moscow. Her experience reminds us that the careers of most Self-Initiated Expatriates (SIEs) are not totally autonomous but are circumscribed by family relationships and commitments.

- In terms of *learning*, both Kate and Paul learn as they go. Kate morphs from an environmental law specialist to a versatile corporate lawyer and Paul from a software salesman to a powerful international manager. They probably learn primarily from novelty—new jobs, new companies, new countries, new cultures, and new systems. They constantly grow their 'career capital,' particularly their 'knowing-how' expertise, utilizing portable skills and discarding location-specific ones as they go. They are, perhaps, "addicted to novelty and learning" (Osland, 1995, p. 152).

- In terms of *chance,* Kate's and Paul's careers, particularly their serial expatriations, are, like most careers but on a more expansive, global scale, subject to chance factors. For example, while their move to Melbourne was planned, their employment wasn't—they took the best chances they could find when they got there. Likewise, moving to Latvia was occasioned by factors far beyond their control. Paul's more organizational career path has reduced the element of chance, but even here Kate and Pauls' global movements were dependent on the chances offered by corporate rotation policies. The 'happenstance' element in careers (Krumboltz & Levin, 2002) and the post-event rationalization of many careers are well-known (Weick, 1996), but in the careers of global nomads, the chances multiply across a geographically expansive stage.

If we look at these five defining features of the two careers under consideration—initiation, motivation, adaptation, learning, and chance, what we notice is their variability and apparent 'flakiness': the five elements combine to make a constant flux, and while we can see some potential stabilizers—Kate's occupational specialization, Paul's companies, the directedness created by the couple's concerns for their children and their children's education—their global movements seem less the result of planning, or of upwardly mobile occupational or organizational careers, than of a 'chaos theory' of careers (Bright & Pryor, 2005). Yet the theme of this chapter is that in international careers, as in other careers, "chaotic careers create orderly fields" (Peterson & Anand, 2002, p.257). That is, the apparent chaos underlying mobility at the individual level somehow assembles into orderly patterns of activity at a societal level so that patterns of 'talent flow' from one country to another can be more clearly seen and understood (Carr, Inkson, & Thorn, 2005). How does this work?

SELF-INITIATED EXPATRIATION AND MOBILITY

Self-initiated expatriation is emerging as an important topic in the mobility literature (Doherty, 2010) and SIEs as important players in the international labor market and potentially valuable human resources for both the countries to which they move and the organizations that they join. Not only are the numbers of internationally mobile people increasing, their patterns of mobility are also becoming more complex. New forms of mobility are developing, including short-term transfers (Fenwick, 2004), very long-distance commuting, and frequent excursions (Flamm & Kaufmann, 2006). The frequency of mobility is also emerging in the literature, with references to the chronically mobile (Nowicka, 2006) or to serial expatriates (Bozkurt & Mohr, 2008).

To date, research on SIEs has tended to consider international mobility in isolation, examining individual moves but failing to consider the relationship of mobility to life events such as employment, partnership, and childbirth and to contextualize all mobility over the life course. The literature on motives for self-initiated expatriation, including factor analytic studies, identifies clusters of key factors termed here as economics, cultural and travel opportunities, affiliations (including family), career, quality of life, and the political environment (Doherty, 2010; Jackson et al., 2005). Similar findings from studies involving different cultural groups suggest there may be some cross-cultural consistency in these factors (Tharmaseelan, Inkson, & Carr, 2010). Motivation is likely to depend on specific circumstances, including national characteristics. For example, economic and political motivation may be higher among those who live in underdeveloped countries, and/or those with autocratic regimes, while the cultural and travel opportunities motive may dominate for those who are geographically isolated (Inkson & Myers, 2003).

Here, we distinguish between SIEs and 'one-shot' migrants. One-shot migrants move from Country A to Country B with the intention of settling permanently in Country B. SIEs move intentionally from Country A to Country B but without the intention of settling permanently in Country B. After a time in Country B, the SIE may move on to Country C and beyond. The one-shot migrant may do the same, thus becoming an SIE. There are fine gradations between the two categories, and both contribute to the global economy through their creation and international diffusion of knowledge (OECD, 2008).

But there is something about the SIEs' potential ongoing mobility that may make them especially important. Due to their education and qualifications, their prior experience, their absorption of work, and cultural knowledge from their previous local and international positions, Kate and Paul are each repositories and diffusers of unique combinations of knowledge. This knowledge, combined with the skills and experiences of others in the host country and host company, enable endless new applications. While this notion of knowledge accumulation through career experience applies to all who pursue work careers (Bird, 1996), it applies in greater measure to those whose careers are mobile—for example, between organizations, between occupations, between industries—and perhaps, most of all, those who move between countries. Benefits to the SIE include the development of individual competencies that might not have taken place had they remained in the same location (Doherty & Dickmann, 2009; Myers & Pringle, 2005), the broadening of work and social networks (Jokinen, Brewster, & Suutari, 2008) and the opportunity of exploring other cultures (Hippler, 2009; Inkson & Myers, 2003), and increasing cross-cultural competence.

Self-initiated expatriation as a phenomenon can be considered at different levels of analysis, according to the 'knowledge interests' (Habermas, 1984; Roper, Ganesh, & Inkson, 2010) involved: for example, those of SIEs and potential SIEs (individual level), those of employers and potential employers of SIEs (organization level), and those of societies and nations which may benefit or otherwise from the presence, retention, and utilization of SIEs within them (society level). Here, we focus primarily on the knowledge interests of SIEs themselves and of their home and host countries. The individual-level mobility of SIEs is generated by their motives and values ('push' factors) and directed to specific outcomes perceived to be available in the new country ('attractors' or 'pull' factors). It is assumed that the aggregation of many internal motives, and attractors perceived to characterize particular countries, will generate a net effect of potential mass migration. This will be moderated by target countries' boundary management in terms of migration policies and procedures. The process thus aggregates individual actions into more predictable 'talent flows' conceptualized as dynamic currents of skill residing in mobile individuals. By noticing and tapping these flows, smart countries (and, most likely, smart organizations) can, if they wish, develop migration policies, employment policies, and human resource practices that enable them to benefit maximally from the new realities of international mobility.

GAINS AND LOSSES

The benefits of mobility are not realized equally by all countries. Some countries gain, while others lose. Some might gain more, or lose less, or utilize available self-initiated expatriation resources more efficiently if they developed better policy and practice. In this chapter, therefore, we provide a brief overview of the concepts of self-initiated expatriation-caused 'brain drain,' 'brain gain,' and 'brain waste.' We then argue that all these are components of talent flow (Carr, et al., 2005). Finally, we show how this mobility can impact on the human resources and competitiveness of organizations and countries.

Brain drain. The term 'brain drain' is used to describe the international transfer of human capital (Beine, Docquier, & Rapoport, 2008). The interest in researching labor movements of the highly educated began in the 1960s with concern that British scientific brains were being lost to the US and elsewhere (Koser & Salt, 1997; Portes, 1976). This emphasis on scientists, or, more recently, technology workers, has remained (Carr, et al.,

2005), even though it is now recognized that self-initiated expatriation and permanent migration cause worldwide shortages in other fields such as health (Dubois & Singh, 2009), accountancy (Jackling & Keneley, 2009), and the trades (Han, Park, Jin, Kim, & Seong, 2008).

A well-educated and well-trained population is part of the 'sunk cost' of investment that any country makes in its own people through their socialization, education, and development, and, particularly in this knowledge-driven era, is important for the social and economic development of that country. A country invests in education, building its human capital, which in turn, drives competitiveness and stimulates foreign interest (Le, Gibson, & Oxley, 2003). However, with international labor markets relatively open for skilled people, and with increasing mobility, there is no guarantee that the return from this investment in education will be realized. Instead, it is possible for one country to make the investment and another to benefit from that investment (Birkinshaw, 2005).

The movement of labor across this increasingly globalized marketplace is, therefore, unevenly distributed. Today, the movement of 'brains' tends to be from developing countries to developed countries (Beine, et al., 2008). These people often choose to migrate to these more developed countries (i.e., their intention is to remain permanently in the host country) to further their career prospects and to take advantage of the opportunities available in a larger economy. Economic disparities between countries are a major driver for the mobility of those with the opportunity to move, and the loss of skills from less developed countries may increase that disparity still further. There are however, a number of developed countries expressing concerns about a perceived loss of talent, including Canada (Docquier & Rapoport, 2008), Finland (Johansson, 2008), Sweden and Denmark (Dumont & Lemaitre, 2005), Australia (Australian Senate, 2005), New Zealand (Inkson et al., 2004), and South Africa (Gwaradzimba & Shumba, 2010). In such expressions, however, we believe these countries may both overestimate the loss of talent, underestimate the potential of incoming talent to offset losses, and ignore some concomitant benefits of perceived brain drain. Research has shown, for example, that brain drain is beneficial not only to the host country but also on occasion to the home or source country. Remittances, particularly from those moving from lesser developed countries, can contribute to the source country's economy (Giuliano & Ruiz-Arranz, 2009). People who 'drain' temporarily but later return to the home country also contribute, bringing additional skills acquired during their time abroad (Agrawal, Kapur, McHale, & Oettl, 2010).

Brain Gain. As implied above, while talent is flowing out of some countries, other countries are benefitting from the infusion of new labor and new skills. This is through a combination of the decisions of the migrants and SIEs to live and work abroad or by the deliberate recruitment of highly educated people (Australian Senate, 2005). Governments have responded to the global movement of labor in a number of ways. The immigration policies of major industrialized countries have been changed significantly to allow open access and/or special consideration to SIEs who are well educated (Mahroum, 2005). The US, UK, Canada, Australia, New Zealand, and many other countries have developed specific immigration policies that target such workers (Iredale, 2005), thus making inflows more dependent on human capital and less on country of origin or ethnic background. International agreements also ease the flow of highly educated people into countries with skill shortages. Citizens of the European Union (EU), for example, are able to obtain employment in other EU countries without the need for formal immigration or visas (Recchi, 2008). Reciprocal agreements operate between North American countries through the North American Free Trade Agreement and New Zealand and Australia through the Closer Economic Relations agreement (Ouaked, 2002).

Some countries have gone further than a passive encouragement of the highly educated to an active enticement of new talent. Denmark, Sweden, and the Netherlands provide tax relief to foreign experts (Mahroum, 2005), while China, Israel, and Malaysia have a range of benefits and scholarships to attract the highly educated (Australian Senate, 2005). Many countries 'prospect' overseas to recruit skilled workers in areas of shortage such as health services. Further, Lowell suggests that skill shortages in the future will result in "aggressive policies to attract skilled migrants," (2005, p.11), thus predicting a more active involvement by governments in order to obtain the skills needed. Even more recently, there has been discussion on the "global war for talent" (Beechler & Woodward, 2009, p. 273), with countries strategizing to obtain maximum advantage (Ng, 2010).

This talent war is also observed at the organization level (Somaya & Williamson, 2008), focusing on skill shortages and the need to attract, retain, and motivate sufficient staff (Wang & Bu, 2004). The competition for workers comes not only from other domestic companies but also from organizations in other parts of the world. Where free movement provisions exist, an employer is able to recruit abroad without difficulty. Searching for and securing human talent is, therefore, increasingly becoming a global industry (Birkinshaw, 2005), with highly educated people circulating between countries and organizations as they contribute to the global economy (Beaverstock, 2005).

Brain Waste. The third component of this international mobility is brain waste, where mobile workers in a new country are not employed, or are employed at a level below that commensurate with their skills. Generally, this waste is more apparent with those who come from lesser developed countries (Özden, 2006) and where the cultural difference between the source and host country is greatest (Carr, et al., 2005). In a global environment where the circulation of talent is a vital part of a competitive economy, it is necessary to evaluate not only the empirical numbers of people joining the labor force, replacing those who leave, but also the contribution and performance of these new workers (Hardy, 2010).

If highly qualified workers are working below their potential, then there is lost performance. There is worldwide anecdotal evidence of doctors and scientists working as taxi drivers and nurses working as nurse aides (Schiff, 2005). Prejudice and discrimination, particularly by local employers more comfortable with culturally similar employees, may be a prime cause. Also, there are difficulties in ensuring that qualifications gained in a home country are equivalent to, and recognized as such by the authorized body in the host country. Here, professional groups that want to protect their members from 'foreign competition' may collude to prevent incomers from practicing the professions and trades that they have most to contribute in. Lack of work experience in the host country creates a 'catch 22' situation where SIEs find they can't get employment without local experience, but they can't get local experience without first finding local employment.

Not all SIEs, however, relocate for career purposes. For example, many young adults from Australia and New Zealand journey abroad to undertake their 'Big OE' or overseas experience—usually a period of two to three years motivated by opportunities for cultural experiences and adventure (Inkson & Myers, 2003). For these people, employment is about earning money to travel to the next destination, and they will often take expedient jobs such as laboring or bar work to do this. Ironically, the skills and competencies developed in these jobs can often contribute to new career directions.

TALENT FLOW AND SIES

The concepts of brain drain and brain gain have developed negative connotations, tend to be considered separately instead of as part of a single process, and ignore the fact that international mobility "changes both the competencies of the people within it and the environments through which it passes" (Carr et al., 2005, p. 388). And 'brain' is a term frequently taken to have the narrow meaning of scientific expertise. We therefore prefer to use the term 'talent flow' to refer to these phenomena.

What do we know then, about SIEs that is likely to have an impact on talent flow? What types of individuals will undertake self-initiated expatriation and what kind of talent flows will they create? SIEs, like corporate expatriates, and increasingly like permanent immigrants, tend to be highly educated. It is the educated, after all, who are likely to have skills-in-demand that provide good 'currency' in the cities to which they relocate.

Research has also shown that SIEs are a heterogeneous group with a broad age range. Younger SIEs, as mentioned above, may live and work abroad as part of their OE (Inkson & Myers, 2003). This mobility is often temporary, bounded by eligibility for work permits, with the nature of the employment being less important than the location. Among SIEs who move abroad when they are in their 30s and 40s, in contrast, the key motivation for men may be career development and financial opportunity, while for women, cultural and travel opportunities and relationships are additional motivations (Thorn, 2009).

Unlike their corporate counterparts, SIEs are not dependent on the company to send them abroad (Inkson, Arthur, Pringle, & Barry, 1997) and, hence, can be more flexible with their mobility, choosing both the country and the timing of the relocation. We would expect, therefore, to find SIEs located in a broader range of countries.

The self-initiated expatriation lifestyle is likely to appeal to those who are independent and free of family constraints, though, as the case of Kate and Paul shows, these are not insurmountable obstacles. And, a person who has successfully relocated once and enjoyed the challenge may be undaunted by the prospect of a further move: in fact, the desire for mobility and novelty may be further stimulated (Osland, 1995). Hence, SIEs may become frequently mobile, moving among countries at will.

SIEs moving without the security of company remuneration packages are also demonstrating a higher level of risk taking (Richardson & Zikic, 2007). Finding accommodation and schooling for children can be a significant stress, especially without the housing and education benefits which usually accompany corporate expatriation, and without the ability to plan long term that permanent migrants enjoy.

Perhaps of even more significance to the SIE is the absence of a social network in the new location to assist with settlement and acculturation, and, often, the temporary status meaning that such networks have to be recommenced in each new location. Most corporations arrange at least a degree of mentorship and support for newly relocated people, providing local knowledge and advice, while permanent migrants can often find support from family members and ethnic communities from their own country. SIEs therefore will tend to be those with less need for social support or with the capacity to build such support quickly in a novel environment. The image of the SIE that is emerging, therefore, is of a flexible, educated person who responds well to the challenges of living abroad and who will, potentially, continue to be mobile.

Other Factors of Relevance. Corporate expatriation has tended to be dominated by men, but research from across the world suggests that SIEs are equally likely to be women (Doherty, Dickmann, & Mills, 2011; Suutari & Brewster, 2003). Tharenou (2010b) suggests that women, particularly those without a partner or children, may self-initiate their own experience to gain the career opportunities and advancement not available in their home country. Gender discrimination and unfair treatment can similarly entice women to look outside their country of residence for employment (Fitzgerald & Howe-Walsh, 2009).

Another issue magnified by the flow of SIE talent is that of dual-career couples such as Kate and Paul. Traditionally, women have given way to the careers of their partners, but Raghuram (2004) suggests this may not always be the situation for SIEs, with women also taking the lead role in mobility. The difficulty, though, is that while one partner may secure career advancement through a move to a new location, finding employment that is of interest to a partner, and at the appropriate level for their career development, may be a problem. One partner may take expedient positions, as Kate did, in order to support the other's career (Ackers, 2004). Some reciprocity may occur, but the long-term implications of such sacrifices on career development are unclear.

It is important to recognize that some of this flow of self-initiated talent does return to live and work in their home countries. Inkson et al. (2004) considered this facet in some detail, examining whether those who do return to the home country are in some way different to those who choose to remain abroad. Their results are significant—those who remain abroad reported a greater desire to excel in competition (achievement motivation), while those who intended returning placed more priority on relationships (affiliation motivation). The implication of these findings is that those with the most drive and ambition, the entrepreneurial ones highly valued in a competitive global environment, are not only the ones most likely to leave, but the ones least likely to return. In a similar vein, research by Myers and Pringle (2005) has shown that women, possibly higher than men on affiliation motivation, are more likely to return to their home country than men. Again there are implications on the special characteristics of the self-initiated that comprise these talent flows.

MANAGING TALENT

We discussed earlier how countries actively entice talent to their country through tax benefits and migration policies, but how do organizations attract, develop, motivate, and retain this talent, particularly SIE talent? And how do they respond to the possibly temporary departure of their own employees who may seek self-initiated expatriation experiences elsewhere? Inkson and King (2011, p.43) suggest that in today's global, knowledge society, there are three key components of an organization which can both attract and manage talented staff and generate added value: culture, capabilities, and connections. The culture of an organization can be an attractant to SIEs, especially if that culture is seen to encompass a global perspective. Human resource practices, which embrace multiculturalism and acknowledgement of international experience, are standard requirements for many SIEs. Ownership of this alignment must be consistent across all levels, from the leader, to the manager and to the Human Resource (HR) Department.

An organization must also be aware of its capabilities and skill deficits so that it can effectively target the required talent. Many organizations are reaching beyond the national boundaries to fill these gaps, using international HR companies. Some organizations, if they are to attract and utilize the best SIE talent, may need to loosen rigidities around recruiting only those who have qualifications, expertise, and language abilities rooted in local institutions. Once SIEs are employed, the organization should focus on developing this talent and their career opportunities further in order to avoid the repatriate failure statistics witnessed in corporate expatriations (Shen & Hall, 2009). But it should also recognize that some SIEs are by nature 'wanderers' and aim to utilize their expertise maximally, while they are available, and, if possible, to institutionalize it as insurance against the wanderer's departure.

Connections are another element for successfully managing talent. Existing connections are important, and many organizations keep track of employees who go abroad with the prospect of enticing them back at some stage in the knowledge that their self-initiated expatriation experiences will have developed their potential still further. In New Zealand, the Kiwi Expatriates Association (KEA: www.keanewzealand.com) has facilitated this on a broader scale, creating a virtual job community that connects New Zealand organizations to the diaspora. The networks of the newly employed talent are also worth promulgating, both in terms of the international connections they offer and the potential for new talent recruitment.

To these factors, we would add a fourth component important when managing talent—creativity. These SIEs have shown a willingness to move throughout the world to get what they want, and the employer must be prepared to do the same. In the knowledge society, organizations need to think laterally and globally and to redesign employment systems to suit the needs of internationally mobile talent (Beechler & Woodward, 2009).

CONCLUSION

Kate and Paul have taken their talents around the world, flowing from developed to developing countries with ease. They have contributed to the skill base in each of the countries, and in return have gained experiences, which, in Kate's words, "have enabled us to grow as people." We have used the example of just one couple to show the dynamics of international talent flow. However, when we expand this to think about all mobility, there are implications not only for the individuals, but for countries and organizations. Countries need to ensure they have the incentives to attract this talent and the legislation to allow them in. To maintain competitiveness, they must also encourage their talent to repatriate, to return their competencies, networks, and international experience to the home economy (Tharenou, 2010a). To capitalize on these flows, both countries and organizations need to ensure they have sufficient capacity to appropriately employ these people and to ease their transition into the renewed environment.

Another point to consider is the decreasing importance, in a networked world, of individuals' physical locations. Nowadays employees can work for a company in another country without leaving home. For many years migrants and SIes have continued to benefit their home countries by remitting earnings: nowadays the existence of national diasporas and the prominence of knowledge rather than money as a precious commodity provides opportunities for patriotic SIes and migrants to provide for their home countries or its organizations with expertise without it being necessary for them to return (Gamlen, 2011). Such efforts, however, need to be organized at a national level.

The long-term implications of self-initiated expatriation are not known. Will international mobility continue to increase? What will happen to the next generation? Will Kate and Paul's children, who have travelled the world all their lives, continue to be highly mobile, or will they seek a more settled existence to re-establish their identities?

In this chapter we have tried to show how the complex minutiae of such individual decision-making concerning the location of working and living self-organize into more stable and predictable larger-scale international flows of talent. These flows are personally initiated but have structural causes and constraints. At the national level, it behooves each jurisdiction to consider carefully how its framework of legislation, incentives, and controls affects the attraction, socialization, retention, and utilization of talented SIes. At the firm level, smart human resource policies and practices are likewise required. The issues we have raised will most likely increase in importance with the growing flows of global nomads. Policy makers at both the national and organizational level would do well to consider the Kate and Pauls of the world and the development of mechanisms that recognize their special character.

REFERENCES

Ackers, L. (2004). Managing relationships in peripatetic careers: Scientific mobility in the European Union. *Women's Studies International Forum*, 27, 189–201.
Agrawal, A., Kapur, D., McHale, J., & Oettl, A. (2010). Brain drain or brain bank? The impact of skilled emigration on poor-country innovation. *Journal of Urban Economics*, 69(1), 43–55.
Australian Senate. (2005). *They still call Australia home: Inquiry into Australian expatriates*. Canberra: Commonwealth of Australia.
Beaverstock, J. V. (2005). Transnational elites in the city: British highly-skilled inter-company transferees in New York City's financial district. *Journal of Ethnic and Migration Studies*, 31(2), 245–258.
Beechler, S., & Woodward, I. C. (2009). The global 'war for talent'. *Journal of International Management*, 15(3), 273–285.
Beine, M., Docquier, F., & Rapoport, H. (2008). Brain drain and human capital formation in developing countries: Winners and losers. *Economic Journal*, 118(528), 631–652.
Bird, A. (1996). Careers as repositories of knowledge: Considerations for boundaryless careers. In M. Arthur & D. Rousseau (Eds.), *The boundaryless career: A new employment principle for a new organizational era* (pp. 150–168).
Birkinshaw, J. (2005). Knowledge moves. *Business Strategy Review*, 16(4), 37–41.

Bozkurt, Ö., & Mohr, A. (2008). *Mobility, connectivity and social capital in multinational enterprises.* Paper presented at the Academy of Management Conference, Anaheim.

Bright, J., & Pryor, R. (2005). The chaos theory of careers: A user. *Career Development Quarterly, 53*(4), 291–305.

Carr, S., Inkson, K., & Thorn, K. (2005). From global careers to talent flow: Reinterpreting 'brain drain'. *Journal of World Business, 40*(4), 386–398.

Doherty, N. (2010, August). *Self-initiated expatriates—Mavericks of the global milieu.* Paper presented at the The Academy of Management, Montreal.

Doherty, N., & Dickmann, M. (2009). Exposing the symbolic capital of international assignments. *International Journal of Human Resource Management, 20*(2), 301–320.

Doherty, N., Dickmann, M., & Mills, T. (2011). Exploring the motives of company-backed and self-initiated expatriates. *The International Journal of Human Resource Management, 22*(3), 595–611.

Dubois, C. A., & Singh, D. (2009). From staff-mix to skill-mix and beyond: Towards a systemic approach to health workforce management. *Human Resources for Health, 7*(87), 1–19.

Dumont, J.-C., & Lemaitre, G. (2005). *Counting immigrants and expatriates in OECD countries: A new perspective.* Paris: OECD.

Fenwick, M. (2004). On international assignment: Is expatriation the only way to go? *Asia Pacific Journal of Human Resources, 42*(3), 365–377.

Fitzgerald, C., & Howe-Walsh, L. (2009). Self-initiated expatriates: An interpretative phenomenological analysis of professional female expatriates. *International Journal of Business and Management, 3*(10), 156–175.

Flamm, M., & Kaufmann, V. (2006). Operationalising the concept of motility: A qualitative study. *Mobilities, 1*(2), 167–189.

Gamlen, A. (2011). Diasporas. In A. Betts (Ed.), *Global migration governance* (pp. 266–286). Oxford: Oxford Universiy Press.

Giuliano, P., & Ruiz-Arranz, M. (2009). Remittances, financial development, and growth. *Journal of Development Economics, 90*(1), 144–152.

Gwaradzimba, E., & Shumba, A. (2010). The nature, extent and impact of the brain drain in Zimbabwe and South Africa. *Acta Academica, 42*(1), 209–241.

Habermas, J. (1984). *The theory of communicative action: Reason and the rationalization of society* (Vol. 1). Boston: Beacon Press.

Han, S. H., Park, S. H., Jin, E. J., Kim, H., & Seong, Y. K. (2008). Critical issues and possible solutions for motivating foreign construction workers. *Journal of Management in Engineering, 24*(4), 217–227.

Hardy, J. (2010). 'Brain drain', 'brain gain' or 'brain waste': East-West migration after enlargement. In O. Drossou & O. Farinde (Eds.), *Mobility and Inclusion: Managing labour migration in Europe* (pp. 48–54). Berlin: Heinrich Böll Stiftung. Retrieved from http://www.migration-boell.de/web/migration/46_2413.asp.

Harvey, M. (1998). Dual-career couples during international relocation: The trailing spouse. *International Journal of Human Resource Management, 9*(2), 309–331.

Hippler, T. (2009). Why do they go? Empirical evidence of employees' motives for seeking or accepting relocation. *International Journal of Human Resource Management, 20*(6), 1381–1401.

Inkson, K., Carr, S., Edwards, M., Hooks, J., Jackson, D., Thorn, K., & Allfree, N. (2004). *From brain drain to talent flow: Views of expatriate Kiwis.* University of Auckland Business Review, 6(2), 29–40.

Inkson, K., & King, Z. (2011). Contested terrain in careers: A psychological contract model. *Human Relations, 64*(1), 37–57.

Inkson, K., & Myers, B. (2003). 'The big OE': Self-directed travel and career development. *Career Development International*, 8(4), 170–181.

Iredale, R. (2005). Gender, immigration policies and accreditation: Valuing the skills of professional women migrants. *Geoforum*, 36, 155–166.

Jackling, B., & Keneley, M. (2009). Influences on the supply of accounting graduates in Australia: A focus on international students. *Accounting & Finance*, 49(1), 141–159.

Jackson, D. J. R., Carr, S. C., Edwards, M., Thorn, K., Allfree, N., Hooks, J., & Inkson, K. (2005). Exploring the dynamics of New Zealand's talent flow. *New Zealand Journal of Psychology*, 34(2), 110–116.

Johansson, E. (2008). Does Finland suffer from brain drain? Helsinki: The Research Institute of the Finnish Economy.

Jokinen, T., Brewster, C., & Suutari, V. (2008). Career capital during international work experiences: Contrasting self-initiated expatriate experiences and assigned expatriation. *The International Journal of Human Resource Management*, 19(6), 979–998.

Koser, K., & Salt, J. (1997). The geography of highly skilled international migration. *International Journal of Population Geography*, 3(4), 285–303.

Krumboltz, J., & Levin, A. (2002). *Planned happenstance: Making the most of chance events in your life and your career*. Atascadero, CA: Impact Publishers.

Le, T., Gibson, J., & Oxley, L. (2003). Cost- and income-based measures of human capital. *Journal of Economic Surveys*, 17(3), 271–307.

Lowell, B. L. (2005). Policies and regulations for managing skilled international migration for work. New York: United Nations Expert Group Meeting on International Migration and Development.

Mahroum, S. (2005). The international policies of brain gain: A review. *Technology Analysis and Strategic Management*, 17(2), 219–230.

Myers, B., & Pringle, J. (2005). Self-initiated foreign experience as accelerated development: Influences of gender. *Journal of World Business*, 40, 421–431.

Ng, P. T. (2010). Singapore's response to the global war for talent: Politics and education. *International Journal of Educational Development*, 31(3), 262–268.

Nowicka, M. (2006). Mobile locations: Construction of home in a group of mobile transnational professionals. *Global networks*, 7(1), 69–86.

OECD. (2008). The global competition for talent: Mobility of the highly skilled. Paris: OECD.

Osland, J. (1995). *The adventure of working abroad*. San Francisco: Jossey–Bass Inc.

Ouaked, S. (2002). Transatlantic roundtable on high skilled migration and sending countries issues. *International Migration*, 40(4), 153–166.

Özden, Ç. (2006). Educated migrants: Is there brain waste? In World Bank (Ed.), *International migration, remittances, and the brain drain* (pp. 227–244).

Parasuraman, S., & Greenhaus, J. H. (1997). *Integrating work and family: Challenges and choices for a changing world*. Westport, CT: Quorum.

Peterson, R. A., & Anand, N. (2002). How chaotic careers create orderly fields. In M. Peiperl & M. Arthur (Eds.), *Career creativity: Explorations in the remaking of work* (pp. 257–279).

Portes, A. (1976). Determinants of the brain drain. *International Migration Review*, 10(4), 489–508.

Raghuram, P. (2004). The difference that skills make: Gender, family migration strategies and regulated labour markets. *Journal of Ethnic and Migration Studies*, 30(2), 303–321.

Recchi, E. (2008). Cross-state mobility in the EU. *European Societies*, 10(2), 197–224.

Richards, G., & Wilson, J. (Eds.). (2004). *The global nomad: Backpacker travel in theory and practice.* Clevedon: Channel View Publications.

Richardson, J., & Zikic, J. (2007). The darker side of an international academic career. *Career Development International,* 12(2), 164–186.

Roper, J., Ganesh, S., & Inkson, K. (2010). Neoliberalism and knowledge interests in boundaryless careers discourse. *Work, Employment & Society,* 24(4), 661–679.

Schiff, M. (2005). *Brain gain: Claims about its size and impact on welfare and growth are greatly exaggerated.* World Bank Publications.

Shen, Y., & Hall, D. (2009). When expatriates explore other options: Retaining talent through greater job embeddedness and repatriation adjustment. *Human Resource Management,* 48(5), 793–816.

Somaya, D., & Williamson, I. O. (2008). Rethinking the 'war for talent'. *MIT Sloan Management Review,* 49(4), 29–34.

Super, D. E. (1990). A life-span, life-space to career development. In D. Brown & L. Brooks (Eds.), *Career choice and development: Applying contemporary theories to practice* (pp. 197–261). San Francisco: Jossey-Bass.

Suutari, V., & Brewster, C. (2003). Repatriation: Empirical evidence from a longitudinal study of careers and expectations among Finnish expatiates. *Journal of Human Resource Management,* 14(7), 1132–1151.

Tharenou, P. (2010a). Identity and global mobility. In S. C. Carr (Ed.), *The psychology of global mobility* (pp. 105–123). New York: Springer.

Tharenou, P. (2010b). Women's self-initiated expatriation as a career option and its ethical issues. *Journal of Business Ethics,* 95(1), 73–88.

Tharmaseelan, N., Inkson, K., & Carr, S. (2010). Migration and career success: Testing a time-sequenced model. *Career Development International,* 15(3), 218–238.

Thorn, K. (2009). The relative importance of motives for international self-initiated mobility. *Career Development International,* 14(5), 441–464.

Wang, B., & Bu, N. (2004). Attitudes toward international careers among male and female Canadian business students after 9/11. *Career Development International,* 9(7), 647–672.

Weick, K. (1996). Enactment and the boundaryless career: Organizing as we work. In M. Arthur & D. Rousseau (Eds.), *The boundaryless career: A new employment principle for a new organizational era* (pp. 40–57). New York: Oxford University Press.

6 Differences in Self-Initiated and Organizational Expatriates' Cross-Cultural Adjustment

Vesa Peltokorpi and Fabian J. Froese

Reflecting changes in the international labor force, more professionals initiate their own expatriation than are assigned abroad by multinational companies (MNCs). For example, a study on expatriated professionals from Western countries shows that 65% of them are self-initiated expatriates (SIEs) and the remaining 35% organizational expatriates (OEs) (Doherty, Dickmann, & Mills, 2008). SIEs are individuals who decide by themselves to live and work in foreign countries (Peltokorpi & Froese, 2009); OEs are individuals who are deployed by MNCs to complete a time-based task or achieve an organizational goal in a country of a company's choice (Edström & Galbraith, 1977). The prevalence of self-initiated expatriating is also shown by the increased international movement of professionals. For example, at least 1.5 million skilled individuals were estimated to migrate to Organisation for Economic Co-operation and Development (OECD) countries in 2004 (OECD, 2006). Therefore, it is not surprising that scholars have started to classify and examine SIEs as a distinctive group of expatriates.

While recently increasing, there is still surprisingly little research on SIEs. Due to their increasing share of the international labor force and notable differences between OEs and SIEs, more research is called for to better understand issues associated with SIEs and their expatriation (Inkson, Arthur, Pringle, & Barry, 1997). In this chapter, we review and extend our research on OEs and SIEs (Peltokorpi, 2008; Peltokorpi & Froese, 2009; Froese & Peltokorpi, 2011). More specifically, we focus on (1) the differences in OEs and SIEs cross-cultural adjustment (Peltokorpi & Froese, 2009) and (2) explore the reasons for different cross-cultural adjustment patterns. Because our studies were conducted in Japan, a brief description of Japanese culture is warranted. In addition to being minorities in terms of language, race, and religion, cultural values of verticality and collectivism influence Western expatriates' cross-cultural adjustment in Japan (Peltokorpi, 2008). Verticality is displayed in strict behavioral norms determined, for example, by age (Nakane, 1972) and collectivism in group-oriented behavior and conformity to group norms (Triandis, 1995). The tendencies for the Japanese to show the 'right' attitudes and behavioral patterns in order to fit into the group increase the in- and out-group categorization

(Triandis, 1995). The low average English proficiency in Japan can also influence cross-cultural adjustment. For example, the Japanese have one of the lowest average Test of English for International Communication (TOEIC) scores in the world (Yoshihara, Okabe, & Sawaki, 2001). Perhaps due to these cultural and linguistic barriers, expatriates are shown to have only a few host country nationals (HCNs) with whom to share their problems and to be isolated from the Japanese society (Skuja & Norton, 1982; Tokyo English Life Line, 2003). The host country influence is taken into account in our studies.

The rest of this chapter is organized as follows. The following section defines and conceptually differentiates SIEs from OEs, sojourners, immigrants, and migrant workers. The third section provides a brief review of SIE research. The fourth section examines differences in SIEs and OEs cross-cultural adjustment and the reasons for different cross-cultural adjustment in Japan. The fifth section discusses the findings, and the sixth section concludes this chapter.

SIES: DEFINITION AND DIFFERENTIATION

SIEs are defined as individuals who decide by themselves to live and work in foreign countries (Peltokorpi & Froese, 2009). SIEs can be distinguished from OEs along various work-related dimensions. While SIEs are argued to make the decision to move and work abroad often with no definite time frame in mind (Tharenou, 2010), OEs are deployed by MNCs to foreign countries to accomplish a specific job or organization-related goal within a pre-designed time period, ranging often from six months to five years (Edström & Galbraith, 1977). SIEs thus do not follow the structured career path of OEs; they tend to perceive their overseas experience as a means of self-development or part of some other personal agenda (Inkson et al., 1997; Jokinen, Brewster, & Suutari, 2008). OEs' motivation to go abroad can be explained by the related financial benefits, increased opportunities for career progression, and personal interests in international experience (Miller & Cheng, 1978; Suutari & Brewster, 2000). Among these career-related factors, the enhanced chances for career progression are most important because international work experience is one of the main requirements for promotion to higher-level managerial positions in MNCs (Carpenter, Sanders, & Gregersen, 2001). SIEs also often fund their own relocation, while OEs tend to receive generous relocation packages. Finally, while OEs have the option to return home and have a job waiting in the home office, SIEs returning back to their home countries or moving on to other countries often have to find jobs by themselves.

SIEs can also be differentiated from sojourners, immigrants, and migrant workers. While sojourners can be classified as any people who stay a short time period in foreign countries, such as foreign students, SIEs are foreign national employees living "ex-patria" (usually 2–5 years) in host countries (Selmer & Lauring, 2010). In contrast to immigrants (i.e., individuals who come to a host country to take a permanent residence), SIEs move to foreign countries for work on their own initiative. They may or may not seek permanent residence in host countries. Accordingly, SIE researchers have focused on the career-related outcomes and motivation of self-initiated professionals from developed countries, such as Australia (Tharenou & Caulfield, 2010), Finland (Suutari & Brewster, 2000), and New Zealand (Inkson et al., 1997). Motivation to live and work in foreign countries and residence status thus separate SIEs from immigrants. One difficulty regarding SIEs however—given the diversity among individuals who decide to pursue their careers abroad—is to differentiate them from migrant workers and those who are expatriating with the intention of staying in the host country for few years and then returning to their home country or moving to other countries (McKenna & Richardson, 2007; Forstenlechner, 2010). In contrast to often low-educated migrant workers (Rodriguez & Tiongson, 2001), SIEs are highly educated (Suutari & Brewster, 2000). Perhaps for these reasons, researchers have focused on university educated SIEs who have returned back to their home countries (Inkson et al., 1997; Inkson & Myers, 2003; Myers & Pringle, 2005; Tharenou & Caulfield, 2010). SIEs are thus (re)defined here as professionals who decide by themselves to live and work for a certain time period in foreign countries.

LITERATURE REVIEW

While being an increasingly important part of the global work force (Tharenou & Caulfield, 2010), little focused research on SIEs exists. In order to differentiate our research, we provide a brief review of SIE research. First, interview studies in New Zealand show that overseas work experiences provides SIEs increased self-confidence, self-reliance, and a clearer career focus when returning back to their home country (Inkson et al., 1997; Inkson & Myers, 2003). Another interview study in New Zealand shows that self-initiated overseas experiences provides accelerated career development opportunities for both female and male SIEs, but females who tend to stay overseas longer have deeper and more integrated work-related experiences than males (Myers & Pringle, 2005). A qualitative study with SIEs in Ireland, England, the Netherlands, and Poland shows further that while SIEs move overseas for professional development, they do little research on their future career and employment opportunities before leaving their home countries (Felker, 2011). Another interview study with American SIEs in East Asian cities shows that a large portion of SIEs are married to HCNs (Vance, 2005). Moreover, an interview study of academics in South Korea shows that many SIEs were motivated to move to Korea partly because they wanted know the country of their spouses better (Froese, 2012). Finally, an interview study of skilled Lebanese in Paris shows that social-, cultural-, economic-, and symbolic capital facilitate SIEs' international mobility (Al Ariss & Syed, 2011, see Al Ariss, 2010; Al Ariss & Özbilgin, 2010, for other studies on Lebanese SIEs in Paris).

In addition to the career-related interview studies, researchers have used surveys to examine differences in SIEs and OEs motivation to live and work abroad. For example, SIEs are found to be younger and more often female than OEs, to have a higher organizational mobility, expect higher benefits from international experiences for their future careers, and that their main motive to work abroad is to gain international experience (Suutari & Brewster, 2000; Biemann & Andresen, 2010). Location and host country reputation motives are also more important to SIEs; OEs place more emphasis on specific career motives, such as job, skills and career impact (Doherty, Dickmann, & Mills, 2011). OEs and SIEs career capital accumulation is further shown to differ because OEs scored higher on several dimensions in knowing-how, knowing-why, and knowing-whom career capital (Jokinen et al., 2008). Studies among SIEs show further that younger expatriate academics are more motivated to live and work abroad due to adventure and travel, career, and financial incentives (Selmer & Lauring, 2010). Married SIE academics have higher work performance than non-married SIEs (Selmer & Lauring, 2011). Moreover, a study among SIEs in Singapore shows that a lack of job autonomy, job suitability, and job variety as well as lack of fit with the psychological contract contribute to the perceived underemployment of SIEs (Lee, 2005). Finally, a recent study with Australian SIEs shows that host country pull (weak embeddedness), home country pull, and shocks explain their intentions to repatriate and that shocks also play a key role in explaining SIEs' job search and repatriation (Tharenou & Caulfield, 2010).

RESEARCH ON SIES AND OES IN JAPAN

In contrast to the career-related consequences and motivational differences in most previous SIE studies, our research focuses on the differences in SIEs and OEs cross-cultural adjustment. Though overlooked in the SIE literature, research in this area is important for several reasons. First, we move a step forward by linking the demographic and motivational differences of OEs and SIEs to cross-cultural adjustment. Indeed, expatriate demographic and motivational factors are shown in OE research to explain significant variance in cross-cultural adjustment (see Hechanova, Beehr, & Christiansen, 2003; Bhaskar-Shrinivas, Harrison, Shaffer, & Luk, 2005, for reviews). In addition to identifying differences in SIEs and OEs cross-cultural adjustment, we also explore the reasons for the different adjustment patterns. Second, research on SIEs and OEs cross-cultural adjustment provides important information to MNC staffing policies. While often dispatched by MNCs to foreign units for control and career-development purposes (Edström & Galbraith, 1977), OEs are expensive and face adjustment difficulties (Bhaskar-Shrinivas et al., 2005). On average, organizations spend over two and a half times more money to send an employee on expatriate assignment than they would to hire locally (McGoldrick, 1997), and a three-year assignment is estimated to cost around US$1 million (Allerton, 1997). SIEs provide a cheaper alternative to staff overseas operations than OEs because they can be hired under local contracts and are not provided pre-departure and on-site training.

Cross-cultural adjustment is defined as the degree to which expatriates are psychologically comfortable and familiar with different aspects of foreign environment (Black & Mendenhall, 1991). Theoretical foundations of cross-cultural adjustment are based on the cultural learning theory that emphasizes the importance of social behavior and practical social skills underlying attitudinal factors (Black & Mendenhall, 1991; Selmer, 2006). In research, cross-cultural adjustment is conceptualized as a multifaceted construct with general, work, and interaction related facets (Black, 1988; Black & Stephens, 1989). General adjustment refers to the degree of psychological comfort with regard to several aspects of the host culture environment, such as climate, food, heath care, housing conditions, and shopping. Work adjustment refers to the degree of comfort regarding different expectations, performance standards, and work values. Finally, interaction adjustment refers to the degree of comfort associated with interacting with HCNs inside and outside of work. This tripartite definition has been operationalized and validated in numerous empirical studies (Hechanova et al., 2003; Bhaskar-Shrinivas et al., 2005). While interrelated, various work and non-work related factors influence general, work, and interaction adjustment in different ways (Bhaskar-Shrinivas et al., 2005). Meta-analyses show further that cross-cultural adjustment is an important predictor of job attitudes and expatriate performance (Hechanova et al., 2003; Bhaskar-Shrinivas et al., 2005). The three facets of cross-cultural adjustment were used as dependent variables in our studies on SIEs and OEs in Japan.

DIFFERENCES IN SIES AND OES CROSS-CULTURAL ADJUSTMENT

Our previous study focused on SIEs and OEs cross-cultural adjustment differences (Peltokorpi & Froese, 2009). Regarding the three cross-cultural adjustment facets, we started by identifying differences in interaction adjustment. First, SIEs who have made the decision to live and work in Japan tend to be more motivated to interact with HCNs and more tolerant of cultural differences during intercultural interactions. SIEs may even seek to interact more with HCNs than OEs due to their personal interest in Japanese culture. Also, HCN spouses or partners can have important roles in introducing SIEs to HCNs (Vance, 2005). SIEs can thus be more aware of the challenges in interactions with HCNs than OEs who seldom receive adequate pre-departure training (Black & Mendenhall, 1990). The interaction and possible formation of relationships with HCNs allows SIEs to gain insights into cultural norms, facilitating intercultural interactions. In contrast, usually living for a restricted period in residential areas with a dense concentration of OEs may limit their non-work interactions to other OEs or to a limited number of HCNs proficient in English and interested in interacting with foreigners. While these interactions can be fulfilling, they reinforce the division between in- and out-group members, reducing interactions with HCNs (Takeuchi, Marinova, Lepak, & Liu, 2005). Thus, we suggested the following hypothesis:

Hypothesis 1: OEs experience a lower degree of interaction adjustment with HCNs than SIEs.

Adjustment to general aspects of the host country was also expected to vary among OEs and SIEs. Though possibly being motivated to live in Japan and interested in Japanese culture, SIEs lack the non-work-related support (e.g., education for their children and housing allowances) that OEs usually receive from their companies (Suutari & Brewster, 2000; Vance, 2005). For example, OEs tend to live in areas with a high concentration of foreign residents and have housing with standard Western utilities. SIEs are often not willing or able to finance such residences. If SIEs seek to rent private apartments in Japan, they are often discriminated against partly since many apartment owners refuse to let their apartments to foreigners (Mori, 1996). In contrast to SIEs, who often need to live in places that are not in demand by HCNs, OEs receive assistance and financial support from their companies so as to maintain the same standard of living abroad as at home (Konopaske & Werner, 2005). Taking these differences into account, we suggested the following hypothesis:

Hypothesis 2: OEs experience a higher degree of general living adjustment than SIEs.

Finally, we identified differences in work adjustment. While OEs are dispatched to accomplish predefined job/organization-related goals, SIEs often have to find a new job at a new company. SIEs thus have to cope with cross-cultural differences and adjust to a new job and organization. However, this does not mean that OEs are better adjusted to interact with HCNs at work. Indeed, Western expatriates are found to be frustrated with low risk taking, lengthy decision making, and high-context communication in Japan (Peltokorpi, 2007), which may interfere with their work-related goals. However, SIEs can be in a worse situation since they often occupy a job that does not suit their educational and professional background, skills, and interests (Lee, 2005). Additional frustration can be caused by limited opportunities for career advancement and differential treatment in Japanese organizations (Kurata, 1990). Some consequences of long-term underemployment in terms of underutilized skills and abilities are increased frustration and negative work attitudes among SIEs (Lee, 2005). Additional factors decreasing work adjustment are created by the lower job security of SIEs usually hired on one-year contracts in Japan (Kurata, 1990). Studies further suggest that SIEs receive less mentoring and social support from their HCN colleagues in Japan than OEs (Kurata, 1990). Thus, we suggested the following hypothesis:

Hypothesis 3: OEs experience a higher degree of work-related adjustment than SIEs.

These three hypotheses were tested with 124 SIEs and 55 OEs in the greater Tokyo area (Kawasaki, Saitama, Tokyo, and Yokohama). On average, OEs were 34.3 years old ($SD = 8.4$) and had worked for 37 months ($SD = 43$) in Japan. Most of them were male (73%), not married (69%), and roughly half held managerial positions. In line with the importance of American and European companies in Japan (Japan Institute of Labour, 2002), most came from the USA, Germany, France, and the UK. In total, the respondents represent 24 different nationalities. Among them, 73% were working for foreign-owned companies, and 33% had a Japanese partner (married or not married). Despite relatively similar age (32.5 years, $SD = 10.2$), percentage of males (67%), and marital status, SIEs had worked longer in Japan (59.7 months, $SD = 61.9$), and only 37% held managerial positions. More SIEs were working for Japanese companies (54%) and also slightly more had Japanese partners (46%).

To test differences in OEs and SIEs cross-cultural adjustment (measured by a Black and Stephen's [1989] 14-item scale for interaction, general, and work adjustment), we conducted MANCOVA and ANCOVA analyses with three control variables (length of stay in Japan [measured in years], job level [staff or manager], and company nationality [domestic or foreign]) as covariates. MANCOVA revealed first that there were significant differences in OEs and SIEs cross-cultural adjustment ($F = 3.82$, $p < 0.01$). Subsequent ANCOVA revealed that SIEs were significantly more adjusted in terms of interaction adjustment ($F = 10.89$, $p < 0.001$). SIEs were further found to express higher levels of general adjustment, while these differences were meaningful only at the $p < 0.10$ level of significance. The result was also in opposition to our original assumptions. Finally, we did not find any significant differences for work adjustment.

REASONS FOR DIFFERENT CROSS-CULTURAL ADJUSTMENT PATTERNS

While the above analyses demonstrated differences in SIEs' and OEs' cross-cultural adjustment, we still do not know why these differences exit. To provide a more fine-grained analysis, we tested first the differences between SIEs and OEs by conducting independent sample t-tests to compare the demographics, personality, job-related characteristics, and cross-cultural adjustment. In addition to the previously examined length of stay in Japan, job level, and company nationality, we added several new variables in our analysis. We included demographic variables: Age (measured in years), gender (0 = female, 1 = male), marital status (0 = not married and 1 = married), education (ranging from 1 = primary school to 5 = master degree or higher), and work experience in Japan and abroad work experience (measured in months). We also dummy coded supervisor nationality (0 = local, 1 = foreign supervisor). Since personality influences cross-cultural adjustment (Van Oudenhoven, Mol, & Van der Zee, 2003), we further measured four dimensions of expatriate personality—cultural empathy, open mindedness, social initiative, and flexibility by 20 items from a shortened multicultural personality questionnaire (MPQ; Froese & Peltokorpi, 2011; Peltokorpi & Froese, 2012).

Statistical tests indicated no differences in age, gender, marital status, and education between SIEs and OEs (see Table 6.1). However, there were significant differences for host country language proficiency and overseas experience. SIEs are more fluent in Japanese than OEs ($t = 4.22$, $p <0.001$). SIEs have also spent more time in Japan than OEs ($t = 2.24$, $p <0.05$), but OEs have more experience working in other foreign countries than SIEs ($t = -2.39$, $p <0.05$). Second, there were no statistically significant differences in SIEs' and OEs' multicultural personality traits. Both SIEs and OEs have relatively high open-mindedness, cultural empathy, and social initiative. Third, job related characteristics differed between SIEs and OEs. More OEs than SIEs occupied managerial positions ($t = -2.40$, $p <0.05$). SIEs worked more often than OEs under Japanese supervisors ($t = -2.42$, $p <0.05$). Though the vast majority of OEs work for foreign companies, many SIEs work for domestic companies ($t = -3.73$, $p <0.001$). Finally, our data shows significant differences in cross-cultural adjustment. However, only interaction adjustment differs significantly between SIEs and OEs. SIEs are better adjusted to interacting with HCNs than OEs ($t = -3.81$, $p <0.001$).

We further conducted a mediation analysis to examine the differences in SIEs' and OEs' interaction adjustment. The mediation analysis is based on the three-step method by Baron and Kenny (1986). More specifically, a mediation is given (1) if the independent variable (SIE vs. OE) affects the mediator (other factors), (2) the independent variable affects the dependent variable (interaction adjustment), and (3) the mediator affects the dependent variable. Full mediation is given if the effect of the independent variables becomes insignificant in a complete regression when both the independent and mediating variable are entered.

Demographics and personality traits, explaining significant variance with interaction adjustment in OE research (Bhaskar-Shrinivas et al., 2005), were used as mediating variables. As shown in Table 6.1, Japanese language, Japanese experience, and abroad experience were related with the dummy

Table 6.1   Differences between SIEs and OEs

	SIE		OE			
	Mean	SD	Mean	SD	t-value	Sig
Demographics						
Age	33.07	7.48	33.83	8.45	-0.59	
Gender	0.67	0.47	0.72	0.45	-0.62	
Marital status	0.30	0.46	0.30	0.46	0.03	
Education	4.46	0.62	4.61	0.60	-1.52	
Japanese language	3.02	0.91	2.39	0.96	4.22	***
Japan experience	57.69	60.64	36.96	44.48	2.24	*
Abroad experience	17.01	29.67	31.53	49.74	-2.39	*
Personality						
Open-mindedness	4.20	0.59	4.12	0.50	0.85	
Emotional stability	3.57	0.68	3.69	0.64	-1.14	
Cultural empathy	3.96	0.57	3.98	0.51	-0.17	
Social initiative	3.85	0.67	3.99	0.60	-1.32	
Social initiative						
Job level	0.30	0.46	0.53	0.50	-2.40	*
Supervisor nationality	0.43	0.50	0.62	0.49	-2.42	*
Company nationality	0.46	0.50	0.75	0.43	-3.73	***
Cross-cultural adjustment						
Interaction	3.77	0.92	3.20	0.92	3.81	***
General	3.92	0.64	3.84	0.51	0.86	
Work	3.97	0.76	3.97	0.82	-0.03	

Note: $*p < 0.05$, $**p < 0.01$, $***p < 0.001$.

variable SIEs vs. OEs, fulfilling Condition 1. We conducted a series of regression analyses with interaction adjustment as the dependent variable to test for the other conditions (see Table 6.2). First, we entered the dummy variable SIEs vs. OEs. In Model 1, SIEs vs. OEs significantly affects interaction adjustment ($\beta = -0.276$, $p < 0.001$), showing that SIEs have higher interaction adjustment. The result satisfies Condition 2. Model 2 shows that Japan experience and Japanese language skills are positively related with interaction adjustment ($\beta = 0.148$, $p < 0.05$; $\beta = 0.534$, $p < 0.001$, respectively), showing that the respondents who have lived longer in Japan and those who speak better Japanese are better adjusted to interact with HCNs. Abroad experience in general was not statistically related with interaction adjustment. Thus, Japan experience and Japanese language skills satisfy Condition 3 of our mediation tests. In Model 3, we entered all variables to test whether Japan experience and Japanese language skills fully or partially mediated the relationship

Table 6.2 Predictors of Interaction Adjustment

	Model 1		Model 2		Model 3	
SIE vs. OE	-0.276	***			-0.084	
Japan experience			0.148	*	0.135	*
Abroad experience			-0.045		-0.029	
Language skills			0.534	***	0.512	***
R^2	0.076		0.341		0.348	
Adjusted R^2	0.071		0.330		0.332	
F	15.495	***	29.698	***	22.509	***

Note: $*p < 0.05$, $**p < 0.01$, $***p < 0.001$.

between SIEs vs. OEs and interaction adjustment. While Japan experience (β = 0.135, p <0.05) and language skills (β = 0.512, p <0.001) remain statistically significantly related to interaction adjustment, the SIEs vs. OEs variable became insignificant suggesting a full mediation effect. In other words, Japan experience and Japanese language experience explain why SIEs were more adjusted to interacting with HCNs.

DISCUSSION

This chapter examined differences between SIEs' and OEs' cross-cultural adjustment and the reasons for the adjustment differences. The findings show that SIEs and OEs differ in terms of host country language skills, overseas experience, job situations, and interaction adjustment. There were no statistically significant differences in expatriates' demographics, personality traits (measured by a shortened MPQ), general and work adjustments. Given the importance of cross-cultural adjustment in OE research (Hechanova et al., 2003; Bhaskar-Shrinivas et al., 2005), we further examined the reasons why SIEs showed higher interaction adjustment than OEs. Mediation analysis showed that this relationship was fully mediated by Japanese language proficiency and Japan experience. In other words, SIEs had greater interaction adjustment because of their better Japanese language proficiency and longer stay in Japan.

These findings are understandable taking into account the low average English proficiency among HCNs in Japan (Yoshihara et al., 2001) and that host country language proficiency is shown to facilitate expatriates' interaction adjustment in China (Selmer, 2006) and Japan (Peltokorpi, 2008). In Japan, Western expatriates face communication difficulties due to the differences in alphabets, grammar, and language syntax (Peltokorpi, 2007; Peltokorpi, 2010). In contrast, host country language proficiency creates and fosters interactions with HCNs and enables to expatriates to understand local culture (Takeuchi, Yun, & Russel, 2002; Selmer, 2006). This increased understanding of the host country culture enables expatriates to get along and communicate more effectively with HCNs. In contrast, insufficient host country language proficiency limits the expatriates' communicative interactions with other foreigners and limited number of host country nationals with adequate skills in English or some other common language (Peltokorpi, 2008). The anxiety-uncertainty management theory posits further that limited host country proficiency decreases the foreign workers' motivation to interact with HCNs (Gudykunst & Nishida, 2001). The higher host country language proficiency of SIEs can be explained by their higher motivations to interact with HCNs and control over their length of stay in host countries.

The positive impact of longer host country experience on SIEs interaction adjustment can be explained in three different ways. First, the interaction is in line with the time-related explanations of expatriate cross-cultural adjustment (Torbiörn, 1982; Black & Mendenhall, 1991). That is, expatriates need time to learn and become familiar to the host country culture. Alternatively, host country experience and host country language proficiency can be subject to spillover effects (Bhagat, 1983). In support, expatriates who stay longer in host countries are found to be more proficient in Japanese (Peltokorpi, 2008). The results can also be due to the attribution effect (Van Oudenhoven et al., 2003). That is, maladjusted SIEs drop out and more adjusted ones to stay in host countries. The attribution effect is relevant with SIEs that tend to stay longer (Suutari & Brewster, 2000) and have more control over the length stay in host countries than OEs (Peltokorpi & Froese, 2009). While some SIEs may perceive self-initiated expatriation as an opportunity for accelerated career development (Myers & Pringle, 2005), the others may seek to stay in host countries for personal reasons (Vance, 2005). In contrast, OEs usually stay in host countries a predetermined time period, ranging from six months to five years (Edström & Galbraith, 1977). This is likely to influence SIEs and OEs motivation to learn host country language and interact with HCNs.

PRACTICAL IMPLICATIONS

The findings can be used to provide managerial recommendations related to expatriate selection and training. First, MNCs may pay more attention to SIEs in their recruiting efforts since they appear to be equally or even better adjusted to work and life in Japan (and other culturally and linguistically complex countries). In particular, MNCs may focus on SIEs who have work experience in the host country. In contrast to OEs, MNCs can reduce cost and meet their talent needs by hiring SIEs. Second, MNCs can select expatriates, either SIEs or OEs, based on their host country language skills or provide language training. Motivation to engage in language studies can be enhanced by specific language acquisition goals and linking improvements in language test scores to performance appraisals (Peltokorpi, 2007). Third, expatriate training is often divided into general cross-cultural training and country-specific training. The research in this chapter suggests that country-specific training is more important in Japan, since Japanese language and Japan experience, not abroad experience or multicultural personality traits, explain why SIEs showed higher interaction adjustment.

CONCLUSION

While SIEs are identified to constitute a significant part of international labor force, surprisingly little research in this area has been conducted. This chapter shows that significant differences in OEs and SIEs cross-cultural adjustment exist that can be explained by their different host country language proficiency and experience of living in the host country. The findings presented are hoped to stimulate and provide several avenues for future research in this area.

REFERENCES

Al Ariss, A. (2010). Modes of engagement: Migration, self-initiated expatriation and career development. *Career Development International, 15*(4), 338–358.

Al Ariss, A., & Özbilgin, M. (2010). Understanding self-initiated expatriates: Career experiences of Lebanese self-initiated expatriates. *Thunderbird International Business Review, 54,* 275–285.

Al Ariss, A., & Syed, J. (2011). Capital mobilization of skilled migrants: A relational perspective. *British Journal of Management, 22*(2), 286–304.

Allerton, H. (1997). Expatriate gaps. *Training & Development, 51*(7), 7–8.

Baron, R. M., & Kenny, D. A. (1986). The moderator-mediator variable distinction in social psychological research: Conceptual, strategic, and statistical considerations, *Journal of Personality & Social Psychology, 51*(6), 1173–1182.

Bhagat, R. S. (1983). Effects of stressful life events on individual performance effectiveness and work adjustment processes within organizational settings: A research model. *Academy of Management Review, 8,* 660–671.

Bhaskar-Shrinivas, P., Harrison, D. A., Shaffer, M. A., & Luk, D. M. (2005). Input-based and timebased models of international adjustment: Meta-analytical evidence and theoretical extensions. *Academy of Management Journal, 482,* 257–281.

Biemann, T., & Andresen, M. (2010). Self-initiated expatriates versus assigned expatriates: Two distinct types of international careers? *Journal of Managerial Psychology, 25*(4), 430–448.

Black, J. S. (1988). Work role transitions: A study of American expatriate managers in Japan. *Journal of International Business Studies, 19,* 277–294.

Black, J. S., & Mendenhall, M. (1990). Cross-cultural training effectiveness: A review and a theoretical framework for future research. *Academy of Management Review, 15,* 113–136.

Black, J. S., & Mendenhall, M. (1991). The U-curve adjustment hypothesis revisited: A review and theoretical framework. *Journal of International Business Studies,* 225–247.

Black, J. S., & Stephens, G. K. (1989). The influence of the spouse on expatriate adjustment and intention to stay in assignments. *Journal of Management, 15,* 529–544.

Carpenter, M. A., Sanders, W. G., & Gregersen, H. B. (2001). Bundling human capital with organizational context: The impact of international experience on multinational firm performance and CEO pay. *Academy of Management Journal, 44,* 439–511.

Doherty, N., Dickmann, M., & Mills, T. (2008, July). *Career activities or active careerists?* Paper presented at the EGOS Colloquium, Amsterdam, the Netherlands.

Doherty, N., Dickmann, M., & Mills, T. (2011). Exploring the motives of company-packed and self-initiated expatriates. *International Journal of Human Resource Management, 22*(3), 595–611.

Edström, A., & Galbraith, J. R. (1977). Transfer of managers as a coordination and control strategy in multinational organizations. *Administrative Science Quarterly, 22,* 248–263.

Felker, J. A. (2011). Professional development through self-directed expatriation: Intentions and outcomes for young, educated Eastern Europeans. *International Journal of Training and Development, 15*(1), 76–86.

Forstenlechner, I. (2010). Exploring expatriates' behavioral reaction to institutional injustice on host country level. *Personnel Review, 39*(2), 178–194.

Froese, F. J. (2012). Motivation and adjustment of self-initiated expatriates: The case of expatriate academics in South Korea. *International Journal of Human Resource Management, 23,* 1095–1112.

Froese, F. J., & Peltokorpi, V. (2011). Cultural distance and expatriate job satisfaction. *International Journal of Intercultural Relations, 35,* 49–60.

Gudykunst, W. B., & Nishida, T. (2001). Anxiety, uncertainty, and perceived effectiveness of communication across relationships and cultures. *International Journal of Intercultural Relations, 25,* 55–71.

Hechanova, R., Beehr, T. A., & Christiansen, N. D. (2003). Antecedents and consequences of employees' adjustment to overseas assignments: A meta-analytic review. *Applied Psychology: An International Review, 52*(2), 213–236.

Inkson, K., Arthur, M. B., Pringle, J., & Barry, S. (1997). Expatriate assignment versus overseas experience: International human resource development. *Journal of World Business, 2,* 351–368.

Inkson, K., & Myers, B. A. (2003). "The Big OE": Self-directed travel and career development. *Career Development International, 8*(4), 170–181.

Japan Institute of Labor (2002). *Survey on work and life among expatriates in Japan.* Tokyo: Japan Institute of Labor.

Jokinen, T., Brewster, C., & Suutari, V. (2008). Career capital during international work experiences: Contrasting self-initiated expatriate experiences and assigned expatriation. *International Journal of Human Resource Management, 19*(6), 979–998.

Konopaske, R., & Werner, S. (2005). US managers' willingness to accept a global assignment: Do expatriate benefits and assignment length make a difference? *International Journal of Human Resource Management, 167,* 1157–1175.

Kurata, Y. (1990). Human resource management of foreign staff employees in Japanese companies. *Hitotsubashi Journal of Social Studies, 22,* 27–36.

Lee, C. H. (2005). A study of underemployment among self-initiated expatriates. *Journal of World Business, 40,* 172–187.

McGoldrick, F. (1997). Expatriate compensation and benefit practices of US and Canadian firms: Survey results. *International HR Journal,* Summer, 13–17.

McKenna, S., & Richardson, J. (2007). The increasing complexity of the internationally mobile professionals: Issues for research and practice. *Cross Cultural Management, 14*(4), 307–329.

Miller, E. L., & Cheng, J. (1978). A closer look at the decision to accept an overseas position. *Management International Review, 3*, 25–33.

Mori, H. (1996). Foreign workers' working and living conditions in Japan. *Journal of International Economic Studies, 10*, 23–64.

Myers, B., & Pringle, J. K. (2005). Self-initiated foreign experience as accelerated development: Influences of gender. *Journal of World Business, 40*, 421–431.

Nakane, C. (1972). *Japanese society*. Berkeley: University of Berkeley Press.

OECD (2006). Immigration rises in OECD countries but asylum requests fall, says OECD. Paris: OECD.

Peltokorpi, V. (2007). Intercultural communication patterns and strategies: Nordic expatriates in Japan. *International Business Review, 16*(1), 68–82.

Peltokorpi, V. (2008). Cross-cultural adjustment of expatriates in Japan. *International Journal of Human Resource Management, 19*(9), 1588–1606.

Peltokorpi, V. (2010). Intercultural communication in foreign subsidiaries: The influence of expatriates' language and cultural competencies. *Scandinavian Journal of Management, 26*, 176–188.

Peltokorpi, V., & Froese, F. J. (2009). Organizational expatriates and self-initiated expatriates: Who adjusts better to work and life in Japan? *International Journal of Human Resource Management, 20*(5), 1095–1111.

Peltokorpi, V., & Froese, F. J. (2012). The impact of expatriate personality traits on cross-cultural adjustment: A study with expatriates in Japan. *International Business Review, 36*, 331–342.

Rodriguez, E. R., & Tiongson, E. R. (2001). Temporary migration overseas and household labor supply: Evidence from urban Philippines. *International Migration Review, 35*(3), 709–725.

Selmer, J. (2006). Language ability and adjustment: Western expatriates in China. *Thunderbird International Business Review, 48*(3), 347–368.

Selmer, J., & Lauring, J. (2010). Self-initiated academic expatriates: Inherent demographics and reasons to expatriate. *European Management Review, 7*(3), 169–179.

Selmer, J., & Lauring, J. (2011). Marital status and work outcomes of self-initiated expatriates: Is there a moderating effect of gender? *Cross-cultural Management: An International Journal, 18*(2), 198–213.

Skuja, I., & Norton, J. (1982). Counseling English-speaking expatriates in Tokyo. *International Social Work, 25*, 30–42.

Suutari, V., & Brewster, C. (2000). Making their own way: International experience through self-initiated foreign assignments. *Journal of World Business, 35*, 417–436.

Takeuchi, R., Marinova, S. V., Lepak, D. P., & Liu, W. (2005). A model of expatriate withdrawal-related outcomes: Decision making from a dualistic adjustment perspective. *Human Resource Management Review, 15*, 119–138.

Takeuchi, R., Yun, S., & Russel, J. E. (2002). Antecedents and consequences of the perceived adjustment of Japanese expatriates in the USA. *International Journal of Human Resource Management, 13*, 1224–1244.

Tharenou, P. (2010). Women's self-expatriation as a career option and its ethnical issues. *Journal of Business Ethics, 95*, 73–88.

Tharenou, P., & Caulfield, N. (2010). Will I stay or will I go? Explaining repatriation by self-initiated expatriates. *Academy of Management Journal, 53*(5), 1009–1028.

Tokyo English Life Line (2003). *Problems faced by foreign women living in Japan: Indicated in the telephone counseling*. Tokyo: Asian Women's Fund.

Torbiörn, I. (1982). *Living abroad*. New York: Wiley.

Triandis, H. C. (1995). *Individualism and collectivism*. Boulder: Westview Press.

Vance, C. M. (2005). The personal quest for building global competence: A taxonomy of self-initiating career path strategies for gaining business experience abroad. *Journal of World Business, 40,* 374–385.

Van Oudenhoven, J. P., Mol, S., & Van der Zee, K. I. (2003). Study of the adjustment of Western expatriates in Taiwan ROC with the Multicultural Personality Questionnaire, *Asian Journal of Social Psychology, 6,* 159–170.

Yoshihara, H., Okabe, Y., & Sawaki, S. (2001). *Eigo de keieisuru jidai—Nihon kigyo no chosen.* Tokyo: Yuhikaku Publishing.

7 Career Concepts of Self-Initiated and Assigned Expatriates
A Theoretical Analysis Based on Coupling and Configuration

Maike Andresen and Torsten Biemann

As companies increase their international operations, the need to develop employees and leaders with global competencies becomes a top priority (Black, Morrison, & Gregersen, 1999b; Black, Gregersen, Mendenhall, & Stroh, 1999a; Connor, 2000; Kohonen, 2005; Suutari, 2003). Globally competent managers are characterized by the ability to interact effectively with people who are culturally different, to deal with various competitive and political environments, and to see rapid change and uncertainty as an opportunity (Early & Ang, 2003; Evans, Pucik, & Barsoux, 2002). International work experience is seen as the most powerful instrument to develop these competencies (Black et al., 1999a; 1999b; Evans et al., 2002). Therefore, international business skill development and foreign work experience are increasingly viewed as part of career progression by both multinational companies (MNCs) and employees (e.g. Evans et al., 2002; Stahl, Miller, & Tung, 2002; Suutari & Brewster, 2000; Vance, 2005) and as a prerequisite to senior management positions (Forster, 2000; Morrison, Gregersen, & Black, 1999).

Inkson and colleagues were among the first to describe an alternative to organizationally initiated international experiences such as expatriate assignments, namely, self-initiated foreign work experiences (Inkson, Arthur, Pringle, & Barry, 1997; see also Suutari & Brewster, 2000). A Self-Initiated Expatriate (SIE) is defined as an employee who migrates voluntarily to a foreign country on his or her own initiative, seeks actively a new employment and is hired by a foreign organization under a local, host-country contract (see Andresen, Bergdolt, & Margenfeld in this volume).

The careers of assigned expatriates (AEs) and SIEs are often characterized by the concepts of traditional and boundaryless careers, respectively (Inkson et al., 1997). However, many careers researchers criticize that most literature on boundaryless careers sees a strong determination of the career by individual agency and free choice and underestimates the importance of structural restrictions and the way in which structures and previous career experiences may influence career behavior (cf. Arnold & Cohen, 2008; Dany, 2003; Mayrhofer, Meyer, Steyrer, & Langer, 2007).

In this chapter, we elaborate on a link between expatriates' employment settings, career concepts, and career decision making. We do so by first integrating boundaryless and traditional careers in a conceptual framework defined by different degrees of coupling and configuration. While coupling refers to the degree to which actors are linked and mutually dependent in their careers, configuration describes the rate of change of the social relationships. Based on this distinction, we then develop a dynamic model of international careers. In essence, we suggest a link between the coupling and configuration in the current employment setting and individuals' career concepts (see Figure 7.1). Moreover, we argue that career concepts are likely to differ between SIEs and AEs. While the upper part of the model in Figure 7.1 describes careers in general terms, the lower part focuses on international mobility in self-initiated or assigned expatriations. In the following, we will elaborate on this framework and discuss its implications. The goal of this chapter is therefore to provide a theoretical framework for international careers, based on the relationships between employment setting, career concept, and career decision making.

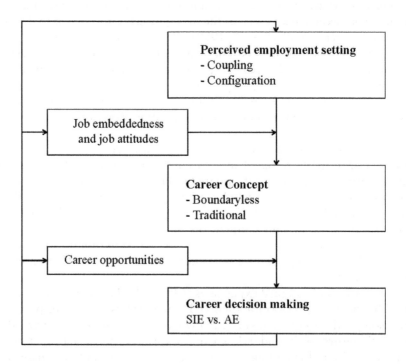

Figure 7.1   Dynamic model of coupling and configuration of international careers.

DIFFERENCES IN CAREER CONCEPTS RELATIONS
BASED ON COUPLING AND CONFIGURATION

Several authors referred to "new careers" in contrast to the traditional career concept in order to contrast the career path of SIEs from the one of assigned expatriates (Cerdin & Le Pargneux, 2010; Crowley-Henry, 2007; Inkson et al., 1997; Inkson & Myers, 2003; Jokinen, Brewster, & Suutari, 2008). The traditional organizational career is characterized by a relatively stable career path in the same profession or area of expertise, sometimes even in the same organization. On the contrary, new careers are often described as boundary-less careers (e.g. Arthur, 1994; Peiperl, Arthur, Coffee, & Morris, 2000), protean careers (Briscoe & Hall, 2006; Hall & Moss, 1998), post-corporate careers (Peiperl & Baruch, 1997), or chronical flexibility (Mayrhofer, Meyer, Steyrer, Iellatchitch, Schiffinger, Strunk, & Mattl, 2002). Among these concepts, the boundaryless career gained most attention by career researchers. It is marked by numerous transitions between jobs, organizations, or fields of professional activity and by individual career management instead of organizational career planning, resulting in a less stable, less predictable career path (Arthur & Rousseau, 1996; Strunk, Schiffinger, & Mayrhofer, 2004). It is argued that boundaryless careers depend increasingly on criteria determined by the external environment (such as marketability of expertise) and external social networks (Arthur & Rousseau, 1996). These relationships between actors and their environments can be delineated by using the dimensions of coupling and configuration (Iellatchitch, Mayrhofer, & Meyer, 2003; Mayrhofer, Meyer, Erten, Hermann, Iellatchitch, & Strunk, 2000). In the following, we will first describe these two dimensions and establish a link to the career concepts of SIEs and AEs in the subsequent section.

Configuration describes the rate of change of the social relationships between an individual and other relevant actors, including the number and composition of these actors (Iellatchitch et al., 2003). In case of frequent changes in the actor configuration, the configuration is unstable, whereas it is stable in case of a low rate of change (Iellatchitch et al., 2003; Mayrhofer et al., 2002). Both international and interorganizational mobility result in a higher change of social relationships along with a number of new and diverse contacts.

Coupling is a conceptual tool that emphasizes relational patterns among elements such as organizational participants (Beekun & Glick, 2001; Orton & Weick, 1990). In the coupling domain of career-related relations between expatriates and organizations, coupling is defined as the closeness of relationship and the degree to which actors are linked and mutually dependent in their career-related actions and decisions (Strunk et al., 2004). That is, the relationship varies in strength along a scale that extends from tight to loose.

Strunk et al. (2004) operationalized the coupling domain in the career context by three aspects: (1) *security* and calculability of career-related prospects, with the coupling dimension ranging from very secure to very precarious (strength of the relationship), (2) subjection of career-related prospects to specific key persons, organizations, and/or system constraints, ranging from very dependent to completely independent (*dependence* in the relationship, i.e. the degree of autonomy of the agents from one another, Beekun & Glick, 2004), and (3) easiness to find *another adequate job* in case of need ranging from very easy to very difficult (consistency of the relationship in terms of the easiness to substitute relations in another domain, Beekun & Glick, 2004).

Accordingly, the relationship of an expatriate to an organization is defined as being tightly coupled if the expatriate experiences, for example, high job security with staff members in general and calculability of career-related prospects. Furthermore, high dependency of career-related prospects is given, e.g. in case of promotions that follow a well-defined career ladder and are linked to seniority or a predefined experience profile. Finally, low availability of adequate job alternatives contributes to tight coupling. Loose coupling, by contrast, is given in a career relationship "where the decisions of one actor have very little consequence for the decisions of the other" (Iellatchitch et al., 2003, p. 740) so that the other's degrees of freedom are kept. This is the case when expatriates experience low security and calculability of career-related prospects, low dependency from key actors, and high availability of alternative jobs.

Coupling is determined by individual *perceptions* of structural career conditions. This means that the effect of factors in the internal and external environment affecting career opportunities on mobility decisions is filtered through individual perceptions (cf. Cappelli & Sherer, 1991). For example, the perception of coupling by expatriates might be influenced by the expatriate's assessment of the current economic situation, which might deviate from the factual situation in the specific company. Moreover, coupling is a *dynamic* process (Andersson, 1992; Snook, 2000) and can change over time or be seen differently depending on the time horizon (Beekun & Glick, 2001).

In this section, we elaborated on coupling and configurations as dimensions to describe perceived employment settings. In the subsequent section, we discuss the suggested link between employment settings and career concepts in international careers.

THE INFLUENCE OF COUPLING AND CONFIGURATION ON THE CAREER CONCEPT

In our model of international careers, we argue that the current employment setting impacts an individual's career concept (see Figure 7.1). The traditional organizational career is linked to a stable configuration with tightly coupled relationships and a high interdependence between actors (Mayrhofer et al., 2000), i.e. (1) career-related prospects are very secure,

(2) career-related prospects are very dependent on specific key persons and/ or constraints, and (3) an alternative job could only be found with major difficulties or not at all should the need arise (Strunk et al., 2004).

Mayrhofer et al. (2002) assume that the traditional career will be complemented increasingly by new careers with higher instability in its configuration and/or looser coupling. Since the concept of the new career endorses the idea that mobility becomes more central to our understanding of how careers develop (Ng, Sorensen, Eby, & Feldman, 2007; Sullivan, 1999), it can be argued that—in case of a boundaryless career or chronic flexibility—the career is marked by a highly unstable configuration due to frequent changes of employing organizations, industries and expertise. In addition, there is a loose coupling in boundaryless careers with respect to the employment setting (DeFillippi & Arthur, 1994; Mayrhofer et al., 2002). Here, the coupling domain can be described as follows: (1) Security and calculability of career-related prospects may be precarious as, for example, organizations may be more inclined to offer opportunities to participate in activities maintaining and enhancing one's career capital to core employees with less psychological and physical mobility (Virtanen, Kivimäki, Virtanen, Elovainio, & Vahtera, 2003). (2) A boundaryless career implies independence of traditional career arrangements (Sullivan & Arthur, 2006) in that career-related prospects are not or hardly subjected to specific actors and/or constraints and is often associated with increased self-determination (Eby, 2001). DiRenzo and Greenhaus (2011) argue that individuals build up career competencies through interorganizational transitions that are positively related to employability, i.e. the capacity to independently create, identify, and realize career opportunities. (3) Employees following a new career have more transferable und less company-specific human capital (Baker & Aldrich, 1996) and, hence, another adequate job can more easily be found.

The degree to which career concepts are influenced by the actual current employment setting is determined by individuals' perceived environmental boundaries, which are defined by the degree of coupling. Examples of environmental boundaries are demographic prerequisites and relevant job market characteristics. For example, employees interested in an international career might be more hesitant to develop boundaryless career concepts when they perceive a high number of barriers to international mobility such as high unemployment rates in a job market and country of interest or, in case of female employees, an anticipated exclusion of women in contemplable positions abroad. Generally, we argue that a higher number of perceived environmental boundaries increases the degree of coupling and, hence, constrains the perceived degrees of freedom to navigate one's own career. Thus, when in the expatriate's view no boundaries might hinder career development, the pursuit of a boundaryless career concept is more likely.

In the boundaryless career literature the delimitation from the organizational career is mainly based on the criterion of frequent changes of employing organizations, industries, and expertise (Arthur & Rousseau, 1996). Although these are signs of an unstable configuration and coupling, the concepts are not referred to (as an exception, see Mayrhofer et al., 2002). Combining the coupling and configuration dimensions with different career concepts results in a differentiation of relationships between actors (see Figure 7.2). The traditional organizational career can typically be found in the career sub-field called 'company world' by Iellatchitch and colleagues (2003) that is characterized by stable configuration and tight coupling, whereas unstable configuration and loose coupling is typical for the career sub-field designated as 'chronic flexibility' characterized by a disappearance of the boundaries of domain of expertise as is typical for the boundaryless career concept (Iellatchitch et al., 2003).

To conclude, employees differ in their degree of coupling and configuration with the organization and these differences are reflected in their career concepts. While individuals in tight coupling and a stable configuration display traditional career concepts, loose coupling and unstable configurations are more likely to result in purely boundaryless career concepts. This implies that the traditional and boundaryless careers are not bipolar concepts (e.g. DeFillippi & Arthur, 1994; Sullivan, 1999) but rather a continuum as described by the degree of coupling and configuration.

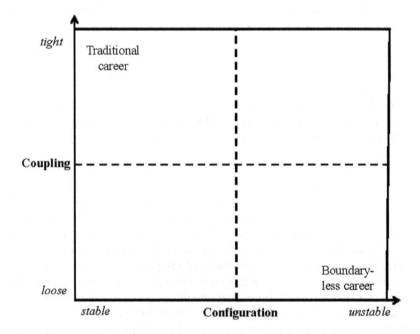

Figure 7.2   The coupling and configuration dimensions characterizing different career concepts.

Proposition 1: The traditional career is characterized by tight coupling and stable configuration, whereas the boundaryless career is characterized by loose coupling and unstable configuration.

High levels of coupling may not be sufficient to generate strong perceptions of interorganizational immobility and to bind employees to an organization, i.e. favoring a traditional career. We argue that moderating effects are of importance, which might impact the strength of the relationship between employment setting and career concepts. Job embeddedness and job attitudes, as potential moderators, represent individuals' internal view on issues in the current employment setting or even off the job and are perceived by the individual to limit or enhance their career mobility and development. Job embeddedness represents a focus on the accumulated, generally non-affective, reasons for mobility, whereas job attitudes such as job satisfaction or organizational commitment include an affective component (Mitchell, Holtom, Lee, Sablynski, & Erez, 2001).

The career concepts suggest that a high level of perceived coupling implies that job alternatives should appear hardly accessible to individuals and that their career may be bound to the organization. In case of loose coupling, by contrast, job alternatives should appear more accessible to individuals and may psychologically pull them away from their current, possibly even well-liked employer (Griffeth, Steel, Allen, & Bryan, 2005; Maertz & Campion, 2004). The belief in attainable viable transition opportunities leads to strong perceptions of mobility and the expectation to be able to find and attain desirable alternatives (DiRenzo & Greenhaus, 2011; Griffeth et al., 2005). However, high levels of coupling may not be sufficient to generate strong perceptions of interorganizational immobility and to bind employees to an organization. And loose coupling is not a guarantor that people are more mobile. It can be assumed that an employee's degree of on-the-job and off-the-job embeddedness moderates the impact of coupling on the choice of the international career mobility pattern.

Embeddedness encompasses several on-the-job and off-the-job facets that affect the extent to which individuals feel embedded in their social networks on the job, in the company and in their community, which is seen as a predictor for voluntary turnover (Lee, Mitchell, Sablynski, Burton, & Holtom, 2004; Mitchell et al., 2001). Mitchell et al. (2001) distinguish three factors—links, fit, and sacrifice. The links reflect the extent to which individuals feel linked to work activities and people they work and interact with. Links to the community are based on being accompanied by their spouse and/or family or owning their home. The fit reflects the level of congruence between their jobs and other important facets of their life such as their skills, talents, values, or preferences. Fit to the community corresponds to whether people like and connect with the community in which they live. Sacrifices indicate what people would incur if they were to leave their position in terms of benefits, opportunities, provisions, autonomy, pay, and security of this job relative to other positions or if they were to leave the community in terms of safety or respect (Mitchell et al., 2001). The greater the fit, links, and sacrifices, the more embedded an individual is in the position.

Whereas "loose coupling also carries connotations of impermanence, dissolvability, and tacitness all of which are potentially crucial properties of the 'glue' that holds organizations together" (Weick, 1976, p. 3) and that may substantiate employees' decision to stay, embeddedness influences employees' decision to leave (Lee, Mitchell, Wise, & Fireman, 1996). Coupling refers to career-related factors that are of relevance for a larger group of employees (Mayrhofer et al., 2002), while embeddedness encompasses more general aspects and conditions in a particular job as well as off the job that are specific to an individual (Lee et al., 2004). Hence, it is to be expected that a comparable group of employees experiencing a similar level of coupling can differ substantially with respect to embeddedness in terms of the content of the connections or attaching factors.

Consistent with Holtom and Inderrieden's (2006) findings, it can be assumed that weak embeddedness in the current job enables loosely coupled individuals to experience mobility because they would not need to sever strong links with coworkers and their community or make great personal sacrifices to transition to a different organization. We assume that this moderating effect is also valid in case of tight coupling, albeit to a lesser extent, in that the higher the degree of embeddedness is the less likely transitions to a different organization will occur. As a result, embeddedness moderates the effects of coupling by creating greater or lower psychological barriers to interorganizational transitions. The more embedded individuals are, the less likely they are to base their decisions to change employers solely on the degree of coupling. In more general terms, we argue that it depends on an individual's job embeddedness and job attitudes whether and to which degree the current employment setting impacts the career concept. Hence, the extent to which individual careers display boundaryless characteristics is likely to vary considerably (DiRenzo & Greenhaus, 2011).

Proposition 2: The relationship between employment setting and career concept is moderated by job embeddedness and job attitudes.

CAREER CONCEPTS AND TYPES OF INTERNATIONAL MOBILITY

The nature of the career concept (i.e. traditional or boundaryless) impacts the type of international mobility that an individual will choose (see Figure 7.1). However, matching the kind of international mobility to the career concepts, differing perspectives can be found in literature. Inkson and colleagues (1997; Inkson & Meyers, 2003) define the career type of expatriate assignments as an organizational career, whereas they refer to the boundaryless career for SIEs (see also Crowley-Henry, 2007; Jokinen et al., 2008). Cerdin and Le Pargneux (2010) counter that an organizational career is compatible with a boundaryless career and interpret from their data that both AE and

SIEs can be engaged in a boundaryless global career. In a comparative study by Andresen, Biemann, and Pattie (forthcoming) of AEs and SIEs pursuing global careers, both groups did not differ in terms of their boundaryless and protean career concepts. Thus, there is no clear evidence on the connection between career concepts and types of international mobility. However, previous research on SIEs and AEs can be used to form a theoretical link between configuration and types of international mobility.

SIEs manage their own careers more independently and change employers in view of better development opportunities (Vance, 2005). Indicative of this difference is that SIEs compared to AEs tend to have a significantly higher international mobility (Jokinen et al., 2008; Suutari & Brewster, 2000) as well as organizational mobility (Biemann & Andresen, 2010; Cerdin & Le Pargneux, 2010). The relation between an SIE and the organization is in tendency short to medium term, leading to a sequence of more or less frequent changes of employers and countries that are likely to extend the breadth of the expatriates' social network with coworkers but also extraorganizational contacts such as suppliers and customers (Jokinen et al., 2008). For SIEs, configuration can be expected to be comparably unstable. AEs, by contrast, are mobile within the same organization and keep the relationship with their home country after they start working abroad due to planned repatriation, albeit they are no longer part of the business networks in the home country (Suutari, 2003). SIEs, on the contrary, usually ultimately leave the organization without having the expectation to return to it after a certain period of working internationally. Hence, there is comparatively little change in terms of actors for AEs leading to a comparably more stable configuration. This leads to

Proposition 3: SIEs are more likely to experience unstable configurations in their employment setting than AEs.

When comparing different career stages and using the example of managers, the degree of coupling is expected to be tight for AEs as well as SIEs in early international careers, as both parties of the employment relationship invest major resources that may even exceed the resources exchanged on a national level. Combining the degree of coupling and configuration, AEs would be situated in the upper left-hand corner in Figure 7.2, whereas SIEs in management positions would be situated in the upper right-hand corner.

Proposition 4: SIE and AE managers are likely to experience tight coupling in their employment setting.

However, with additional international moves, coupling is expected to decrease for AEs as well as SIEs. This is due to the effect that the degree of coupling in terms of the (perceived) structure of career-related risks and opportunities; the opportunities to influence one's career path and the availability of job alternatives is co-determined by career competencies, i.e. the actor's skills, attributes, and action. International experience gained through an assigned or self-initiated expatriation can only to a limited extent be considered as company-specific knowledge since higher responsibility, international perspective, and international contacts help the employees after their work experience abroad not only in their current but also in other organizations (Daily, Certo, & Dalton, 2000). The experiences in a foreign country and in addition in a new organization, as is the case of self-initiated expatriation, produce new knowledge that help to develop career competencies in terms of knowing-whom, know-how, and knowing-why competencies. In case of management-level employees, for whom international experience is highly valued (e.g. Evans et al., 2002; Stahl et al. 2002; Suutari & Brewster, 2000; Vance, 2005), the acquired competencies lead to a decrease in the degree of coupling in that the security of career prospects increases, the dependency decreases and adequate job alternatives become more numerous. International careers in contrast to national careers can be expected to involve an even higher commitment from both parties and represent a very specific career step characterized e.g. by a higher involvement in employees' personal lives (Dowling, Festing, & Engle, 2008). This peculiarity may cease over time with an increase in the number of international and interorganizational experiences. The dynamic process with respect to coupling is described in the following:

(1) Career-related prospects are by tendency secure in all phases as both AEs and SIEs in management positions can be expected to be included in organizational career planning. Before the first international move, the security of career prospects can be expected to be similar. When being abroad, AEs may be in a comparably more favorite position than SIEs as they are even included in long-term career plans, especially if the foreign assignment serves personnel development purposes and international experience is required for internal upward mobility (Cerdin, 2008). Careers of SIEs, by contrast, are most likely managed at a local level. Moreover, SIEs tend to have a weaker intraorganizational network of promoters (Jokinen et al., 2008) and run the risk of discontinuance of the employment relationship related to an employment probation period due to changing employers in the first and each following interorganizational and/or international transitions.

(2) AEs and SIEs can be expected to be dependent on specific external actors and/or constraints in their career-related prospects at all phases, especially if international mobility is a normal career advancement pattern within the organization. During and after the working period abroad, AEs need to cope with imponderables of their employing organization, especially as they are frequently not guaranteed a job upon repatriation or dissatisfied with long-range planning of their repatriation (e.g. Stahl & Cerdin, 2004; Tung, 1998). SIEs' career progression is comparably less predictable due to more frequent changes of organizations and a comparably lower career support by their employer. Thus, the career orientation remains stronger for SIEs than for AEs (Biemann & Andresen, 2010). Although the overall goal of SIEs might be the increase of independence, especially through expertise that can be transferred between companies, for the (limited) period of

stay with an organization the link is tight, and interdependence is high (cf. Inkson et al., 1997). AEs as well as SIEs are likely to profit from new social contacts within the organization as well as externally, e.g. with suppliers and customers, that help to decrease dependencies. Whereas knowing-whom capital increases less through SIE than AE experience (Jokinen et al., 2008), the breadth of SIEs' social network can be expected to be comparably higher due to the interorganizational transitions.

(3) The chances to find another adequate job are assumed to be comparable for managers before the foreign work experience. Over the course of the international career, AEs might be advantaged on the internal labor market, whereas SIEs might build up additional opportunities on the external labor market. It can be argued that both profit from their large external network when searching for a job and from comparably higher career competencies due to learning about different organizations (Mirvis & Hall, 1994). Empirical studies show that SIEs and AEs show equal levels of development of knowing-how and knowing-why career capital, but knowing-whom capital increases less through SIE than AE experience (Jokinen et al., 2008). Moreover, studies show that even in case of missing significant difference regarding the level of academic achievement, there are notably less senior managers among SIEs than there are among AEs (Cerdin & Le Pargneux, 2010; see also Jokinen et al., 2008, Suutari & Brewster, 2008), which might be a sign that adequate jobs are more difficult to find for SIEs. However, the actual coupling between the actors might deviate from its perception by the expatriates. For example, the significantly higher organizational and international mobility of SIEs (Biemann & Andresen, 2010; Cerdin & Le Pargneux, 2010; Jokinen et al., 2008; Suutari & Brewster, 2000) implies that SIEs are more strongly characterized by a career identity that is independent of the employer (Banai & Harry, 2004; Crowley-Henry, 2007; Inkson et al., 1997) and interpret their foreign experience as a valuable competitive asset on the external labor market, concomitant with a perceived higher number of available job alternatives. In sum, AEs and SIEs differ with respect to single coupling dimensions, but their overall degree of coupling is comparable.

Considering the dynamic evolvement of international careers, career pathways might emerge over time, depending on initial career decisions. In essence, we argue that for both SIEs and AEs the degree of coupling decreases with each international work experience due to an increase of career competencies concomitant with international mobility.

This leads to

Proposition 5: Coupling decreases with an increase in the number of foreign experiences as either an AE or SIE.

Based on the criteria of coupling and configuration, we argue that SE and SIE managers differ in their career-related decisions due to differences in their career concept. AEs pursue a traditional organizational career as long as their career pathway is defined by one employer and SIEs tend to pursue most frequently an attenuated form of the boundaryless career. Coupling in case of core employees in similar positions can be expected to be comparable. The main difference is that SIEs more often seek new fields of activity abroad than AEs, which is reflected in an unstable configuration. These differences in career decisions are not only likely to influence the current position but the entire career pattern. To conclude, SIE and AE managers belong to different career sub-fields. Therefore, we argue

Proposition 6: A self-initiated expatriation is more likely to be sought by individuals following a (attenuated form of the) boundaryless career concept, whereas individuals with traditional career concepts favor an assigned over a self-initiated expatriation.

The link between career concept and type of international experience presumes that there are opportunities for an individual to follow one way or another. However, the career pathway is not only determined by an individual's preferences, as indicated in the career concept, but also in the career opportunities that are available. For example, an individual with a traditional career concept might only be able to follow the desired assigned expatriation pathway if there are opportunities in the organization to do so.

Proposition 7: The relationship between career concepts and career decision making is moderated by career opportunities.

IMPACT OF UNFOLDING INTERNATIONAL CAREERS ON FUTURE EMPLOYMENT SETTINGS, JOB EMBEDDEDNESS AND ATTITUDES, AND CAREER OPPORTUNITIES

The dynamic model of international careers that was outlined above argues that career pathways might emerge over time, depending on initial career decisions. This argument is extended in this section. Career opportunities are only partly externally given, but also depend on previous career experiences. In a broader sense, we argue that an individual's decision for an international experience of the type assigned expatriation or self-initiated expatriation can affect further employment settings, job embeddedness and attitudes, and career opportunities. The framework in Figure 7.1 states that decisions for specific types of international experiences impact the later career in several ways. As has been argued, coupling decreases as an expatriate gains further foreign work experiences. Moreover, decisions for a self-initiated or assigned expatriation are further related to later job embeddedness and attitudes.

Proposition 8: SIEs and AEs develop different job embeddedness and attitudes.

Similarly, the choice whether a self-initiated or assigned expatriation is chosen impacts the career experiences that evolve from this position. For example, an expatriate sent abroad to an organization with the purpose of know-how transfer generates experiences that might be advantageous when, after repatriation, a similar position must be filled in another foreign subsidiary. Also, choosing an assigned expatriation might signal the sending organization motivation and commitment (Edström & Galbraith, 1977), which might increase the chance to get further expatriate assignment opportunities. Similarly, self-initiated foreign work experiences might create the necessary knowledge and competencies to effectively deal with problems stemming from self-initiated moves into foreign countries and therefore facilitate further self-initiated expatriations. Following this line of argument, assigned expatriation and self-initiated expatriation career pathways are created, which support the notion of path dependency in careers (Rosenbaum, 1979).

Proposition 9: SIEs and AEs gain different forms of career competencies and experiences, which impact future career opportunities.

SUMMARY

In this chapter we outlined a dynamic model of international careers. We elaborated on a link between expatriates' employment settings as defined by different degrees of coupling and configuration, individuals' career concepts in terms of traditional and boundaryless careers, and career decision making concerning the choice between assigned and self-initiated foreign work experiences.

We argued that employees' differences in their degree of coupling and configuration with the organization are reflected in their career concepts: While individuals in tight coupling and a stable configuration display traditional career concepts, loose coupling and unstable configurations are more likely to result in boundaryless career concepts. By implication, traditional and boundaryless careers are not bipolar concepts but rather a continuum as described by the degree of coupling and configuration. We assumed that the strength of the relationship between the perceived employment setting and career concepts is moderated by job embeddedness and job attitudes representing individuals' internal view on general as well as career-related issues in the current employment setting as well as off the job and that are perceived by the individual to limit or enhance their career mobility and development.

We reasoned further that the nature of the career concept (i.e. traditional or boundaryless) impacts the type of international mobility that an individual will choose. It can be expected that AEs pursue a traditional organizational career as long as their career pathway is defined by one employer and career opportunities are given. SIEs tend to pursue most likely only an attenuated form of the boundaryless career due to their differences with respect to configuration. Whereas SIEs are more likely to experience unstable configurations in their employment setting, AEs tend to experience stable configurations. Considering the example of core management-level employees, coupling in the employment setting can be expected to be tight for both SIEs and AEs. Hence, other factors besides coupling as defined by stability, dependency, and job alternatives are important for understanding interorganizational mobility.

Taking into consideration the dynamic evolvement of international careers, career pathways might emerge over time depending on initial career decisions. We argued that for both SIEs and AEs the degree of coupling decreases with each international work experience due to an increase of career competencies concomitant with international mobility. However, career competencies and experiences developed through foreign work experience are likely to differ between SIEs and AEs, which impact future career opportunities. Career pathways as either AE or SIE are likely to be created, which support the notion of path dependency in careers.

Due to differences in international and interorganizational mobility patterns with concomitant tight coupling with the employer, it is likely that AE managers are included into the group of core employees, whereas SIE managers develop to be part of the core peripheral employees. SIE mangers' skills might be employed by the organization contingent on its demand for them, or individuals can use these skills to pursue other opportunities in the job market, including self-employment and contracting. This segmentation of AEs and SIEs risks to become a self-enforcing mechanism starting from the first international career step in case that employers connotate a higher international mobility propensity to employees who self-initiated their foreign work experience and invest less in these people in terms of salaries and personnel development in order to reach an acceptable return on investment. In order to substantiate and question this (implicit) exclusive segmentation strategy, a deeper knowledge about coupling and configuration of different groups of employees within the organizational system helps to identify different career sub-fields of internationally mobile employees. Based on this information, differences in career concepts can be determined even within the group of tightly coupled employees who can be expected to be involved and committed to both their job and company and represent a valuable company asset. In order to canalize individual international career decision making as either AE or SIE that is related to the career concepts, organizations are well-advised to alter career opportunities according to organizational needs, as we argue that these moderate the career decision making and can help to bind employees. In case that a long-term maintenance of the working relationship plays a minor role for the employer, the tightness of coupling of the organization and the employee and the canalization of international career pathways might be less crucial.

REFERENCES

Andersson, P. (1992). Analysing distribution channel dynamics: Loose and tight coupling in distribution networks. *European Journal of Marketing*, 26(2), 47–68.

Andresen, M., Biemann, T., & Pattie, M. (forthcoming). What makes them move abroad? Reviewing and exploring differences between self-initiated and assigned expatriation. International Journal of Human Resource Management.

Arnold, J., & Cohen, L. (2008). The psychology of careers in industrial and organizational settings: A critical but appreciative analysis. *International Review of Industrial and Organizational Psychology, 23*, 1–44.

Arthur, M. B. (1994). The boundaryless career: A new perspective for organizational inquiry. *Journal of Organizational Behavior, 15*(4), 295–306.

Arthur, M. B., & Rousseau, D. B. (Eds.) (1996). *The boundaryless career. A new employment for a new organizational era.* New York: Oxford University Press.

Baker, T., & Aldrich, H. E. (1996). Prometheus stretches: Building identity and cumulative knowledge in multiemployer careers. In M. B. Arthur and D. M. Rousseau (Eds.), *The Boundaryless Career. A New Employment Principle for a New Organizational Era* (pp. 132–149). Oxford: Oxford University Press.

Banai, M., & Harry, W. (2004). Boundaryless global careers. *International Studies of Management & Organization, 34*(3), 96–120.

Beekun, R. I., & Glick, W. H. (2001). Organization structure from a loose coupling perspective: A multidimensional approach. *Decision Sciences, 32*(2), 227–250.

Biemann, T., & Andresen, M. (2010). Self-initiated foreign expatriates versus assigned expatriates: Two distinct types of international careers? *Journal of Managerial Psychology, 25*(4), 430–448.

Black, J. S., Gregersen, H. B., Mendenhall, M. E., & Stroh, L. K. (1999a). *Globalizing people through international assignments.* New York: Addison-Wesley.

Black, J. S., Morrison, A. J., & Gregersen, H. B. (1999b). *Global explorers: The next generation of leaders.* London: Routledge.

Briscoe, J. P., & Hall, D. T. (2006). The interplay of boundaryless and protean careers: Combinations and implications. *Journal of Vocational Behavior, 69*(1), 4–18.

Cappelli, P., & Sherer, P. D. (1991). The missing role of context in OB: The need for a meso-level approach. *Research in Organizational Behavior, 13*, 55–110.

Cerdin, J.-L. (2008). Careers and expatriation. In M. Dickmann, C. Brewster and P. Sparrow (Eds.), *International Human Resource Management: A European Perspective* (pp. 192–216). London: Routledge.

Cerdin, J.-L., & Le Pargneux, M. (2010). Career anchors: A comparison between organization-assigned and self-initiated expatriates. *Thunderbird International Business Review, 52*(4), 287–299.

Connor, J. (2000). Developing the global leaders of tomorrow. *Human Resource Management, 39*(2/3), 147–157.

Crowley-Henry, M. (2007). The protean career. *International Studies of Management and Organization, 37*(3), 44–64.

Daily, C. M., Certo, S. T., & Dalton, D. R. (2000). International experience in the executive suite: The path to prosperity? Strategic Management Journal, *21*(4), 515–523.

Dany, F. (2003). "Free actors" and organizations: Critical remarks about the new career literature, based on French insights. *International Journal of Human Resource Management, 14*(5), 821–838.

DeFillippi, R. J., & Arthur, M. B. (1994). The boundaryless career: A competency-based perspective. (Special issue on boundaryless careers) *Journal of Organizational Behavior, 15*(4), 307–324.

DiRenzo, M. S., & Greenhaus, J. H. (2011). Job search and voluntary turnover in a boundaryless world: A control theory perspective. *Academy of Management Review, 36*(3), 567–589.

Dowling, P. J., Festing, M., & Engle, A. D. Sr. (2008). *International human resource management. Managing people in a multinational context.* London: Cengage Learning.

120   *Maike Andresen and Torsten Biemann*

Early, P. C., & Ang, S. (2003). *Cultural intelligence: Individual interactions across cultures.* Stanford: Stanford University Press.

Eby, L. T. (2001). The boundaryless career experiences of mobile spouses in dual-earner marriages. *Group and Organization Management, 26*(3), 343–368.

Edström, A., & Galbraith, J. R. (1977). Transfer of managers as a coordination and control strategy in multinational organizations. *Administrative Science Quarterly, 22*(2), 248–263.

Evans, P., Pucik, V., & Barsoux, J.-L. (2002). *The global challenge: Frameworks for international human resource management.* New York: McGraw-Hill.

Forster, N. (2000). The myth of the "international manager." *International Journal of Human Resource Management, 11*(1), 126–142.

Griffeth, R., Steel, R., Allen, D., & Bryan, N. (2005). The development of a multidimensional measure of job market cognitions: The employment opportunity index (EOI). *Journal of Applied Psychology, 90*(2), 335–349.

Hall, D. T., & Moss, J. E. (1998). The new protean career contract: Helping organizations and employees adapt. *Organizational Dynamics, 26*(3), 22–37.

Holtom, B. C., & Inderrieden, E. J. (2006). Integrating the unfolding model and job embeddedness model to better understand voluntary turnover. *Journal of Managerial Issues, 18*(4), 435–452.

Iellatchitch, A., Mayrhofer, W., & Meyer, M. (2003). Career fields: A small step towards a grand career theory? *International Journal of Human Resource Management, 14*(5), 728–750.

Inkson, K., Arthur, M. B., Pringle, J., & Barry, S. (1997). Expatriate assignment versus overseas experience: Contrasting models of international human resource development. *Journal of World Business, 32*(4), 351–368.

Inkson, K., & Myers, B. A. (2003). "The big OE": Self-directed travel and career development." *Career Development International, 8*(4), 170–181.

Jokinen, T., Brewster, C., & Suutari, V. (2008). Career capital during international work experiences: Contrasting self-initiated expatriate experiences and assigned expatriation. *International Journal of Human Resource Management, 19*(6), 979–998.

Kohonen, E. (2005). Developing global leaders through international assignments: An identity construction perspective. *Personnel Review, 34*(1), 22–36.

Lee, T. W., Mitchell, T. R., Wise, L., & Fireman, S. (1996). An unfolding model of voluntary turnover. *Academy of Management Journal, 39*(1), 5–36.

Lee, T. W., Mitchell, T. R., Sablynski, C. J., Burton, J. P., & Holtom, B. C. (2004). The effects of job embeddedness on organizatonal citizenship, job performance, volitional absences, and voluntary turnover. *Academy of Management Journal, 47*(5), 711–722.

Maertz, C. P., & Campion, M. A. (2004). Profiles in quitting: Integrating content and process turnover theory. *Academy of Management Journal, 47,* 566–582.

Mayrhofer, W., Steyrer, J., Meyer, M., Erten, C., Hermann, A., Iellatchitch, A., & Strunk, G. (2000, August). *Towards a habitus based concept of managerial careers.* Paper presented at the Academy of Management, Toronto, Canada.

Mayrhofer, W., Meyer, M., Steyrer, J., Iellatchitch, A., Schiffinger, M., Strunk, G., & Mattl, C. (2002). Einmal gut, immer gut? Einflussfaktoren auf Karrieren in "neuen" Karrierefeldern. *Zeitschrift für Personalforschung, 16*(3), 392–414.

Mayrhofer, W., Meyer, M., Steyrer, J., & Langer, K. (2007). Can expatriation research learn from other disciplines? The case of international career habitus. *International Studies of Management and Organization, 37*(3), 89–107.

Mirvis, P. H., & Hall, D. T. (1994). Psychological success and the boundaryless career. *Journal of Organizational Behavior, 15*(4), 365–380.

Mitchell, T. R., Holtom, B. C., Lee, T. W., Sablynski, C. J., & Erez, M. (2001). Why people stay: Using job embeddedness to predict voluntary turnover. *Academy of Management Journal, 44*(6), 1102–1121.

Morrison, A., Gregersen, H., & Black, S. (1999). What makes savvy global leaders? *IVEY Business Journal, Nov–Dec,* 44–51.

Ng, T., Sorensen, K., Eby, L., & Feldman, D. (2007). Determinants of job mobility: A theoretical integration and extension. *Journal of Occupational and Organizational Psychology, 80*(3), 363–386.

Orton, J. D., & Weick, K. E. (1990). Loosely coupled systems: A reconceptualization. *Academy of Management Review, 15*(2), 203–223.

Peiperl, M., Arthur, M. B., Coffee, R., & Morris, T. (Eds.) (2000). *Career frontiers: New conceptions of working lives.* Oxford: Oxford University Press.

Peiperl, M., & Baruch, Y. (1997). Back to square zero: The post-corporate career. *Organisational Dynamics, 25*(4), 7–22.

Rosenbaum, J. E. (1979). Tournament mobility: Career patterns in a corporation. *Administrative Science Quarterly, 24*(2), 220–241.

Snook, S. A. (2000). *Friendly fire: The accidential shootdown of U.S. Black Hawks over northern Iraq.* Princeton: Princeton University Press.

Stahl, G. K., & Cerdin, J.-L. (2004). Global careers in French and German multinational corporations. *Journal of Management Development, 23*(9), 885–902.

Stahl, G. K., Miller, E. L., & Tung, R. L. (2002). Toward the boundaryless career: A closer look at the expatriate career concept and the perceived implications of an international assignment. *Journal of World Business, 37*(3), 216–227.

Strunk, G., Schiffinger, M., & Mayrhofer, W. (2004). Lost in transition? Complexity in organisational behaviour—The contributions of systems theories. *Management Revue, 15*(4), 481–509.

Sullivan, S. (1999). The changing nature of careers: A review and research agenda. *Journal of Management, 25*(3), 457–484.

Sullivan, S., & Arthur, M. B. (2006). The evolution of the boundaryless career concept: Examining physical and psychological mobility. *Journal of Vocational Behavior, 69*(1), 19–29.

Suutari, V. (2003). Global managers: Career orientation, career tracks, life-style implications and career commitment. *Journal of Managerial Psychology, 18*(3), 185–207.

Suutari, V., & Brewster, C. (2000). Making their own way: International experience through self-initiated foreign assignments. *Journal of World Business, 35*(4), 417–436.

Tung, R. L. (1998). American expatriates abroad: From neophytes to cosmopolitans. *Journal of World Business, 33*(2), 125–144.

Vance, C. M. (2005). The personal quest for building global competence: A taxonomy of self-initiating career path strategies for gaining business experience abroad. *Journal of World Business, 40*(4), 374–385.

Virtanen, M., Kivimäki, M., Virtanen, P., Elovainio, M., & Vahtera, J. (2003). Disparity in occupational training and career planning between contingent and permanent employees. *European Journal of Work & Organizational Psychology, 12*(1), 19–36.

Weick, K. E. (1976). Educational organizations as loosely coupled systems. *Administrative Science Quarterly, 21*(1), 1–19.

8 Self-Initiated Expatriation
Drivers, Employment Experience, and Career Outcomes

Noeleen Doherty and Michael Dickmann

There has been a recent surge in interest in the self-initiated expatriation experience evidenced in an increasing number of published articles exploring this topic. Despite the growing interest in this population, there is still relatively little published work on self-initiated expatriation and Self-Initiated Expatriates (SIEs; Inkson & Richardson, 2010). This is a fact recognized by many academics (for a review, see Doherty, 2010).

SIEs remain a largely unspecified population, and there are as yet no definitive studies of how many individuals undertake self-initiated expatriation, though anecdotally we know that many people chose to spend time living and working abroad on their own initiative. In stark contrast to the traditional company supported expatriate experience, we have a limited academic knowledge base on SIE, their experiences, career development, and the long-term career consequences (Begley, Collings, & Scullion, 2008; Bonache, Brewster, & Suutari, 2007; Brewster & Suutari, 2005; Doherty, Dickmann, & Mills, 2011; Jokinen, Brewster, & Suutari, 2008; Suutari & Brewster, 2001; Thorn, 2009).

While the SIE pool has been acknowledged as a considerably heterogeneous collection of individuals, some typologies have identified groupings based on demographics, motivations, type of role undertaken while abroad, and career aspirations (Inkson, Arthur, Pringle, & Barry, 1997; Suutari & Brewster, 2000; Thorn, 2009). SIEs characteristically appear driven by a desire for exploration, adventure, excitement, and experimentation and are often prompted by family and social connections or to escape from current way of life or job (Inkson et al., 1997). The self-initiated seem to have a very personal interest in developing international experience and may be motivated by the poor employment situation at home (Suutari & Brewster, 2000). They tend to pursue idiosyncratic cultural, personal, and career development experiences (Myers & Pringle, 2005) with complex allegiances and patterns of commitment to the home and host countries (Richardson & McKenna, 2006; Tharenou & Caulfield, 2010). Thus, the cultural exposure, work, and career experiences seem important motivators to SIEs (Thorn, 2009). While they are geographically mobile, self-supporting, and curiosity driven, they have strong personal learning agendas and weak company attachments (Mayrhofer, Sparrow, & Zimmerman, 2008). Perhaps it is unsurprising that the SIE populations studied comprise a variety of individuals from a range of backgrounds, nationalities, host locations, and professional status, undertaking different types of role while abroad and experiencing diverse career outcomes (e.g. Lee, 2005; Suutari & Brewster, 2000).

Some aspects of the characteristics of the SIE have been studied in detail, for example, the gendered nature of the experience (Tharenou, 2009, p. 2010) where it is apparent that the motivation to expatriate for females may be career driven but often more family oriented than for men. Women appear to give more weight to family circumstances in their decision making and more commonly seek less risky destination environments (Richardson, 2006; Tharenou, 2008).

Studies on SIE have tended not to consider educational or professional level of the respondent populations as a factor for describing or explaining the experience in detail. In published works SIE respondents are commonly portrayed in general as highly educated individuals (Thorn, 2009), professionals (Tharenou & Caulfield, 2010), or graduate populations (Jokinen et al., 2008). As such SIEs are intimated as having a high level of educational attainment or professional qualification or experience, thus the career potential of an SIE experience may be significant. A resource-based view has been often adopted in the study of modern careers. In times of highly dynamic competition and labor market insecurity, it is argued that individuals should be striving to maximize their own attractiveness to employers (DeFillippi & Arthur, 1994) and become career capitalists (Inkson & Arthur, 2001). The 'intelligent career' approach (Arthur, Claman, & DeFillippi, 1995) of knowing-how (performance capabilities), knowing-whom (networks and social capital), and knowing-why (work motivation, personal beliefs, and values) has been applied in the fields of international mobility and global careers (Dickmann & Baruch, 2011). Individuals are encouraged to maximize their knowing-how, knowing-why, and knowing-whom as this would ultimately impact on their career patterns and perceived career success in the knowledge economy (Khapova, Arthur, & Wilderom, 2007). Career investments can be made across the career capital areas and given the diverse challenges that SIEs encounter their career capital may benefit. Knowing-how acquisition through working abroad is likely to develop as it does for corporate assignees (Dickmann & Doherty, 2010), knowing-why career capital investments may relate to the drive to develop international working skills through living and working abroad (Doherty, Dickmann, & Mills, 2008), and given the opportunities to develop social and professional relationships, the SIE experience can have an impact on knowing-whom capital (Jokinen et al., 2008).

This chapter reviews the characteristics, which appear to impact SIE and the individual experiences of the event. It explores in more detail the educational background of a sample of SIEs in relation to the decision to expatriate, the expatriation experience, and the career impact of a self-initiated stay abroad. These experiences are analyzed within the career capital framework to provide a more detailed picture of the relevance of educational and professional credentials to individuals who undertake an SIE.

SIE MOTIVATIONS—PERSONAL AND CAREER DRIVERS

What motivates individuals to leave their home country and jobs to move abroad under their own volition, for a period of time? Previous studies have provided some evidence of the range of factors impacting the mobility of SIEs; see, for example, studies by Carr, Inkson, and Thorn (2005), Doherty et al. (2011), Inkson and Myers (2003), Richardson and Mallon (2005), Suutari and Brewster (2000), and Thorn (2009). Many of these are at the personal level. The most salient personal reasons for self-initiated expatriation have been highlighted as cultural exposure, travel, and relationship and family reasons (Thorn, 2009). Also important are the attractiveness of a particular location, the lure of the host culture and lifestyle, and perceived ability to adapt. Motivators relating to the desire for adventure, challenge, and travel opportunities are also key to the decision to move abroad (Doherty et al., 2011). These non-work, more holistic life experience drivers appear to be significant to the desire to move abroad for the self-initiated. Therefore, we know that for SIEs the decision to move abroad is often underpinned by a complex range of factors not purely for work or a career impetus (Doherty, Brewster, Suutari, & Dickmann, 2008; Doherty et al., 2011; Inkson, Thomas, & Barry, 1996).

However, SIEs regularly find a job or work experience while in a foreign location. Given that SIEs have considerable agency, the degree of latitude in decision making means that they can chose where they will travel to, the length of time they will spend abroad, and the type of employment they take up. This high level of personal agency and personal investment in the choice of destination (Doherty et al., 2011) may facilitate the better adjustment and integration with the host culture found among some SIEs (Peltokorpi, 2008). Also, since SIEs invest heavily in the experience, they may be very likely to go to a location where they are more familiar with the culture and language (Suutari & Brewster, 2000). On the other hand, the SIE event is often unplanned and opportunistic, so unlike company-backed expatriates, they are less likely to have a pre-arranged job or position and face a risky situation (Richardson & Zikic, 2007). They appear to more often find a job on arrival once they are in the host destination rather than before going (e.g. Felker, 2011; Peltokorpi, 2008). Studies of SIEs indicate that they do perceive a career benefit from the experience, rating career-related issues in the top 10 reasons for moving. For example, better remuneration, career challenges and opportunities for career advancement (Thorn, 2009), and professional challenge and skills development (Doherty et al., 2008) are motivators.

SIE AND EDUCATIONAL BACKGROUND

Previous studies of SIEs have had a predominant focus on well-educated individuals as the population of interest. These have included university alumni (Inkson et al., 1996), graduate engineers (Suutari & Brewster, 2000), business school graduates (Tharenou, 2003), managers (Suutari & Taka, 2004), professionals (Bozionelos, 2009; Jokinen et al., 2008; McKenna & Richardson, 2007; Tharenou & Caulfield, 2010), and academics (Richardson, 2006; Richardson & McKenna, 2006; Richardson & Zikic, 2007). Where data pertaining to educational level of SIE samples have been collated, many of those SIE populations appear to have attained a graduate-level education or qualification, with a prevalence of professionals who self-initiate (Tharenou & Caulfield, 2010). Inkson and Myers (2003) indicated that their sample of New Zealanders were relatively well educated with nearly three quarters having had some tertiary education and nearly half holding a degree qualification. Thorn's (2009) study of 2,608 highly educated New Zealand SIEs comprised over a third (36.2%) with postgraduate qualifications, 44.5% with a first degree, and the remaining 9.3% holding a certificate from a tertiary institution. In the main it would appear that the study of SIEs has focused on people with the requisite skills, knowledge, and abilities, which would leverage 'professional' job opportunities in the host location and which it might be anticipated, facilitate a positive career experience.

Since SIEs often acquire a job after they arrive, their professional credentials and qualifications are potentially a key determinant of the types of work opportunities that would be available to them. Being well qualified may facilitate opportunities more easily for those who seek work before moving and may also mitigate the somewhat rather risky experience of seeking work on entry to the host country. Educational and professional qualifications may therefore be a determining factor in the decision-making process, providing the wherewithal to be more employable, to help secure a good position and, while providing for economic security in the short term, may also determine any career benefit that can be realized longer term. Suutari and Brewster (2000) in their study of graduate Finnish engineers suggested that those who self-initiated may select countries near to their own due to ease of travel and the types of jobs available. But this may limit the job roles they can command and the typical tasks they carry out and potentially impact their ability to realize a career-enriching experience. So it is important to consider what job roles are undertaken by SIEs.

SIE—TYPE OF JOB ROLE UNDERTAKEN WHILE ABROAD

Among the few studies that have looked in detail at the role taken up during an SIE (Doherty et al., 2011; Jokinen et al., 2008; Lee, 2005; Suutari & Brewster, 2000), Suutari and Brewster (2000) studied Finnish graduate engineers while abroad. They identified a range of roles undertaken, including positions in international organizations, expert roles or project-type roles and middle or lower management levels. SIE populations are often employed at operational levels or in a technical-type position, for example, nursing (Bozionelos, 2009) or engineering (Suutari & Brewster, 2000). Although in the main, highly qualified, such research suggests that SIEs appear to engage in lower level organizational roles than those they held in their home country. Compared with company-backed expatriates, SIEs do not typically hold managerial jobs while abroad (Inkson & Myers, 2003; Richardson & McKenna, 2006; Suutari & Brewster, 2000) and the role in the host country appears to be perceived as less challenging with more variation in financial reward (Doherty et al., 2011; Suutari & Brewster, 2000).

In some instances it is probable that SIEs may encounter a less career-enhancing situation since they often seem to take up a job or position that is neither commensurate with their educational and professional background nor in line with their skills and interests. This can be potentially because of local human resource (HR) practices. For example, as highlighted by Peltokorpi and Froese (2009), in the Japanese context the fundamental impact of social networks on hiring practices may mean that SIEs are not able to secure particular positions and may accept roles below their capabilities, such as positions in language teaching or consultancy (Kurata as cited in Peltokorpi & Froese, 2009). Therefore, Peltokorpi and Froese (2009) suggest that although SIEs appear more cross culturally adjusted than company-backed expatriates, they tend to secure lower employment opportunities, often below their qualifications and experience, potentially hampering the career capital benefit of the experience. This may indicate that the self-initiated can be subject to conditions of underemployment; a topic considered next.

UNDEREMPLOYMENT AND THE SIE EXPERIENCE

Underemployment can be defined in terms of wage loss or employment gaps and at a subjective level as the perception of underutilization relative to the individual's expectations of their career. This state is associated with decreased job satisfaction and decreased psychological well-being. Bolino and Feldman (2000) associated underemployment among corporate expatriates with factors relating to the job level such as authority, status, and power. They found that those in higher level positions are likely to be more fully exploiting their education, experience, and abilities. For those in lower level positions, the resultant underemployment situation may result in underutilization of individuals' skills causing frustration, dissatisfaction, and negative work attitudes. Bolino and Feldman (2000) suggested that underemployment is higher among those who did not have free choice in accepting an assignment and that mentoring can help alleviate underemployment.

A compounding factor for the SIE may be the increased likelihood that they will work in smaller organizations (<1,000 employees) and are significantly more likely to take up what they perceive to be a less challenging role than corporate sponsored expatriates (Doherty et al., 2011) at lower organizational levels (Jokinen et al., 2008). These employment patterns could mean that the SIE experience is likely to result in underemployment while in the host country. For SIEs there has been little focus on the potential impact of underemployment; therefore, the full picture on underutilization of skills for these individuals is still unclear.

Lee (2005) focused on underemployment among SIEs and suggested that a lack of job autonomy, job suitability, job variety, and fit to the psychological contract were contributory factors. On the other hand, SIEs who enjoyed autonomy on their job assignments and those who perceived that their psychological contract was fulfilled were less likely to experience underemployment. Lee (2005) suggested that insufficient variety in the jobs of SIEs causes perceptions of underemployment, which are linked to a negative effect on job satisfaction, potential work alienation, a negative effect on career satisfaction, and frustration about the lack of opportunities to experience advancement. This can lead to a decline in positive career behaviors and attitudes as evidenced among corporate expatriates (Bolino & Feldman, 2000). The topic of underemployment among SIEs has not been extensively researched to date.

SIE AND REPATRIATION

Repatriation has been flagged as a challenging aspect of the expatriation journey (Doherty et al., 2008) with the potential to prompt a disruption to career, certainly for corporate repatriates where they may experience a career wobble, a temporary glitch in their perceived career trajectory, when they return from an expatriation (Doherty & Dickmann, 2007). Studies exploring the repatriation of SIEs have found that those who are less embedded abroad have fewer barriers to repatriating and, when prompted by a shock such as a relative falling ill, will focus their efforts on finding a job in the home country (Tharenou & Caulfield, 2010). Not unlike the corporate repatriate who can experience a career wobble, self-initiated repatriates can also experience problems on repatriation. Begley et al. (2008) found that for SIEs, securing employment on return is a challenge made more difficult by the perceived negative value of the international experience among employers in developed countries. Returning SIEs suffered a negative impact on their careers, which meant that they were able to secure employment only at lower-level positions with decreased responsibility and authority. They were sometimes unable to secure full-time, permanent employment and had to take temporary work to regain local experience or return to education, despite being well-qualified professionals.

While the corporate expatriate can benefit from an array of support mechanisms and practices designed to assist them and their family through the various transitions precipitated by expatriation and help them to accommodate to the new environment, work requirements, and career implications (Collings, Doherty, Leuthy, & Osborn, 2011), SIEs do not benefit from such organizational practices. The SIE, in general, must rely on their own resources to deal with the move and its implications both personally and career-wise, unsupported and alone. Not only would this impact the move, in general, but it may also impact on the career experience of SIE and the ability to realize the career capital benefit of the experience.

STUDY BACKGROUND

As part of a larger web-based survey of expatriates (Doherty, Dickmann, & Mills, 2007), a sample of SIE respondents was captured between December 2006 and March 2007. The study was designed to explore the motivations impacting the decision to work abroad and the perceived outcomes of such an experience. A web-based questionnaire was hosted by the Expatica website (an online English-language news and information source for expatriates living, working in, or moving to the Netherlands, Germany, France, Belgium, or Spain [www.expatica.com]). The target population was limited to those who had access to the Internet and who self-selected to participate.

The survey instrument comprised items on demographics and attitudinal items polling views on the motivational factors underpinning the decision to work abroad following Dickmann, Doherty, and Mills (2005). Respondents were also asked about their experiences of employment, the impact on networks, skills, motivations and career goals.

RESULTS/FINDINGS[1,2]

The SIE Sample

The total study sample comprised 522 useable responses of which 324 registered as SIEs, (having self-defined as *I went on my own initiative without company backing*; 65% of the total respondents). This proportion of approximately two-thirds to one-third company-supported to self-initiated respondents may indicate that there is a considerable number of SIEs operating within the global labor market. These are predominantly unidentified individuals who because of the ways in which they enter an organizational context are often a low profile, unknown entity (Jokinen et al., 2008).

The sub-sample of SIEs contributing to this analysis comprised 53% females and 47% males. Respondents were on average 38 years of age. Just over half of respondents recorded themselves as living with spouse or partner (55%), while 45% said they were single. The majority (74%) indicated that they had no dependents. Just under half of those responding (49%) were unaccompanied on their trip. These findings support previous work, which explored the demographics of SIE populations (Tharenou, 2009).

In the main most respondents who indicated nationality, were of Western origin; therefore, this is a population who were mobile between developed countries, perhaps reflecting the wider opportunity to move from one developed country to another and potentially impacted in the EU context by the reduction in institutional and geographical as well as organizational boundaries (Doherty, Dickmann, & Mills, 2010).

Sectors most popular as employment in the host setting, where indicated, were IT/computing (20%); education (12%); finance/banking (5%); with business/consultancy, marketing, media, and local/national government all attracting 4% of respondents. This reflects substantial movement within the IT sector, where there may be more openings for skilled individuals and where there are fewer barriers to the transfer of skills and the use of technical knowledge.

The majority of respondents were well educated. While only 20% indicated that they had been educated to less than degree level, 32% of respondents were graduates, and 48% identified themselves as post graduates.

Slightly more individuals (55%) had no prior international work experience than those who did have prior work experience abroad (45%). The vast majority (93% of respondents) of those who had previously worked internationally indicated that it had been a positive experience. This reflects the potential impact of prior positive experiences on the motivation to undertake further work episodes abroad as highlighted in previous work (for example, Selmer & Lam, 2003; Tharenou, 2003).

The average length of stay recorded was 7.5 years. A large proportion (86% of respondents) was still abroad, and these individuals expected to stay at least another 12 months. While corporate expatriates are normally time limited as determined by the organization, length of stay abroad can distinguish the SIE. In general SIEs appear to stay abroad longer since they are much less constrained and can determine the time frame themselves (Doherty et al., 2011).

SIE MOTIVATIONS

The range of motivations that have been identified as important to prompting an international experience range from the very personal; lifestyle

Table 8.1   Motivational Factors Impacting Expatriation—Mean Response

Items Influence on decision to work abroad 1 = No influence—7 = Very great influence	Self-initiated (N = 324) Mean response
Desire for adventure	5.35
Confidence in your ability to work/live abroad	5.34
To see the world	5.26
Professional challenge of working abroad	4.89
Potential for skills development	4.82
Desire to live in the host country	4.75
Impact on career	4.61
Having the relevant job skills	4.5
Desire to live in host city/location	4.45
The opportunity to improve your language skills	4.38
Standard of living in host country	4.36
Your ability to adapt to the host country	4.35
The job you were offered	4.01
Host culture	4.01
Balance between work and social life	3.93
Personal financial impact	3.78
Potential role(s) available after your work abroad	3.63
Reputation of host country being open to foreigners	3.61
Successful previous experience in a foreign environment	3.54
Prestige of working in the host country	3.27
Superior career opportunities in the host country	3.23
Opportunities to network in the host country	3.07
Expected length of stay	2.88
Willingness of family/partner to move	2.81
Poor employment situation at home	2.76
Personal safety	2.73
Maintaining personal networks	2.72
To be with/near loved persons	2.59
Reputation of host country in your area of work	2.53
Pre-departure preparation	2.47
Close ties to your country of origin with host country	2.32
Possibility of gaining permanent residency in host country	2.26
Maintaining work networks with the home country	2.24
To distance yourself from a problem	2.06
Better opportunities for your family	2.06
Ability to support your family better abroad	2.05
For health reasons	1.53
Following friends	1.42

drives, through to defined career motives. Respondents were invited to indicate the level of influence a range of factors had on their decision to work abroad (Dickmann, Doherty, Mills, & Brewster, 2008). These items were rated on a 7-point Likert scale from no influence to very great influence. (Mean scores are contained in Table 8.1.)

The motivational drivers reported as having a considerable influence on the decision to take up SIE careers were topped by the *'desire for adventure,'* the individual's perceived *'confidence in their ability to work/live abroad,'* and their desire *'to see the world.'* Motivators rated as more moderate in their influence on the decision to move abroad included skills and career development potential such as *'professional challenge of working abroad,' 'potential for skills development,' 'desire to live in the host country,' 'impact on career,'* and *'having relevant job related skills.'*

SIEs appear driven by a holistic approach to the experience. While work and career are important, the more rounded developmental experience of the event seems paramount certainly relative to corporate individuals (for further details of comparisons of corporate and SIE motivations, please see Doherty et al., 2008; Doherty et al., 2011). The importance given to lifestyle and adventure as drivers supports previous work on the SIE motivations being grounded in a non-work mode (Thorn, 2009). Issues such as proximity to family, balancing work and life outside work as well as personal skills development (language skills and confidence in the ability to live and work abroad), the reputation of the host country, and the poor employment situation at home have been found to be significantly more important to SIEs (Doherty et al., 2011). Thus, the self-initiated appeared swayed by a holistic set of criteria and are influenced by factors, as suggested by Thorn (2009), which are often outside the gift of institutional or organizational influence.

POSITION WHILE ABROAD

Just over half (54%) of SIE respondents indicated that they had a job to go to, while 46% had no pre-arranged position before moving. It has been suggested that there is a propensity for SIEs to travel abroad and then find a job when in the host location (Felker, 2011; Peltokorpi, 2008); however, the current sample comprised a considerable number who were proactive in securing employment prior to their travels.

The most prevalent size of organization within which this sample of SIEs worked was small companies of less than 100 employees (39% of respondents). Thirty-four percent of respondents (34%) took up positions in larger organizations (employing 1,000 or more employees), and 28% of respondents held positions in medium-sized organizations (between 100 and 1,000 employees).

While 75% of those responding indicated that they held a more responsible role, and 58% responded that they held a more challenging role, a substantial minority (42% of respondents) indicated that they were in a lower-salaried position. This is in contrast to the experience of company-backed expatriates in that they are often both very well financially rewarded and are significantly more likely to hold a more responsible role while abroad than SIEs. These findings may hint at the potential for SIEs to experience underemployment while abroad as alluded to by previous research (Lee, 2005).

Perhaps unsurprisingly, most of those SIEs responding (76%) indicated that they did not have an existing network of work contacts in the destination country before departure, while 24% did have work contacts. There was a fairly even split between those self-initiated individuals who did not have personal contacts in the destination country before departure (51%) and those who did have personal contacts (49%). Some people were motivated to develop networks of work contacts (32%) and personal contacts (36%) in the destination country before departure. The importance of knowing-whom capital to the expatriation experience has been highlighted by Jokinen et al. (2008) who indicated that SIEs tend to develop their knowing-whom capabilities to a lesser degree than corporate expatriates partially because they have fewer contacts on arrival within the organization and potentially because they have fewer social contacts through which to develop their social capital.

The majority of respondents (81%) did not have a mentor. Of those who did, 6% had a mentor before departure, and 12% had a mentor when they got to the destination country. Given that the SIE often has little or no organizational support, it is likely that having a mentor would prove beneficial particularly for career-related issues and also for the adjustment of the SIE in the host location as indicated by previous research (Peltokorpi, 2008).

Within this sample of SIEs, perhaps unsurprisingly, most responding (94%) had no guarantee of employment with a home country employer on return. Of those who had some guarantee of a position on return, the best level was 'no guarantee of employment but best endeavor to find a job' (24% of those responding). Many individuals undertake an SIE without a specific time frame and only engage in job search processes after returning home (Begley et al., 2008).

With respect to their attitude and views on career and career planning, over half of those responding (56%) indicated that they had specific career plans; however, 29% indicated a neutral tendency toward having specific career goals. The majority of those responding (74%) wanted an international career, but some (20%) were neutral to this notion. There was a generally high level of career self-awareness with many (85% of respondents) indicating that they were aware of how strengths and weaknesses in their capabilities impacted their career. A number (59% of respondents) indicated that they were satisfied with the success they had achieved in their career, but 23% were neutral, and 18% disagreed on this point. The respondents did show a level of proactive tendency as 70% agreed that they take the initiative on starting new projects and a large proportion of respondents (87%) agreed that they like trying out new ideas. These results may be indicative of the risky situation that the SIE experience embodies. This would require a certain level of proactivity on the part of the SIE since they rely almost entirely on their own initiative and resources to proceed with the move abroad. SIEs display a significant amount of subjective desire to control their own careers (Krieger, 1995) but appear to opt for a less-planned and more non-work-oriented experience. They appear to operate as career activists, motivated to achieve a more holistic development experience (Doherty et al., 2008). The findings may also flag some degree of dissatisfaction with career success, which could be indicative of potential underemployment experiences. This is an area that merits further exploration beyond that which the current data allow.

EDUCATIONAL ATTAINMENT AND THE SIE EXPERIENCE

Educational attainment prior to self-initiating an expatriation event may have an impact on a range of variables that have yet to be explored. Therefore, the responses of SIEs taking part in the current study were analyzed by educational level to ascertain any patterns. The respondents were grouped according to their recorded level of educational attainment (Group 1: Less than degree level, Group 2: Degree level, and Group 3: Postgraduate degree level; see Table 8.2 below).

With respect to the motivational drivers, the responses of the three groups were compared. There were significant differences in the influence of motivational drivers of *'having the relevant skills'* and *'impact on career'* across the three levels of educational attainment. Both these items were rated as significantly more influential to those with postgraduate qualifications, than those with less than degree-level qualifications ($p < .000$) perhaps indicating the salience of a potential career benefit to more highly educated people.

Professional challenge was significantly more influential to the decision to go abroad for those with a first degree than those without a degree ($p < .001$). This may reflect a difference in motivation to undertake a SIE, with those holding higher-level qualifications being more attuned to the potential career benefits of a stay abroad. It may also suggest that those individuals with a degree-level education may seek out roles, which provide a professional challenge, while they are in a foreign location.

Having had *'successful previous experience'* was reported as significantly more influential to those with a postgraduate degree, than those with less than degree-level qualifications ($p < .001$). This may reflect the impact of a previous experience on potential career prospects. Although, there were no significant differences between the three qualification groups in terms of whether they had a job to go to or not prior to expatriating, for

Table 8.2   Educational Attainment and the SIE Experience—Significant Differences across Educational Groups

	Group	Mean rank	U Test	z	Significance level
Confidence in your ability to work/ live abroad	1	52.99	1371.5	-2.942	.003
	2	72.36			
To see the world	1	54.12	1427	-2.687	.007
	2	71.66			
To see the world	2	115.63	3510	-3.224	.001
	3	89.5			
Professional challenge of working abroad	1	51.4	1296	-3.372	.001
	2	74			
Impact on career	1	62.64	1830.5	-3.682	.000
	3	92.62			
Having the relevant job skills	2	63.04	1864	-3.794	.000
	3	93.97			
The job you were offered	1	66.29	2023	-3.122	.002
	3	91.36			
Successful previous experience in a foreign environment	2	64.07	1899.5	-3.436	.001
	3	91.40			

*Group 1: Less than degree level; Group 2: Degree level; Group 3: Postgraduate degree level.

the item *'The job you were offered,'* significant differences were apparent in the level of influence on those without a degree and those with postgraduate qualifications. The job offered was significantly more influential to postgraduates (p = .002).

The topic of previous experiences while abroad and the impact of these on the decision to embark on a subsequent foreign stay, is relatively underresearched and is an area worthy of further investigation, particularly for the SIE who may use the experience as an alternative to the traditional corporate route to enter multinational companies (MNCs; e.g. Vance, 2005). Overall, a large percentage of the current sample (97% of respondents) indicated that being abroad had developed their willingness to go again. Receptivity to expatriation for SIEs has been linked to high outcome expectations (Tharenou, 2003), suggesting that anticipated career benefits may be a precursor to openness to making the move abroad.

The motivation *'to see the world'* was rated as significantly more influential to the decision to move abroad for those who had a degree-level education, relative to both those with less than degree level (p = .007) and those who had a postgraduate qualification (p = .001). In addition '*Confidence in the ability to work/live abroad*' was rated as significantly more influential to the decision to move abroad, among those with a degree-level qualification than those with less than degree level (p = .003).

As the motivational gestalt of issues which underpin a decision to go abroad is based on a complex mix of influences particularly for the SIE (Doherty et al., 2011; Thorn, 2009), it would be beneficial to explore, in more depth than the current study can facilitate, the relationship between educational level, professional qualifications, and other related demographic variables in driving SIE behavior.

OUTCOMES OF THE SIE EXPERIENCE

An overwhelming majority of respondents (86% of respondents) indicated that the international experience makes it easier to get a job afterwards. This finding underlines the perceived potential career capital of the expatriation experience as suggested by previous research where many individuals undertaking a foreign work experience regularly report a potential career benefit (Jokinen et al., 2008; Dickmann & Doherty, 2010). There were no significant differences across educational levels, possibly reflecting a general perceived benefit of the international experience to future work opportunities.

Respondents were asked to indicate the impact of the international experience on their career capital; single-item scales for their career networks (knowing-whom), their capabilities and skills (knowing-how), and their motivation and sense of purpose (knowing-why) were rated on a 5-point Likert scale from very negative impact to very positive impact (see Table 8.3). Overall, respondents were positive about the impact of the experience. This sample of SIEs reported an overwhelmingly positive impact on their knowing-why (87% of respondents). Many (85%) indicated a positive impact on knowing-how and 63% reported a positive impact on their knowing-whom. These findings lend support to previous work, which suggested that the SIE experience can facilitate varying levels of development for each of the three aspects of career capital, where knowing-whom is perceived to be less impacted by the foreign experience (Jokinen et al., 2008).

In addition to career capital outcomes, respondents were asked to indicate the impact of the international experience on their future career opportunities. Over three quarters of the sample (76% of respondents) indicated that the experience had a positive/very positive impact on future career opportunities, reflecting the general trend for a foreign experience to be perceived as generally favorable to careers (Dickmann & Doherty, 2008; Doherty & Dickmann, 2009). A summary of the perceived career capital impact of the SIE experience is included at Table 8.3.

Table 8.3 SIE Perceptions of the Career Capital Impact of the International Experience

Career capital	Perceived capital
Knowing how	
(Your capabilities, work related skills, expertise)	85% positive impact
Knowing-why	
(Understanding yourself, your motivation, personal beliefs, sense of purpose)	87% positive impact
Knowing-whom	
(Your work relationships, career relevant networks)	63% positive impact
Career impact	
(Your future career opportunities)	76% of respondents indicated that the experience had a positive impact on future career opportunities 86% of respondents indicated it makes it easier to get a job afterwards

DISCUSSION

The SIE experience remains a topic in which there is a limited evidence base on individuals' motivations, experiences, and perceived career outcomes. The SIE experience appears less gendered than corporate expatriation, and in particular the populations studied as SIEs in published works tend to be those who are well educated or of professional status.

The current study highlights the high level of qualifications apparent among SIEs with the majority being educated to a graduate level or beyond, indicating a highly educated, potentially elite population. Many had a pre-arranged job prior to departure and reported very positive previous experiences. Although reflecting more holistic life experience as indicated in previous work (Doherty et al., 2011), highly educated individuals in particular appeared more attuned to the potential skills and career impacts of the event.

The greater importance of professional challenge to those holding a degree, and the career development potential of jobs for postgraduates signals a salient, positive career orientation among these individuals. In addition the job offered was important to the decision to move abroad for highly qualified individuals, and those more highly qualified tended to secure jobs at a comparable level to their home country positions. These findings suggest that individuals with higher-level qualifications employed predominantly within IT/computing, education and finance, (comparable to

Lee [2005] who studied IT, finance, consulting, healthcare, and education sector roles), may be less vulnerable to underemployment than previously indicated. In tandem with and interrelated to educational background, the industry sector in which SIEs operate may be a contributory factor to potential perceptions of underemployment, an area that would benefit from further investigation.

Although career may not be a paramount concern for SIEs, they are still afforded an opportunity to acquire career capital while working abroad (Doherty et al., 2011). While previous research on SIE focuses on particular professional subgroups such as engineers (Suutari & Brewster, 2001) or academics (Richardson & Mallon, 2005) or studies individuals from a particular country of origin (Inkson & Myers, 2003), our study is broader and investigated SIEs employed in a large number of industries in five host locations.

In the current study, there was a generally high level of perceived positive impact of the experience on career capital across knowing-how, knowing-whom, and knowing-why with the most positive impact recorded at the individual level, knowing-why. These SIEs perceived a highly positive impact on their self-understanding, motivation, personal beliefs, and values. The differences in drivers between traditional, company-sponsored expatriates and SIEs have been detailed elsewhere (Doherty et al., 2011), and the data presented here contributes to a more in-depth understanding of the motivational patterns of individuals who decided to go it 'on their own.' The SIE experience supports career capital development in particular for knowing-why, to some extent knowing-how but to a lesser degree knowing-whom, reflecting the findings of previous research in this area where restricted access to networks may dampen the ability to develop knowing-whom capital (Jokinen et al., 2008). Previous research on SIE considers phenomena such as the difficulties and insecurities that they face (Richardson & Zikic, 2007) or the activities associated with the experience on return (Begley et al., 2008; Tharenou & Caulfield, 2010). The intelligent career approach allowed us to investigate perceived outcomes broadly relating to career capital development adding to the emerging picture of the impact of SIE. In fact, our career capital outcomes are substantially positive and serve to nuance some of the qualitative findings of the darker sides of SIE as outlined by writers such as Richardson and Zikic (2007). This study highlights the potential value of SIE as a career capital development experience in its broadest sense of a life's journey (Doherty et al., 2008). With respect to the level of educational attainment or professional qualifications, the current study applied a crude differentiation, which could be refined in future work to explore the impact of particular types of educational attainment or professional qualification in more depth. These data could usefully include finer detail on the type, level, and subject area of qualifications attained. In addition since there is a sparse evidence base on type of role taken up while abroad, these data would allow greater depth of analysis to explore links between educational type and level and underemployment while abroad and on return.

Our study has a range of practical implications. At the individual level, the data show what career capital areas are likely to benefit and that people may have to consciously work on preserving their country-of-origin networks and building their social capital in their host country. Moreover, initiatives such as the European Union's (EU's) 'Year of International Worker Mobility' indicate the active interest in Europe to encourage company-sponsored and self-initiated international moves (cf. Doherty et al., 2010). The current data could be used to demonstrate the perceived career capital advantages.

At an organizational level, there is a potential wealth of implications. First, some sectors and firms are more global or transnational than others (Bartlett & Ghoshal, 1998). Thus, pressures for organizations to balance the dualities of global integration and local responsiveness are high (Evans, Pucik, & Björkman, 2011). It will be especially important for companies in the oil and exploration, banking, engineering, and fast-moving consumer goods sectors to have access to the international insight that SIE appear to develop. Second, some professional expertise is easier to transport across borders than others; for example, the technical competencies of finance and engineering are often more easily applicable in a nationally diverse context than legal or human resource insights. MNCs with a higher need for the former professional skills would be well advised to explore a talent sourcing approach that includes SIEs. Third, and related, many SIEs are highly educated, apparently flexible and gain cross-cultural insights. Global and transnational firms in particular are likely to benefit substantially in terms of cost and unique resources when they attract SIEs. However, specific international branding and approaches to work and career seem to be underdeveloped as shown in the Internet discourse of some of the top German and French companies (Point & Dickmann, 2012). Fourth, it is well-known that company-sponsored expatriates are more expensive to their employers (Doherty & Dickmann, forthcoming). Hiring, developing, and retaining SIEs could therefore be a substantial cost advantage to MNCs. It would then be up to the organization and the individual to find positions in which the particular cross-cultural skills and abilities could be used most effectively. Roles could entail a liaison with the country of origin of the employee, a global manager role in which a professional travels frequently (Cappellen & Janssens, 2005) or a long-term plan to repatriate the individual to their home country division (Dickmann & Baruch, 2011).

On a governmental or supra-state level, our research may also have implications. The study was located within the EU, which has made concerted efforts to reduce the barriers to international mobility. Citizens of the community have a right to live and work in other member countries and our respondents were mostly from EU countries. The regulatory context may have stimulated the highly positive perceptions of SIEs. Our data did not show the 'darker sides' of international working in which SIEs, often professionals, encounter problems and barriers (Min Toh & Gunz, 2009; Richardson & Mallon, 2005). This is an indication of what individuals can gain from deregulation and shows the importance of legal context. It should also remind governments of some of the advantages in doing so.

CONCLUSION

SIEs remain a significant but little understood population, which can contribute to talent flow throughout the globe. It is important to future research endeavors to collect pertinent data on independent variables, including home and host destinations, educational level, professional qualifications, and type of role before, during, and after, to expand our evidence base on the SIE employment and career experience.

In particular potential employing organizations would benefit from increased awareness of SIEs, their motivations, and possible contribution as employees in the global context both while in a host country and on return home. This increased awareness and understanding may be a motivator to develop tailored, yet flexible, resourcing, career and development as well as retention policies geared to SIEs. After all, these highly talented people represent a valuable resource that may have cost benefits to alternative staffing policies, especially vis-à-vis company-sponsored expatriation.

ACKNOWLEDGMENTS

The authors would like to thank Natasha Gunn for facilitating access to the Expatica website, which hosted the survey, and all those individuals who took the time to respond and share their expatriation experiences.

NOTES

1. All percentages quoted are rounded to the nearest whole number.
2. Percentages quoted are of the sample of SIEs.

REFERENCES

Arthur, M. B., Claman, P. H., & DeFillippi, R. J. (1995). Intelligent enterprise: Intelligent careers. *Academy of Management Executive, 9*(4), 7–20.
Bartlett, C. A., & Ghoshal, S. (1998). *Managing across borders: The transnational solution*, 2nd ed. Boston: Harvard Business School Press.
Begley, A., Collings, D. G., & Scullion, H. (2008). The cross-cultural adjustment experiences of self-initiated repatriates to the Republic of Ireland labour market. *Employee Relations, 30*(3), 264–282.

Bolino, M., & Feldman, D. (2000). The antecedents and consequences of under-employment among expatriates. *Journal of Organizational Behavior, 21,* 889–911.

Bonache, J., Brewster, C., & Suutari, V. (2007). Knowledge, international mobility and careers. *International Studies of Management and Organization, 37*(3), 5–21.

Bozionelos, N. (2009). Expatriation outside the boundaries of the multinational corporation: A study with expatriate nurses in Saudi Arabia. *Human Resource Management, 48*(1), 111–134.

Brewster, C., & Suutari, V. (2005). Global HRM: Aspects of a research agenda. *Personnel Review, 34*(1), 5–21.

Cappellen, T., & Janssens, M. (2005). Career paths of global managers: Towards future research. *Journal of World Business, 40*(4), 348–360.

Carr, S. C., Inkson, K., & Thorn, K. (2005). From global careers to talent flow: Reinterpreting "brain drain." *Journal of World Business, 40*(4), 386–398.

Collings, D. G., Doherty, N., Luethy, M., & Osborn, D. (2011). Understanding and supporting the career implications of international assignments. *Journal of Vocational Behavior, 78*(3), 361–371.

DeFillippi, R. J., & Arthur, M. B. (1994). The boundaryless career: A competency-based perspective. *Journal of Organizational Behavior, 15*(4), 307–324.

Dickmann, M., & Baruch, Y. (2011). *Global careers.* London: Routledge.

Dickmann, M., & Doherty, N. (2008). Exploring the career capital impact of inter-national assignments within distinct organizational contexts. *British Journal of Management, 19*(2), 145–161.

Dickmann, M., & Doherty, N. (2010). Exploring organizational and individual career goals, interactions and outcomes of developmental international assign-ments. *Thunderbird International Review, 52*(4), 313–324.

Dickmann, M., Doherty, N., & Mills, T. (2005). *Understanding mobility—In-fluence factors in the decision to accept international assignments.* Report for PwC Geodesy. Cranfield: Cranfield University Press.

Dickmann, M., Doherty, N., Mills, T., & Brewster, C. (2008). Why do they go? Individual and corporate perspectives on the factors influencing the decision to accept and international assignment. *International Journal of Human Resource Management, 19*(4), 731–751.

Doherty, N. (2010, August). *Self-initiated expatriates—Mavericks of the global milieu?* Paper presented at the Academy of Management Symposium, Montreal, Canada.

Doherty, N., Brewster, C., Suutari, V., & Dickmann, M. (2008). Repatriation: The end or the middle? In M. Dickmann, C. Brewster and P. Sparrow (Eds.), *International HRM Contemporary Issues in Europe* (pp. 174–191). London: Routledge.

Doherty, N., & Dickmann, M. (2007). Managing the career wobble of repatriates. *Developing HR Strategy, 15,* 17–21.

Doherty, N., & Dickmann, M. (2009). Exposing the symbolic capital of interna-tional assignments. *International Journal of Human Resource Management, 20*(2), 301–320.

Doherty, N., & Dickmann, M. (forthcoming). Measuring the return on investment in international assignments: An action research approach. *International Jour-nal of Human Resource Management.*

Doherty, N., Dickmann, M., & Mills, T. (2007). *Are you a hero or a heroine: An exploration of the expatriation journey.* Report for Expatica. Cranfield: Cran-field University Press.

Doherty, N., Dickmann, M., & Mills, T. (2008, July). *Career activists or active careerists? Upsetting the status quo of expatriate career management.* Paper presented at EGOS Colloquium, Amsterdam, the Netherlands.

Doherty, N., Dickmann, M., & Mills, T. (2010). Mobility attitudes and behaviours among young Europeans. *Career Development International*, 15(4), 378–400.

Doherty, N., Dickmann, M., & Mills, T. (2011). Exploring the motives of company-backed and self-initiated expatriates. *International Journal of Human Resource Management*, 22(3), 595–611.

Evans, P., Pucik, V., & Björkman, I. (2011). *The global challenge: International human resource management*, 2nd ed. Boston: McGraw-Hill.

Felker, J. A. (2011). Professional development through self-directed expatriation. *International Journal of Training and Development*, 15(1), 76–86.

Inkson, K., & Arthur, M. (2001). How to be a successful career capitalist. *Organizational Dynamics*, 30(1), 48–61.

Inkson, K., Arthur, M., Pringle, J., & Barry, S. (1997). Expatriate assignment versus overseas experience: Contrasting models of international human resource development. *Journal of World Business*, 32(4), 351–368.

Inkson, K., & Myers, B. A. (2003). "The big OE": Self-directed travel and career development. *Career Development International*, 8(4), 170–181.

Inkson, K., & Richardson, J. (2010, August). *Self-initiated expatriation and career development: Diversity across cultures and genders.* Paper presented at the Academy of Management Symposium, Montreal, Canada.

Inkson, K., Thomas, D. C., & Barry, S. (1996). Overseas experience: Increasing individual and national competitiveness. *University of Auckland Business Review*, 1(1), 52–61.

Jokinen, T., Brewster, C., & Suutari, V. (2008). Career capital during international work experiences: Contrasting self-initiated expatriate experiences and assignees expatriation. *International Journal of Human Resource Management*, 19(6), 979–998.

Khapova, S. N., Arthur, M. B., & Wilderom, C. P. M. (2007). The subjective career in the knowledge economy. In H. Gunz and M. Peiperl (Eds.), *Handbook of Career Studies* (pp. 114–130). Thousand Oaks, CA: Sage Publications.

Krieger, W. D. (1995). *Career activism: The role of individual activity in career management (personal control).* Unpublished PhD dissertation, New York: New York University.

Kurata, Y. (1990). Human resource management of foreign staff employees in Japanese companies. *Hitosubashi Journal of Social Studies*, 22, 27–36. Quoted in V. Peltokropi and F. Froese (2009). Organizational expatriates and self-initiated expatriates: Who adjusts better to work and life in Japan? *International Journal of Human Resource Management*, 20(5), 1096–1112.

Lee, C. H. (2005). A study of underemployment among self-initiated expatriates. *Journal of World Business*, 40(2), 172–187.

Mayrhofer, W., Sparrow, P., & Zimmermann, A. (2008). Modern forms of international working. In M. Dickmann, C. Brewster and P. Sparrow (Eds.), *International Human Resource Management—A European Perspective* (pp. 219–239). London: Routledge.

McKenna, S., & Richardson, J. (2007). The increasing complexity of the internationally mobile professional: Issues for research and practice. *Cross Cultural Management*, 14(4), 307–320.

Min Toh, S., & Gunz, H. (2009, July). *Career-damaging relationships in the workplace: How new immigrants cope with social undermining.* Paper presented at the EGOS Colloquium, Barcelona, Spain.

Myers, B., & Pringle, J. K. (2005). Self-initiated foreign experience as accelerated development: Influences of gender. *Journal of World Business*, 40(4), 421–431.

Peltokorpi, V. (2008). Cross-cultural adjustment of expatriates in Japan. *International Journal of Human Resource Management*, 19(9), 1588–1606.

Peltokorpi, V., & Froese, V. (2009). Organizational expatriates and self-initiated expatriates. *International Journal of Human Resource Management, 20*(5), 1096–1112.

Point, S. and Dickmann, M. (2012). Branding International Careers: An analysis of multinational corporations' official wording. *European Management Journal,* 30(1): 18–31.

Richardson, J. (2006). Self-directed expatriation: Family matters. *Personnel Review, 35*(4), 469–486.

Richardson, J., & Mallon, M. (2005). Career interrupted? The case of the self-directed expatriate. *Journal of World Business, 40*(4), 409–420.

Richardson, J., & McKenna, S. (2006). Exploring relationships with home and host countries. A study of self-directed expatriates. *Cross cultural management, 13*(1), 6–22.

Richardson, J., & Zikic, J. (2007). The darker side of an international career. *Career Development International, 12*(2), 164–186.

Selmer, J., & Lam, H. (2003). "Third-culture kids": Future business expatriates? *Personnel Review, 33*(4), 430–445.

Suutari, V., & Brewster, C. (2000). Making their own way: International experience through self-initiated foreign assignments. *Journal of World Business, 35*(4), 417–436.

Suutari, V., & Brewster, C. (2001). Expatriate management practices and perceived relevance: Evidence from Finnish expatriates. *Personnel Review, 30*(5), 544–77.

Suutari, V., & Taka, M. (2004). Career anchors of managers with global careers. *Journal of Management Development, 23*(9), 833–847.

Tharenou, P. (2003). The initial development of receptivity to working abroad: Self-initiated international work opportunities in young graduate employees. *Journal of Occupational and Organizational Psychology, 76*(4), 489–515.

Tharenou, P. (2008). Disruptive decisions to leave home: Gender and family differences in expatriation choices. *Organizational Behavior and Human Decision Processes, 105*(2), 183–200.

Tharenou, P. (2009). Self-initiated international careers: Gender differences and career outcomes. In S. G. Baugh and S. E. Sullivan (Eds.), *Maintaining Focus, Eenergy, and Options over the Career* (pp. 197–226). Charlotte: Information Age Publishing.

Tharenou, P. (2010). Women's self-initiated expatriation as a career option and its ethical issues. *Journal of Business Ethics, 95*(1), 73–88.

Tharenou, P., & Caulfield, N. (2010). Will I stay or will I go? Explaining repatriation by self-initiated expatriates. *Academy of Management Journal, 53*(5), 1009–1028.

Thorn, K. (2009). The relative importance of motives for international self-initiated mobility. *Career Development International, 14*(5), 441–464.

Vance, C. M. (2005). The personal quest for building global competence: A taxonomy of self-initiated career path strategies for gaining business experience abroad, *Journal of World Business, 40*(4), 374–385.

9 Tax and Salary Issues in Self-Initiated Expatriation

Thomas Egner

International tax competition arising out of globalization has so far been discussed solely from the point of view of corporate taxation and the taxation of groups of companies and has mainly been focused on the rates of corporation tax. In legal literature scholars have also considered the tax consequences of seconding workers abroad, albeit mainly from the aspect of the tax cost (Elschner & Schwager, 2007; Endres, Spengel, Elschner, & Schmidt, 2005). In the meantime it has also been recognized that, "there is considerable evidence that the relative taxation of highly skilled expatriates has an impact on the location decisions of multinational investors" (Jacobs, Endres, Spengel, Elschner, Höfer, & Schmidt, 2005, p. 9). The tax consequences of a "self-initiated expatriation"—something which is usually done for personal and professional reasons and therefore does not form part of a company's considerations—have hardly been discussed, although the tax consequences differ considerably.

When deciding on expatriation, the employees concerned do not usually consider, or do not fully consider, the tax consequences. However, this can give rise to a considerable extra tax burden on the individual concerned. Therefore, additional tax burdens should be taken into account in salary negotiations.

This article will endeavor to demonstrate the tax consequences of expatriation on the basis of various possible scenarios. The connecting factor, from which the applicable tax law derives, is initially the question of residence. A distinction must then be made between

(a) the employee's ongoing tax burden in the respective host country and
(b) the possible one-off tax consequences triggered by his move abroad.

To round off, social security issues are discussed. Since expatriation is an internationally relevant topic, an attempt is made to demonstrate the tax consequences as generally as possible without portraying individual countries, though examples refer to taxation in Germany.

RESIDENCE AS THE CONNECTING FACTOR FOR TAX PURPOSES

The dominant type of tax for an employee is income tax. An employee's liability to pay income tax depends initially on the individual's residence (De Broe, 2010). If an employee is a resident in a country, the employee is subject to unlimited taxation there. This means that his globally earned income is taxable in his country of residence (worldwide income principle) (Eden & Taboada, 2010). An individual also has an unlimited tax liability if he has his habitual abode in a country. This is to be assumed if he continually spends more than 183 days in that country (Prokisch, 2010). Apart from this, an individual has a limited tax liability if he has no residence or habitual abode but earns income in that state (territoriality principle; De Broe, 2010). A limited tax liability arises in the country, in which an individual works, if he lives in another country. This is often the case in the border area between two countries.

Particularly expatriates often have more than one place of residence because they maintain their residence in their home country or because their family remains in their home country for a certain transitional period or even permanently. In such cases there is a double unlimited tax liability. To avoid double taxation, it is often possible to turn to a Double Taxation Agreement ("DTA"), which allocates the right to levy taxes to only one country; there may also be unilateral provisions in the national income tax laws for offsetting foreign taxes against the domestic income tax.[1]

The starting point for the further tax considerations in this article will be a taxable employee, who initially has both his place of residence and his place of work in his home country and then wishes to take up work in a host country. In doing so, the employee can

(a) also change his place of residence to the host country
    (aa) while giving up his former place of residence or
    (bb) while maintaining a place of residence in his home country,
(b) not establish a place of residence in the host country and regularly return from the foreign place of work to his place of residence in his home country.

Another distinction must be made for tax purposes, namely whether or not a DTA exists between the home country and the host country.

The scenarios given each lead to different tax burdens, which must be taken into account when a self-initiated expatriate chooses a host country. It is assumed that the self-initiated expatriation is to cover a lengthy period of time; short stays abroad of less than six months are excluded. In such cases the tax liability usually remains in the employee's home country and does not shift to the host country (Prokisch, 2010).[2]

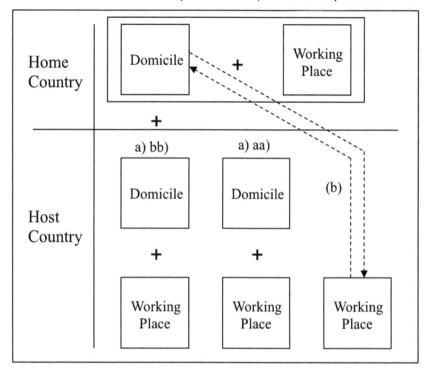

Figure 9.1 Possible scenarios of expatriation.

TAXATION OF INCOME

The Individual Changes his Place of Residence and his Place of Work

In the first scenario to be considered, it is initially assumed that the employee changes his place of residence and his place of work to the host country. The employee thereby becomes subject to unlimited taxation in the host country. The tax liability ends in his home country. The amount of the level of taxation levied on earned income is of crucial importance to the employee.

The differences in the levels of taxation between the individual's home country and his host country must particularly be taken into account in salary negotiations. It is the net salary that must be considered—and possibly, as the case may be, corrected by the differences in purchasing power—so that the individual does not have to suffer a drop in his available income. If the secondment is initiated by the employer, this is usually achieved in the form of a "net-of-tax remuneration agreement" (Endres et al., 2005). If, in addition, other sources of income are also moved to the host country (e.g. capital assets), they can also give rise to either greater or less taxation, which can affect the available net income.

In order to be able to estimate a host country's level of tax, it is possible to refer to tax burden comparisons made by various institutions. The most commonly used comparative data, which are updated each year, derive from the OECD. The European Union (EU) offers corresponding comparisons for the European area.

However, since the employee's tax burden depends on his respective individual situation, the OECD and the EU can only offer standardized comparisons for typical employee situations: single—married—with/without children. The tax burden refers in each case to a standardized income as a percentage of the country's typical average income (100–167%). In the case of married taxpayers without children, it is assumed that the one spouse earns 100% of the average income and the other one 33%. In the case of married taxpayers with children, it is assumed the taxpayer is the sole earner. As can be seen from the following table, the tax burden varies considerably.

The clear differences in the case of married employees are quite noticeable in this comparison. An unmarried taxpayer with an average income is subject to a tax burden of 4.3% in Mexico, 18.7% in Germany, and 21.6% in Australia. In Germany children particularly have a strong impact (–0.6%), whereas in Australia and New Zealand the resulting burden is greater if there are children than without.

Table 9.1   Tax Burden of Workers with Income-Related Taxes in Selected Countries

Family type	Single		Married	
	No children		No children	2 children
Wage level	100%	167%	100%–33%	100%–0%
Australia	21.6%	27.5%	17.6%	20.4%
Austria	14.7%	21.8%	10.8%	12.5%
Canada	14.9%	21.5%	11.9%	8.0%
France	14.1%	20.2%	12.2%	8.2%
Germany	18.7%	27.1%	13.7%	-0.6%
Mexico	4.3%	11.9%	0.3%	4.3%
New Zealand	16.9%	23.2%	15.8%	17.0%
Switzerland	10.0%	14.7%	7.4%	4.6%
UK	16.3%	22.8%	14.5%	14.8%
US	15.3%	21.8%	12.7%	0.6%
OECD[2]	14.2%	20.5%	11.1%	8.8%

Source: OECD, 2011.
[1]In % of the country's average gross wage.
[2]Unweighted average.

Table 9.2 Marginal First and Top Income Rates in Selected Countries[1]

	Marginal first income tax rate		Marginal top income tax rate	
	%	Tax free (personal allowance)	%	Income above
Australia	15.0	6,000 AUD	45.0	180,000 AUD
Austria	36.5	€11,000	50.0	€60,000
Canada	15.0	0	29.0	127,021 CAD
France	13.0	€5,875	45.8	€69,783
Germany	14.0	€8,004	47.5	€250,730
Mexico	1.9	0	30.0	392,842 MXN
New Zealand	12.5	23.2%	39.0	75,000 NZD
Switzerland	5.2	10,500 sfr	40.0	712,500 sfr
UK	20.0	6,475 £[2]	50.0	150,000 £
US	16.2	$8,000	43.2	$500,000

Source: OECD, 2011.
[1]Tax burden, including federal income tax, state and local income taxes, and income tax-related surcharges.
[2]Only for individuals with income below 100,000 £.

However, the meaningfulness of these comparisons is limited because the tax burden is, in each case, stated for an employee with average earnings. If the income of the taxable person concerned differs considerably, it is not possible to make a comparison. For this the trends of the marginal tax rates would have to be taken into account.[3]

The same applies if the average incomes in the countries compared differ greatly. It is not meaningful to make a comparison between a high-income country (e.g. Switzerland) and a developing country because the taxable person will not be prepared to work in a developing country for that country's average remuneration. The comparison might be meaningful only in cases of adventure-seeking Self-Initiated Expatriates (SIEs) as they would agree to the local average remuneration and focus on different criteria for their decision.

Furthermore, the income comparisons only partly take into account differences in the basis for the assessment of income. However, the amount of income that is taxable will usually differ from country to country because

(1) part of the income may be tax-free in some countries or
(2) the amount of the employee's own business expenses, which he can deduct, may differ.

Relevant questions regarding (1) above, which the employee must check are, for example, the taxation of a company car, severance payments, or certain allowances. In the case (2) above, namely, the employee's own business expenses, various items can be significant such as, for instance, the deduct-ibility of a home office, the cost of travelling between home and work, or the cost of further education (Eden & Taboado, 2010).[4]

However, these statistical comparisons do at least offer an initial point of reference for the tax burden. In order to ascertain the individual burden in a specific case, one can refer to an assessment simulation. The expected tax burden is thereby ascertained on the basis of the (expected) amount of income, the income tax rate specific to the country and the person's indi-vidual circumstances. If there are other income-related taxes, they must likewise be taken into account as must local income taxes, as is the case in, for example, the US.[5,6]

Such standardized and individualized comparisons should also encom-pass the social security contributions (unemployment insurance, health insurance, and pension insurance) as well as the state subsidies (e.g. child benefit) in addition to the tax burden. This appears to be necessary because the social security systems in the individual countries are financed differ-ently. On the one hand—as is the case in Germany—independent contri-butions may be payable in addition to the taxes; on the other hand, in many countries these social subsidies are already covered by the taxes, which then tend to be higher. Both systems can also exist in parallel within

Table 9.3   Tax Burden of Workers with Income-Related Taxes and Social Security Contributions in Selected Countries

Family type	Single		Married	
	No children		No children	2 children
Wage level	100%	167%	100%–33%	100%–0%
Australia	21.6%	27.5%	17.6%	6.6%
Austria	32.7%	37.4%	28.1%	18.1%
Canada	22.2%	26.5%	18.7%	7.7%
France	27.8%	33.3%	25.9%	17.5%
Germany	39.2%	43.8%	34.2%	19.6%
Mexico	5.6%	13.4%	1.6%	5.6%
New Zealand	16.9%	23.2%	15.8%	-1.1%
Switzerland	16.0%	20.6%	13.4%	2.8%
UK	25.5%	30.2%	22.8%	19.0%
US	22.9%	29.5%	20.4%	8.2%
OECD[2]	24.3%	30.0%	21.0%	12.5%

Source: OECD, 2011.
[1]In % of the country's average gross wage.
[2]Unweighted average.

one state. Again the OECD and the EU also provide information on these corresponding levels of burden.

Clear differences can be seen in the tax burdens between countries but also between the taxable person's marital status: In Mexico the tax burden of an unmarried taxpayer is 5.6% and in Germany 39.2%. When comparing tax burdens, direct state subsidies (e.g. child benefit) are taken into account. In New Zealand, in the case of a married spouse with two children, this leads to a surplus of the subsidies over and above the tax payments and social security contributions.

Apart from the limitations due to tax interpretation, it must also be noted with regard to the social security systems that it is not possible to make a direct comparison because the level of security diverges greatly in the individual countries. If, taking into account the social security contributions, the level of security provided is inadequate (e.g. below that provided in the person's home country), and the contributions for additional private insurances must be included in any comparison.

The "Human Resource Tax Analyser" of the Centre of European Economic Research allows a more far-reaching analysis to be made of the tax burden on employees. This is "a multi-period forward-looking approach based on individual data" (Jacobs et al., 2005, p. 9). However, the corresponding levels of burden for current periods are not freely available.

The Individual Maintains a Place of Residence in his Home Country

In the second scenario, it is assumed that the taxable person maintains a residence in his home country in addition to a new residence in the host country.

In this case the individual's global income is subject to unlimited taxation in both the home country as well as the host country. This leads to double taxation if no DTA exists between the home country and the host country and if there are also no national unilateral relief measures (De Broe, 2010).

If there is a DTA, the so-called "tie-breaker rule" (Art. 4(2) OECD Model Tax Convention) usually applies. This determines the dominant place of residence in a four-step process. First, one seeks to establish (1) where the person has the center of his/her personal life. This is usually where the taxable person's family (spouse, children) lives. If this does not lead to a clear result, then (2) his economic interests (situs of income sources and capital) must be considered. The next step (3) is the question of his habitual abode. This is usually assumed to be where the taxable person spends more than 183 days. The last criterion to be applied is (4) his nationality (Stuart, 2010).

If it follows from the tie-breaker rule that the taxable person is still subject to unlimited taxation in his home country but is employed in the host country, one must examine on the basis of the DTA—if one exists—which country has been allocated the right to levy tax in this scenario. In Art. 15(1) the OECD Model Tax Convention provides that the right to levy tax vests in the state where the professional occupation is exercised (host country). However, the specific DTA applicable can also allocate the right to levy tax differently—either generally or for individual cases. Thus, for example, the DTA between Germany and Switzerland includes a special provision that Germany may, under certain conditions, when an individual moves to Switzerland continue to levy tax on income derived from German sources even in the year of his move and in the following five years even if he is no longer subject to unlimited taxation and the right to levy taxes has passed to Switzerland.[7,8]

Double taxation will result if there is no DTA between the home country and the host country. However, in such cases the national tax laws usually provide for the foreign tax to be offset against the domestic tax. The employee's tax burden will then be determined by the higher level of tax (Endres et al., 2005).

Against this background, determining one's place of residence is a significant organizational question that arises in the course of „self-initiated expatriation." One should check in the individual case whether maintaining a place of residence in one's home country may be an advantage for tax purposes or whether this place of residence should absolutely be relinquished in order to avoid additional tax burdens (including the cost of submitting tax declarations). If, for personal reasons, the former home in the home country is not to be given up, it is possible to avoid being subject to unlimited taxation by renting the home to a third party because a person has a place of residence for tax purposes only if the home is available to him at all times.

The Individual Returns Daily to his Home Country

There is a particular tax scenario if only the place of work is moved abroad and the taxable person returns regularly—daily—to his residence in his home country (a so-called cross-border commuter). Such a scenario usually only occurs in the border area of two neighboring states. In such a scenario, the tax claims from the tax liability in the country of residence and the tax claims of the country of employment compete with one another. The OECD Model Tax Convention does not provide for any particular regulation for cross-border commuters, so tax would be levied in the country of employment. However, a number of DTAs do include particular rules for this situation (Litwinczuk, 2010).

For example, Germany has incorporated a regulation for cross-border commuters in the DTA with France, Austria, and Switzerland. The cross-border commuter regulation applies to taxable persons who have their place of work and their place of residence within a zone of 20 to 30 km on different sides of the border (e.g. Art. 15(6) DTA Austria; Art. 13(5) DTA France).

The region, which is considered to have the greatest cross-border worker mobility, is the border area between Germany, France, Luxembourg, and

Belgium. While the Double Taxation Agreement with France expressly governs the residency of cross-border commuters, there is no corresponding provision in the DTA with Luxembourg. The provision on the taxation of workers in the DTA with France, in principle, corresponds to the provision in Art. 15 of the OECD Model Tax Convention. The right to levy taxes is allocated exclusively to the country of employment. However, if the definition of a cross-border worker is fulfilled, the right to levy taxes is allocated to the country of residence. In the DTA with Luxembourg, the right to levy taxes is likewise allocated to the country of employment (Art. 10(1)), but there is no derogating cross-border commuter rule.

The DTA between Germany and Switzerland provides a particularly good example for the complexity of possible tax agreements. Under Art. 4(1) of the DTA, the right to levy taxes on income from employment vests in the country of employment. However, under Art. 15a of the DTA, the right to levy taxes in the case of cross-border commuters vests in the country of residence. Nevertheless the country of employment may tax the income from employment up to a maximum of 4.5% of the gross income and said tax is to be credited against the income tax levied in the country of residence. A special rule also applies to senior executives. If the taxable person is resident in one country and at the same time acts as a board member, managing director or procurator *("Prokurist")* of a corporation in another country, he is taxed in his country of employment (Art. 15(4) of the DTA). However, this rule only applies if the cross-border commuter rule under Art. 15a DTA does not apply.

METHODOLOGY FOR AVOIDING DOUBLE TAXATION

The allocation of the right to levy taxes to the country of residence or the country of employment is the formal basis for avoiding double taxation. Methodologically double taxation is avoided by applying the exemption method and credit method. With the exemption method (Art. 23A OECD Model Tax Convention), only the state to whom the right to levy taxes has been allocated may impose taxes. With the credit method, each state can impose taxes but the state to whom the right to levy taxes has been allocated must allow the tax that has been levied in the other state to be credited against its taxes. The tax to be credited can, however, only be credited if the pro rata tax on said income in the state in which it is credited is not exceeded. In order to avoid an excess foreign tax credit the allowable tax at source is therefore also often limited.[9]

Example: An employee resides in State A and works in State B. There he earns income from employment in the amount of $150,000, which is subject to tax at a rate of 20% in the country of employment. Tax is levied in State A together with tax on his other income in the amount of $50,000. The tax rate is 40%.

Table 9.4   Tax Burden of Workers with Income-Related Taxes and Social Security
Contributions in Selected Countries

Income country A		$50,000
Income country B	+	$150,000
Gross income amount	=	$200,000
Income tax – country A	-	$50,000
Tax at source – country B	-	$30,000
Net income amount	=	$120,000

Solution: In State B tax at source of $30,000 (20% of $150,000) is levied.
In State A the taxable income amounts to $200,000. The tax due on this
is $80,000. The pro rata tax apportionable to the foreign income amounts
to $60,000 (150/200 of $80,000). The tax at source to be credited can be
credited in full because the amount of $60,000 is not exceeded. The tax

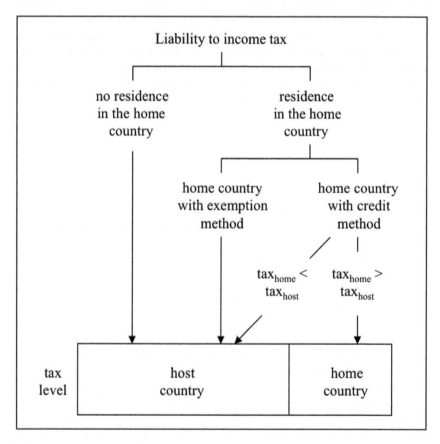

Figure 9.2   Tax level and residence.

still payable in State A still amounts to $50,000. The net income amounts to the results shown in Table 9.4.

The credit method always gives rise to problems if the tax at source to be credited is greater than the pro rata income tax in the crediting country. This can, for example, occur if in that country losses from other sources of income reduce the income tax or the tax rates in the source country are higher than those in the crediting country.

Which of the two methods applies in an individual case is governed by the respective DTA. Either the level of tax of the taxable person's home country or of his host country is relevant for him depending on residency and the applicable method of relief.

TAX BENEFITS FOR EXPATRIATES

When choosing a host country for expatriation—in the sense of giving up residency in one's home country—countries that provide special tax benefits for expatriates are of particular interest. Such benefits are usually only limited in time or available to certain professions.

Methodologically, such benefits ensue from, on the one hand, the scale of taxation (more favorable tax rates) and, on the other hand, a limitation of the worldwide income principle by the fact that only the income earned in the respective country, and income transferred to said country, is subject to taxation ("remittance basis"). Furthermore in some countries such as Sweden or China, the tax base is reduced by exempting parts of the income and/or by a higher exemption threshold (Deloitte, 2011; Pakarinen, 2011a).

A disadvantage is, however, that such benefits do not always apply in the case of a self-initiated expatriation. Often they only apply if the employee has been seconded abroad. The conditions that then apply must in any event be checked in each individual case.

For example, in the GB, taxation on the remittance basis takes effect only if the taxable person is only resident there but not if he is ordinarily resident or domiciled there (Dirkis, 2010).[10] The distinction between these three types of residence is not without its problems and is not clearly regulated by statute. A taxable person is only domiciled if he has close personal connections to GB, e.g. he has British nationality and has lived in the GB for most of his life (HM Revenue & Customs, 2010). By contrast, a person becomes resident if he spends more than 183 days in GB (Lemos, 2010). In the case of ordinary residence, the permanency of the stay in the GB is relevant. The following criteria must be fulfilled:

Basically, a person is taxed in GB on the basis of the worldwide income principle if the taxable person is resident in GB (Obuoforibo, 2011). However, the income tax law provides taxable persons who are not domiciled or ordinarily resident the option to be taxed only on the basis of income derived in GB (GB-source income; HM Revenue & Customs, 2010). The

Table 9.5   Criteria of Ordinary Residence in GB

(1) Your presence here has a settled purpose. This might be for only a limited period, but has enough continuity to be properly described as settled. Business, employment, and family can all provide a settled purpose, but this list is not exhaustive.	+
(2) Your presence in the UK forms part of the regular and habitual mode of your life for the time being. This can include temporary absence from the UK. For example, if you come to live in the UK for three years or more, then you will have established a regular and habitual mode of life here from the start.	+
(3) You have come to the UK voluntarily. The fact that you chose to come to the UK at the request of your employer rather than seek another job does not make your presence here involuntary."	+

Source: HM Revenue & Customs, 2010, p. 9.

foreign income may not, however, be transferred to GB. Conversely, the taxable person loses his claim to his personal tax allowance and must pay a Remittance Basis Charge.[11]

It clearly follows from this that an individual must plan his residency carefully if he is to be taxed on the remittance basis. The idea of leaving one's family in one's home country is usually not helpful because in that case the foreign income—which is tax free in GB—is usually subject to unlimited taxation in one's home country.

Similar rules can be found in China and Israel. In China non-domiciled individuals are subject to personal tax only on income sourced in China (Deloitte, 2011).[12] In Israel the taxation on the remittance basis takes effect if the taxable person is either a new immigrant or a returning resident (Israel Ministry of Immigrant Absorption, n.d.).

Further examples of countries offering tax benefits for foreign nationals are Denmark and Sweden. However, in contrast to the British system, the benefits are not granted on the basis of domicile but mainly on the basis of tax residency and the kind of employment (Pakarinen, 2011a; Pakarinen, 2011b). Compared with this, the situation in Belgium is clear.[13] The benefits under the "special expatriate tax regime" are reserved for employees (academics and people with specialist skills) who are seconded by their employer in their home country to an affiliate in the host country for a limited period of time. The secondment must furthermore be based on a secondment agreement (De Broe & Bammens, 2010; Offermanns, 2011a).

EXTRAORDINARY SALARY COMPONENTS

The taxable person's place of residence is also of significance in the case of severance payments that are payable by the employer upon termination of an employment relationship. If the self-initiated expatriation occurred after the individual lost his job in his home country and if the severance payment is made until after he has relocated to the host country, the question arises as to where the tax obligation lies. The same applies if the taxable person is planning to return to his home country after he has spent a certain period of time in the host country and a severance payment is expected.

Under the OECD Model Tax Convention, severance payments do not constitute a salary component, so the tax would be levied in the state of residence at the time the severance payment is paid out. If the tax levels in the host country and in the home country are very different, the timing of the severance payment (before/after relocation) can lead to considerably divergent tax burdens. However, many DTAs contain regulations that differ from the OECD Model Tax Convention. Thus, it is often the case with severance payments that an allocation is made according to the economic cause of the severance payment and the right to levy taxes is allocated to the country of employment—even if the individual no longer has a residence in that country at the time when the severance payment is made. However this usually only applies if the severance payment is understood to be compensation for the loss of the individual's employment (lost future wages). If the severance payment has the characteristics of a pension (pension claim settlement), the right to levy taxes vests in the state of residence (principle of residence).

The taxation of stock options, which qualify as remuneration, can also give rise to difficulties. This is because with stock options it can be assumed that the income flows in at different points in time (at the time of grant, vesting, exercise, sale of the shares; Jacobs et al., 2005). In Germany the inflow is basically upon exercise of the options. However, in other countries it can be assumed that the date of taxation will be when the stock options are granted.[14] This can lead to double taxation when the options are granted and when they are exercised. Furthermore, some countries assume that they have been earned on a pro rata temporis basis during the term of the employment relationship (as with severance payments), so taxation can also occur, retrospectively, upon exercise even if the taxable person in the meantime no longer resides in and/or works in that country.

EXPATRIATION TAXATION

If an individual gives up his residence in his home country and thereby ends his unlimited tax liability in that country, this can additionally trigger one-off tax burdens. The cause for this is that the home country loses direct access to the taxable person when he moves abroad. If, in the course of relocating, assets, which are subject to tax in the individual's home country, are shifted abroad, undisclosed reserves are usually deemed to have been realized (De Broe, 2010).

Example: A German taxpayer has a shareholding of more than 1% in a German corporation. This means that if said shareholding—or part thereof—is disposed of any gain on disposal is taxable.[15] Existing undisclosed reserves are deemed to be subject to tax in Germany. Because the taxable person relocates abroad, the German fiscal authorities lose the ability to check when and whether the taxable person disposes of his shareholding. A legal fiction is, therefore, created whereby the shares are deemed to have been disposed of at the time when the individual relocated abroad and the undisclosed reserves are taxed.[16]

If the taxable person moves to an EU Member State, payment of the tax is deferred without interest accrual up until actual disposal of the shareholding. The taxable person must, however, prove to the German fiscal authorities (federal tax administration) each year that he still holds the shareholding; otherwise the tax becomes due.

In individual cases this problem can also exist in the case of shareholdings that have been built up during the course of an employment relationship, e.g. because a correspondingly high shareholding accrued due to employee shares or stock options.

All tangible and intangible assets, which are transferred abroad in the course of the relocation and are thereby removed from the reach of the tax authorities of the country of origin, can be affected by such "expatriation taxation."

Expatriation taxation exists in many countries in various forms and extents.[17] If, when moving his residence abroad, a taxable person is affected by expatriation taxation, he must consider whether it is sensible to maintain a residence in his home country. If residence is still maintained, the undisclosed reserves remain subject to tax because the unlimited tax liability in the individual's home country continues to exist—they are not disclosed. However, this only applies if any DTA that may exist continues to allocate the right to levy taxes on the undisclosed reserves to the country of residence.

A corresponding expatriation taxation can also be triggered if the individual later relocates from the host country to another host country or back to his home country.

SOCIAL SECURITY ISSUES

Apart from the tax consequences, expatriation also gives rise to legal issues concerning social security. Expatriation usually has the effect of ending the social security obligation in the individual's home country, which then starts anew in the host country (territoriality principle) (OECD, 2011).[18] In this context the extent to which claims still exist against a state social security authority following expatriation is of importance. This can, for example, concern unemployment insurance and the state pension insurance. As far as unemployment insurance is concerned, one must check to what extent claims can be made in the individual's home country if he becomes unemployed after moving abroad. With regard to the state pension insurance, the extent to which claims arising out of the former state pension insurance exist upon attainment of the retirement age will require clarification. In addition there is the question of the extent to which former periods of having paid contributions are relevant for possible claims in the event that the individual returns to his home country.

If an employee has paid contributions into the German state pension insurance and the employee subsequently moves abroad because of his job, the pension claim that has already been acquired survives. Upon attainment of the retirement age, the pension benefits are remitted abroad. The pension benefits paid by the statutory pension insurance are, however, subject to limited taxation in Germany. If, in addition, there is no possibility of continuing the insurance on a voluntary basis, the employee can also have the contributions he has already paid reimbursed.

Unlike the pension insurance, with unemployment insurance the entitlement to any benefits ends when the individual emigrates. This is particularly problematic if the job abroad is for a limited duration. However, there is the possibility of continuing to pay contributions on a voluntary basis so as to be entitled to make a claim after returning to Germany. There are, however, exceptions to this in the context of the EU. Thus, for example, someone who is unemployed can receive benefits under the German unemployment insurance for a period of up to six months if he emigrates to an EU country.

It should be noted that because of the territoriality principle of social security, the respective qualifying periods for any entitlement to benefits begin to run anew if an individual changes system by virtue of emigration.

Since the social security systems diverge even more than tax law, it is not possible to make generally valid statements on this. Each case must be considered on an individual basis.

OTHER ASPECTS

In addition to the immediate income tax impacts, longer term tax implications must also be taken into account. A relevant question can for example be what inheritance tax law applies in the case of subsequent inheritances. This too—as with income tax—can result in double taxation if inheritance tax accrues both in the home country of the person who makes the bequest as well as in the home country of the heirs. Moreover, double taxation conventions covering inheritance tax are considerably rarer than double taxation conventions covering income tax.[19]

SUMMARY

It has been shown that in the case of a self-initiated expatriation, the tax conditions in the host country should absolutely be analyzed before the expatriation so that when negotiating one's salary one has a proper idea about the gross income necessary to result in a given target net income.

158   *Thomas Egner*

Furthermore, if the individual is resident in more than one country, a check must be made in which countries the individual is subject to taxation or, if he is subject to taxation in more than one country, whether a DTA exists, which avoids additional tax burdens.

Apart from the periodic tax liability of ongoing salary payments, expatriation can also give rise to one-off tax burdens if the unlimited tax liability in the individual's home country ends.

Social security issues should also absolutely be clarified before expatriation in order to, as the case may be, secure claims for the future—e.g. by making voluntary contributions while away in the host country.

NOTES

1. Germany: Sec. 34c Income Tax Act.
2. Art. 15 (2) OECD Model Tax Convention.
3. For income tax rates, also see www.taxrate.cc or the IBFD tax surveys (www.ibfd.org).
4. For detail information, see OECD (2011), Part III: country details.
5. In Germany, e.g. the solidarity tax (5.5% of the income tax). Similar surcharges exist in a lot of countries, e.g. France or Luxembourg.
6. The tax burden includes federal income tax, state income tax, and local income tax.
7. No nationality of Switzerland and resident in Germany for more than four years.
8. Art. 4 (4) of the DTA between Germany and Switzerland.
9. E.g. Sec. 34c German Income Tax Act.
10. Similar regimes exist, e.g. in Japan or Singapore.
11. For users of the remittance basis who have been resident in GB for seven out of the last nine years.
12. The benefit applies only to non-domiciled individuals who do not stay longer than five consecutive tax years.
13. In the Netherlands a special expatriate tax regime also applies only to employees who are seconded by their employer (Offermanns, 2011b).
14. For the problem of cross-border income taxation of stock options, see OECD (2006).
15. Sec. 17 German Income Tax Act.
16. Sec. 6 German Foreign Transaction Tax Act.
17. E.g. in Austria, France, and the Netherlands.
18. For detail information, see IBFD country surveys (www.ibfd.org).
19. Germany has signed only five DTAs covering inheritance tax but about 90 covering income tax.

REFERENCES

De Broe, L. (2010). The relevance of residence under EC tax law. In G. Maisto (Ed.), *Residence of individuals under tax treaties and EC law* (pp. 107–132). Amsterdam: IBFD.
De Broe, L., & Bammens, N. (2010). Belgium. In J. M. Mössner (Ed.), *Taxation of workers in Europe* (pp. 109–140). Amsterdam: IBFD.

Deloitte (2011). *Taxation and investment guide: China, China highlights.* Retrieved from http://www.deloitte.com/assets/Dcom-Global/Local%20 Assets/Documents/Tax/Intl%20Tax%20 and%20Business%20Guides/2011/ dtt_tax_highlight_2011_China.pdf.

Dirkis, M. (2010). The expression 'liable to tax by reason of his domicile, residence' under Art. 4 (1) of the OECD Model Convention. In G. Maisto (Ed.), *Residence of individuals under tax treaties and EC law* (pp. 135–152). Amsterdam: IBFD.

Eden, S., & Taboado, C. P. (2010). General report on the taxation of workers in Europe. In J. M. Mössner (Ed.), *Taxation of workers in Europe* (pp. 25–37). Amsterdam: IBFD.

Elschner, C., & Schwager, R. (2007). A simulation method to measure the effective tax rate on highly skilled labor. *Public Finance Analysis,* 63(4), 563–582.

Endres, D., Spengel, C., Elschner, C., & Schmidt, O. (2005). The tax burden of international assignment. *Intertax,* 33, 490–502.

HM Revenue & Customs (2010). *Residence, domicile and the remittance basis.* Retrieved from www.hmrc.gov.uk/cnr/hmrc6.pdf.

Israel Ministry of Immigrant Absorption (n.d.). *Tax reform.* Retrieved from http://www.moia.gov.il/Moia_en/TaxReform/Introducinginnovativereforms. htm?SearchText=.

Jacobs, O. H., Endres, D., Spengel, C., Elschner, C., Höfer, R., & Schmidt, O. (2005). *International taxation of expatriates—Survey of 20 tax and social security regimes and analysis of effective tax burdens on international assignments.* Frankfurt: Fachverlag Moderne Wirtschaft.

Lemos, M. (2010). United Kingdom. In G. Maisto (Ed.), *Residence of individuals under tax treaties and EC law* (pp. 583–642). Amsterdam: IBFD.

Litwinczuk, H. (2010). Taxation of cross-border workers and EC tax law. In J. M. Mössner (Ed.), *Taxation of workers in Europe* (pp. 71–94). Amsterdam: IBFD.

Obuoforibo, B. (2011). United Kingdom—Individual taxation, country surveys IBFD. Amsterdam: IBFD.

OECD (2006). *The taxation of employee stock options.* Paris: OECD Publishing.

OECD (2011). Taxing wages 2010. Paris: OECD Publishing.

Offermanns, R. (2011a). *Belgium—Individual taxation, country surveys IBFD.* Amsterdam: IBFD.

Offermanns, R. (2011b). *Netherlands—Individual taxation, country surveys IBFD.* Amsterdam: IBFD.

Pakarinen, L. (2011a). Sweden—*Individual taxation, country surveys IBFD.* Amsterdam: IBFD.

Pakarinen, L. (2011b). Denmark—*Individual taxation, country surveys IBFD.* Amsterdam: IBFD.

Prokisch, R. (2010). Double taxation conventions on taxation of workers. In J. M. Mössner (Ed.), *Taxation of workers in Europe* (pp. 51–70). Amsterdam: IBFD.

Stuart, E. (2010). Art. 4 (2) of the OECD Model Convention: Practice and case law. In G. Maisto (Ed.), *Residence of individuals under tax treaties and EC law* (pp. 181–194). Amsterdam: IBFD.

10 Self-Initiated Repatriation at the Interplay between Field, Capital, and Habitus
An Analysis Based on Bourdieu's Theory of Practice

Maike Andresen and Matthias Walther

Research about careers upon repatriation has largely focused on the intra-company return of traditional assigned expatriates (AEs) who have been sent abroad by their employer (e.g. Thomas, 2002; Richardson & Mallon, 2005). Professionals nowadays often initiate their own expatriation (Myers & Pringle, 2005) and leave their country without company aid (Suutari & Brewster, 2000). These Self-Initiated Expatriates (SIEs) of whom many thousands are circulating around the global economy (e.g. Howe-Walsh & Schyns, 2010; McKenna & Richardson, 2007) have become a focal point of interest in the last few years. While the area of foreign experiences initiated by the individual is now rudimentarily understood, the area of self-initiated repatriation, i.e. the repatriation without company support at the behest of the individual (Begley, Collings, & Scullion, 2008) is an under-researched area (Tharenou & Caulfield, 2010). In this chapter, we aim to enlarge our understanding about this heretofore neglected topic in academic research by investigating the modification of highly skilled[1] expatriates' habitus and career capital, i.e. economic, cultural, and social capital, while abroad and its effect for the re-entry into the Danish, French, and German home labor market. As theoretical framework, we use Bourdieu's (1972) theory of practice since it allows a context-sensitive view of careers (Mayrhofer & Schneidhofer, 2009). It considers institutional and organizational factors as well as individual aspects (Iellatchitch, Mayrhofer, & Meyer, 2003; Mayrhofer, Meyer, Steyrer, & Langer, 2007) of international careers and therefore permits a holistic approach, which is crucial for understanding (Ng, Sorensen, Eby, & Feldmann, 2007).

Our research is significant for several reasons. First, it enlarges our understanding about Self-Initiated Repatriates' (SIRs) attributed value upon return into the home country labor market (see e.g. Doherty & Dickmann, 2009 for the symbolic capital of AEs). This is of special interest for SIRs since they have to compete for jobs with local applicants as they are not repatriated into a sending institution and have to seek a job back home. Second, highly skilled SIRs can represent a valuable human resource in filling key positions (Begley et al., 2008). Home country companies seeking valuable employees should have an interest to know in how far SIRs' career capital meets their requirements. Last, the debate surrounding the concept of self-initiated repatriation goes well beyond the frontier of business organizations (Forstenlechner, 2010). Our theoretical framework allows us to investigate to what extent the re-entry value of SIRs' modified habitus and career capital differs with respect to the country of return. Comparative career research being virtually non-existing (Mayrhofer & Schneidhofer, 2009), we hereby contribute to a better understanding of career fields, especially in a European context.

The rest of this chapter is structured as follows. We start by briefly reviewing the pertinent literature on self-initiated repatriation and career fields on the basis of Bourdieu's Theory of Practice (1972) and deduce our research questions. Subsequently, we present our study and its results. We finish with implications for theory and practice and limitations of our research.

SELF-INITIATED REPATRIATION

SIRs have been defined as SIEs repatriating on their own behalf and without company aid (e.g. Tharenou & Caulfield, 2010). For our research purpose, we enlarge this definition and define self-initiated repatriation as the repatriation of former expatriates who initiate their return on their own without company support. This broadened definition allows us to include former SIEs as well as AEs.

Studies about SIRs investigated reasons and motives for a return of expatriates that are characterized by a mix of weak host country pull and strong home country pull factors (Tharenou & Caulfield, 2010). Governments were only found to be able to incentivize repatriation or ease its process (Forstenlechner, 2010). Begley et al. (2008) analyzed the career re-entry to the Republic of Ireland and worked out that compared to repatriating AEs, SIRs are likely to suffer greater financial and emotional pressure as they have to seek themselves a job in their home country. The authors showed that employers did not fully value the SIRs' international experience. In order to make themselves more attractive to potential employers, SIRs downplayed their international experience and tuned down their curriculum vitae (CV). In the following, the role of career fields in the valuation of career capital and career habitus is explored by applying Bourdieu's theory of practice to careers.

APPLICATION OF BOURDIEU'S THEORY OF PRACTICE TO CAREERS

Applying Bourdieu's Theory of Practice (1972) to the career context, careers unfold in career fields with specific logics and where certain rules apply. Agents endowed with field-relevant career capital try to maintain or improve their position by acquiring and applying career capital wherefore a specific habitus is required (Mayrhofer, Meyer, Steyrer, Maier, Langer, & Hermann, 2004c). The global or general habitus consists of a system of dispositions and refers to a person's way of thinking, feeling, evaluating, speaking, and acting that pre-formats all the expressive, verbal, and practical manifestations and utterances (Lindh & Dahlin, 2000; Krais, 1988). The career habitus is that one habitus that fits to a specific career field. It is developed through socialization and experience and ensures that actors act according to the rules and invest the 'right' combination of career capital on the respective field (Mayrhofer, Iellatchitch, Meyer, Steyrer, Schiffinger, & Strunk, 2004a). If all actors believe in the field-specific illusio (Bourdieu & Wacquant, 1992), i.e. the sacred value of the stake of the career field and act "intentionally without intention" in conformity with the rules of the game (doxa; Bourdieu, 1998), the structure and basic assumptions within the field are confirmed and reproduced (Bourdieu, 1992a; Crossley, 2001). The fact that involvement in a field shapes the habitus (modus operandi), which, in turn, shapes the actions reproducing the field (opus operatum), shows the circular relationship between the two Bourdieuian elements 'field' and 'habitus' (Iellatchitch et al., 2003). In addition to the career habitus, agents also own a set of capital (Bourdieu, 1986), which, depending on the rules of the game, gets a certain value and thus becomes (symbolic) career capital. It is the amount of capital as well as the composition of the portfolio, i.e. the relative parts of the different sorts of capital, which determines, where each agent is located in the career field (Schneidhofer, Schiffinger, & Mayrhofer, 2010). Economic capital, e.g. income, appears in the form of general, anonymous, all-purpose convertible money and can be more easily converted into social and cultural capital than vice versa (Postone, LiPuma, & Calhoun, 1993). Social capital involves relationships of mutual recognition and acquaintance and is based on networks (Mayrhofer et al., 2004a), whereas cultural capital takes the form of incorporated cultural capital, e.g. competences or skills, objectified cultural capital, e.g. books, and institutionalized cultural capital, e.g. academic titles and degrees (Iellatchitch et al., 2003).

BOUNDARIES OF CAREER FIELDS—A COUNTRY PERSPECTIVE

Boundaries of career fields have to be investigated by empirical research (Mayrhofer, Meyer, Iellatchitch, & Schiffinger, 2004b). Bourdieu considers a boundary to be situated where its effects end, i.e. where the stakes of the game lose their impact. Within Europe, we can find cultural differences between different clusters, e.g. the Nordic cluster, the Germanic cluster, or the Latin cluster. Careers are influenced by national culture (e.g. Thomas &

Inkson, 2007). It has even been suggested that the very concept of careers has different meanings across cultures (Derr & Laurent, 1989; Laurent, 1986). In France, internal labor markets are highly important and traditional organizational career paths are far from having disappeared (Dany, Mallon, & Arthur, 2003). According to the French career model, the selection of potential top managers takes place at entry and is mostly based on elite educational qualifications gained in "Grandes Ecoles" (Evans, Lank, & Farquhar, 1989), which are considered as "talent hotbed" (Alexandre-Bailly, Festing, & Jonczyk, 2007). Networks (Burt, Hogarth, & Michaud, 2000), which are often built up during study period (Barmeyer & Mayrhofer, 2007), are determinant factors to succeed in the French (political) tournament career (Rosenbaum, 1979; see Dany, 2003). This French career model is based on elitist values and appears to be unique in Europe (Hartmann, 1997; 2007). It has been suggested that recruitment and career development in Germany is more based on expertise and functional competences and is rather egalitarian in nature (Evans, Pucik, & Barsoux, 2002). However, in the last few years, this has to some extent been questioned. Especially Hartmann (2007) argued that the German initiative of excellence (2004) has lead to a distinction between "excellent" and "average" universities in the German education system (p. 81), which is likely to lead to a more elitist recruitment in the future. Hence, the heretofore existing Germanic career model needs to be confirmed by further empirical research. In Denmark, the labor market is characterized by flexible hiring and firing rules (Datta Gupta & Smith, 2002), active labor market policy, and a generous social safety net (Andersen & Svarer, 2007). Compared to France and Germany, job tenure in Denmark is low and job mobility is rather high (Andersen, Haahr, Hansen, & Holm-Pedersen, 2008), which is why especially the external labor market plays an important role. Management development is generalist (Ramirez and Mabey, 2005), and recruitment in Scandinavian countries takes place for technical or functional jobs (Evans et al., 1989).

Considering the cultural dependency of careers and the labor market specificities in Denmark, France, and Germany, we expect to find differing rules of the game on the respective national career fields. Hence, we have reasons to believe that national borders represent virtual boundaries of career fields.

SIRS AT THE INTERPLAY BETWEEN FIELD, CAPITAL, AND HABITUS: THE RESEARCH FOCUS

If self-initiated repatriation represents a move between career fields, SIRs are likely to face different re-entry conditions depending on their country of return. Figure 10.1 shows the self-initiated repatriation process through the lens of our theoretical framework.

The individual's re-entry success on the native career field depends on the fit of the habitus as well as the amount and composition of career

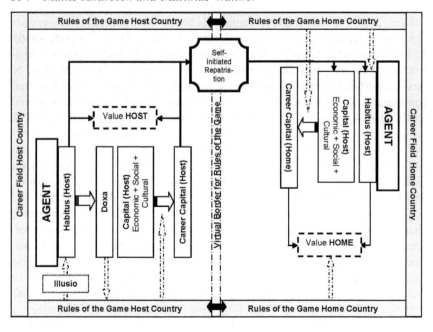

Figure 10.1 Applying Bourdieu's theory of practice on self-initiated repatriation.

capital, i.e. the relative parts of economic, cultural, and social capital in the entire career capital portfolio, to the career field (see Al Ariss & Syed, 2011 for SIEs' application of career capital in a French context). Its value is defined by the specific rules of the career field, which are likely to be different within our investigated countries. Hence, we expect the international experience in general as well as the habitus and the career capital portfolio to be valued differently with regard to the country of return.

When moving abroad, agents are endowed with a career capital portfolio of economic, cultural, and social capital. During expatriation, the agent's set of capital is likely to change (e.g. Jokinen, Suutari, & Brewster, 2008) also leading to a change of the respective capital fractions. Further, Iellatchitch et al. (2003) have argued that "habitus has a dynamic quality" (p. 739) and will develop. Abroad, the agent's career capital portfolio and habitus is evaluated based on host country-specific rules resulting in the value of the expatriate's career capital and habitus in the foreign career field. Upon return, however, SIRs import their (modified) career capital portfolio and habitus, which is evaluated based on the rules of the native career field and which then results in the re-entry value on the home country career field.

In summary, agents endowed with (modified) career capital and habitus continue their careers under home country rules and are therefore in competition with local employees. In our study, we focus on three main research questions:

1. How do the career capital portfolio and the (global and career) habitus develop abroad?
2. Do national frontiers represent virtual borders of career fields?
3. In how far do the SIRs' international experience and (modified) habitus and portfolio of career capital affect the return into the Danish, French, and German career field?

SAMPLE AND DATA ANALYSIS

For our comparative study, we adopted a qualitative research design (King, 2004) based on semi-structured interviews with 22 highly skilled SIRs to Denmark (N = 3), France (N = 10), and Germany (N = 9). A qualitative approach was chosen in order to get an in depth understanding (Denzin & Lincoln, 2008) that is required due to a dearth of studies and a lack of theory about self-initiated repatriation. Our sample is constituted of 17 male and 5 female respondents; the average age is 39.5 years. Seventeen respondents held a master's or MBA degree, 4 interviewees held a doctoral degree and one held a bachelor's degree. All respondents were SIRs, i.e. they had repatriated on their own volition without company support. Nine of them had gone abroad with company support, whereas 13 respondents were SIEs. On average, SIRs had expatriated 2.9 times during their working lives.

All interviews were conducted via telephone or Skype. We followed a pre-tested semi-structured interview guide, which had been elaborated in English, French, and German. As ideally, interviews should be conducted in the respondents' mother tongue (Kruse, 2010), we conducted all interviews with German SIRs in German and all interviews with French returnees in French. As one Dane's (Interviewee 10) German level was almost equal to that of a native speaker, we conducted the interview with this respondent in German. The interviews with the remaining Danish SIRs were conducted in English, which represented a foreign language for both the interviewees and the interviewers. Our interviews lasted between 37 and 113 minutes (69 minutes on average) and were type-recorded, transcribed verbatim, and fully anonymized. Verbatim quotations were translated into English by the authors if necessary.

We used qualitative content analysis (QCA; Mayring, 2003) to analyze our collected data. MaxQDA-software was used to arrange and code the interview transcripts (Kuckartz, 2009). For generating and structuring our coding frame, we combined the concept-driven (deductive) way with the data-driven (inductive) approach (Schreier, 2012). In a first step, we drew upon our theoretical framework, which provided our main categories, e.g. the creation of cultural capital during expatriation or the role of social capital for re-entering the native labor market and subcategories. Additional main- and subcategories emerged inductively from the data, which allowed an in-depth description of our material.

RESULTS

Self-Initiated Repatriation—A Career Capital and Habitus Perspective

Expatriation modified the absolute amount and relative parts of the different types of career capital of our respondents. Hence, SIRs were endowed with a different capital structure upon return than before expatriation. We found mixed results vis-à-vis the development of economic capital. The majority of our respondents (N = 16) reported a positive development of their economic capital basis. Most mentioned was the fact of receiving an attractive income that was due to a higher base salary (N = 7), allowances granted by their employer (N = 4), and lower tax-levels (N = 5). Two former expatriates mentioned lower expenses than in their native country due to lower living costs. During their time abroad, some expatriates (N = 7) were able to save money. By contrast, a minority reported low salary levels abroad (N = 6; all former SIEs) and that being abroad made them spend more money than at home due to a more extraverted lifestyle (N = 2) or higher living costs than in the native country (N = 6). Another emerging topic especially pertinent for one former SIE was a negative effect on the pension at home as she did not pay into the home country pension scheme during her time abroad.

As expected, our data show a positive effect of expatriation on the cultural capital basis, especially vis-à-vis the incorporated cultural capital. Following Fink, Meierwert, and Rohr's (2005) typology, which has also been applied by e.g. Berthier and Roger (2011), we found out that expatriates had acquired market-specific knowledge (e.g. foreign language skills, especially with regard to English as this was often their working language, or knowledge about the legal and system differences; N = 11), job-related management skills (e.g. professional, communication, and leadership skills; N = 16), personal skills (e.g. international and intercultural skills, self-confidence, especially due to challenging tasks abroad, and social competences; N = 20), and general management capacities (N = 5). The latter were mentioned less often because only a few of our sample worked on higher management level and had the opportunity to acquire this type of competences. Interestingly, one person (Interviewee 19) also reported that expatriation had had a negative effect on his incorporated cultural capital. This former French AE illustrated that his English skills had been negatively affected due to the fact that he had to interact in English with other non-native speakers on a day-to-day basis.

> At the age of 25, I spoke four languages: French, English, Italian, and Spanish. At the age of 50, I still speak French, my mother tongue, but my English level is weaker than when I was 25. The reason is quite simple. The English which is spoken on an international level needs

to be applicable to everybody. (…) you have to speak Globish, i.e. English with a simple, limited vocabulary, basic English. (Interviewee 19, French)

In order to document their international experience, SIRs mainly reported to have received employers' references or certificates (N = 12). Two persons also received a letter of recommendation from their former employer. However, several respondents (N = 7) indicated not to have received any written acknowledgment of their work abroad. Hence, these expatriates had not acquired any institutionalized cultural capital. In order to demonstrate what their work had been about, a few (N = 3) decided to describe their tasks in their CV in a very detailed way as it was the case for one German manager:

> I wrote it down for myself in my CV. My CV is very descriptive. I have one short version and one long version where I document everything since I have no written acknowledgement from my employer. (Interviewee 9, German)

Investigating social capital issues, we found mixed results vis-à-vis the maintenance of the existing network. A couple of SIRs (N = 11) indicated they had maintained their old network during their time abroad, whereas others (N = 9) were not able to or interested in keeping their network alive. Of special pertinence for SIEs seemed to be to stay in contact with (former) colleagues (N = 4) and former fellow students (N = 5) or friends at home (N = 3). While only one respondent had not created any new professional network at all, the majority (N = 21) of the respondents illustrated they had been able to create an international network within (N = 4) and particularly outside (N = 17) the employing organization, i. e. with other expatriates in the host country, locals or they built up an international network across countries.

Our data also show a modification in the respondents' global habitus and career habitus abroad. Some expatriates (N = 5) adapted their mindset and behaviors to the host country and even reported to have changed their identity:

> I also had this experience that I started to dream in English and my identity changed because indirectly, I was forced to because I used to have this very national thinking and naïve way of behaving with honesty here from Denmark and that didn't help me a thing (…). So I quickly found out how to become another (name of the person). (Interviewee 12, Dane)

For some of the respondents (N = 4), the career habitus also changed or was clarified during their time abroad. One German manager (Interviewee 9) who worked in the US and UK illustrated that instead of planning everything into great detail as it is common in Germany, she is now more willing to take risks.

Self-Initiated Repatriation—A Career Field Perspective

Re-entering the Danish Career Field. All Danes of our sample adopted the strategy to repatriate and seek employment when already back at home. One (Interviewee 10) engaged a coach for his job hunting on the Danish career field. International mobility appeared to be valued very negatively by Danish employers. All Danes (all former SIEs) had serious re-integration problems into the Danish career field.

> In Denmark, strange enough, it is quite commonly known among us who have been working overseas that you cannot get a job in Denmark. They don't want you. (Interviewee 8, Dane)

One returning Dane (Interviewee 10) thought that due to his experience abroad, he would be an interesting candidate for international Danish companies. Therefore, he was all the more surprised when he recognized that his profile was not sought after at all. This can to some extent be explained by the 'Janteloven,' which is an implicit law deeply rooted in the Danes' habitus.

> Because of this phenomenon, I don't know if you have heard it, but it is something called the Jante Law. They have it in many different countries, but most of it exists in Scandinavia. It is a rule, it is a hidden rule like, because the country is very national. So it is like you cannot stand out, you cannot be stronger than others, you know. You have got to be like everyone else and that sort of mental thinking. (Interviewee 12, Dane)

Especially the fact of having expatriated on their own behest seemed to be very detrimental for Danish returnees. One Danish SIR (Interviewee 10) had the impression that if a Danish company had sent him abroad, he would have had an "excuse" for having left the country. On the other hand, he also reports that having repatriated on his own initiative was seen very positively as it was perceived as final comprehension that it is best at home.

Another Dane (Interviewee 2) who had been in America explained that due to her expatriation she did not have enough networks in Denmark anymore, which made her re-entry problematic. Acquired incorporated cultural capital seemed not to be valued upon return, which sometimes led to frustration. A specific problem was that Danish companies were not open to things, which were not familiar to them. Therefore, acquired incorporated cultural capital was apparently difficult to express.

So it was more like a work-life experience that I could put on my CV. In Denmark, they are not that open to things they don't know, "what is this work, what is this school, what is this course?" (Interviewee 12, Dane)

Finally, all Danes reported habitus-related difficulties upon return. Their habitus, i.e. their way of thinking and acting was not appropriate upon return to Denmark. While specific career habitus-related problems were not mentioned, respondents especially reported difficulties re-adapting to the Danish global habitus.

That is tough, because you have to put yourself into a box again. But repatriates, they don't fit into boxes, because they have another identity, another image, they have a triangle identity (. . .). Now I am not (name of the person) the Dane, now I am (name of the person) the British-American Dane. (Interviewee 12, Dane)

Re-entering the German Career Field. The majority of the German SIRs (N = 5) searched a job from abroad and did not wait until coming home. One respondent (Interviewee 9) took a sabbatical upon return and only started her job search after one year. Contrary to the return into the Danish career field, the German SIRs' international experience was seen a lot more positively by home country employers. Almost all German SIRs (N = 8) reported that, regardless of the country or the sector of activity, their international experience had a positive effect on their re-integration into the German labor market.

It was very important for the fact that I finally got a job at (name of employer). One of the requirements in the job advertisement was that the candidate had studied or worked abroad, ideally both. (Interviewee 15, German)

While the majority of the respondents had to justify their self-initiated repatriation during job interviews (N = 7), almost all (N = 6) reported a positive or at least no negative effect. For one German manager (Interviewee 21), it was seen as an intelligent decision to quit his old employer as the image of this company had deteriorated. However, one German engineer (Interviewee 6) also pointed out that, due to the fact of having changed company, he had to make his proofs again. His positive professional reputation he had built up abroad was of no use anymore and he had to start over again.

Only for one respondent (Interviewee 21), financial issues had an effect on his re-entry into the German labor market. This former AE illustrated that his high salary abroad represented an obstacle to finding a new job since home country firms had difficulty keeping up with such high salaries. Regarding the pertinence of social capital, we found mixed results. Four of our nine German SIRs reported not to have used social capital for their re-entry into the native labor market at all, whereas five respondents clearly expressed to have drawn on their network, especially on contacts they had already had before expatriating.

> And they (former fellow students of responding engineer) talked to the respective firms and said "he is a fellow student of ours. He is very able; you should have a closer look at him." So they campaigned for me. (Interviewee 6, German)

Incorporated cultural capital issues, which were mentioned by all German SIRs, were especially pertinent for re-entering the German career field. Acquired personal skills, market-specific knowledge, e.g. language skills, and job-related management skills, mainly intercultural and professional skills were found to play an important role for a successful re-entry. One former SIE (Interviewee 17) reported that his foreign language skills and intercultural skills were specifically tested during his job interview and were the major reason why he got his job. Interestingly, this same person also mentioned a negative effect of absent institutionalized cultural capital for finding work. The fact of not having any detailed written confirmation of his international experience led to skepticism among his future employer. Another former AE (Interviewee 21) said one major reason why he had been selected was that he had acquired product-related and selling competences. Acquired project management or communication skills were further pertinent competences, which emerged during our interviews.

One German manager who had been to the US (Interviewee 16) reported that his modified career habitus was not applicable back home in the native career field. While in the US it is quite common to publish good (financial) results one has achieved and to highlight one's incorporated cultural capital, this is not appropriate on the German career field. However, this manager did not report to have had any re-adaptation difficulties. Two persons reported they were somehow missing the German global habitus and back at home, things went more easily for them again.

> ... and I have to say, I came back home to Germany after six years and I never had the feeling I had been away for six years. (...) And this gave me a lot of security. Here, life is simply easier, you know the rules and you do not need to pay attention to everything. (Interviewee 9, German)

Re-entering the French Career Field. Similarly to the German respondents, five French SIRs searched a new job already from abroad, whereas only two started their job search back at home. Mixed results were found about the value of international experience on the native career field. For half of the respondents having worked abroad was valued positively. The value of the international experience apparently depends on the sector of activity and the country where the expatriate was. It came up that having worked for big prestigious companies abroad was seen positively whereas having worked as a volunteer in a non-governmental organization (NGO) was penalized upon return. One French engineer (Interviewee 1) reported that his international experience in an NGO was considered as having been on holidays. Another French engineer (Interviewee 13) illustrated that French private-sector companies did not understand the activities of former expatriates in NGOs abroad. Hence, they somehow tried to translate their experience into a more comprehensible language.

> So I did this translation work behind. You are partner. You are always partner during your development project. But you don't say you were partner, you talk about CLIENT. So when you said CLIENT, they didn't ask. (. . .) You need to adapt (your language) so that your dialog partner understands. (Interviewee 13, French)

The value of the international experience also depended on the host country. While it was reported that African countries were sometimes considered to be a little bit *"olé olé"* (Interviewee 1) as French employers had the impression that the expatriate had more focused on enjoying the sun and the swimming pool rather than working (Interviewee 3), one respondent (Interviewee 11) reported that expatriating into other French-speaking European countries was not valued either as it was considered not to be different enough to the host country. More appreciated seemed to be host countries such as Germany, GB, or the US as reported by Interviewee 13.

During job interviews some of the respondents had to justify their self-initiated expatriation (N = 3) and their self-initiated repatriation (N = 4). Whereas one respondent (Interviewee 1) reported that his self-initiated expatriation was seen skeptically as French companies considered him as instable and quickly willing to leave the company again, another French engineer (Interviewee 3) illustrated self-initiation to be more valued than an assignment because SIEs were supposed to have been more challenged. Four respondents reported their self-initiated repatriation did not have any negative effect on their re-entry. However, one French engineer (Interviewee 13) also illustrated it meant he had to make his proofs again, whereas one French manager (Interviewee 19) reported about his difficulties to find a new job due to his age.

While economic capital was not mentioned to play any role in the re-entry into the French labor market, social capital issues were pertinent and mentioned by the majority (N = 7) of the respondents. While three French SIRs did not use social capital, the rest especially drew on their already existing network, e.g. family members, friends, or former fellow students. One French engineer (Interviewee 20) was hired by a former professional contact in France she had worked with during her time in Senegal, i.e. a contact she had built up abroad.

Interestingly, only about half of the respondents mentioned incorporated cultural capital as pertinent for getting or not getting a job upon return. Acquired personal skills, e.g. open-mindedness, language skills, or job-related management skills, e.g. autonomy or professional skills were valued for the re-entry. Problematic was the fact of having acquired too general competences as reported by one French engineer (Interviewee 13) or the fact that due to a change of industry, the acquired competences were not pertinent any more as mentioned by another engineer (Interviewee 19). Four respondents reported that institutionalized cultural capital, e.g. in form of diplomas, played an important role for the re-entry into the French labor market. One French engineer reported that one needs to have a diploma from a prestigious 'Grande Ecole,' otherwise the acquired competences and the international experience is not valued:

> I have all that (international experience), but I did not study at a Grande Ecole. (. . .) So to say, you have to study at (name of a prestigious French engineering school) or you have to study at the big Grandes Ecoles of engineering in France, elite schools. This is the silver bullet. (Interviewee 13, French)

This same person also complains that in France, competences are not valued as careers are elitist, which is also confirmed by the majority of the other French respondents (N = 7) who consider the value of the diploma as a critical key success factor for careers in the French career field. Furthermore, it was reported that those company representatives having graduated from one specific Grande Ecole tend to hire primarily graduates from this same school.

> . . . it is limited by the network. People are seeking that. It has nothing to do with the competences. The network of those having studied at (name of the Grande Ecole), as soon as there is a CEO who has studied at (name of the Grande Ecole), he will prefer that his VPs have also studied at (name of the Grande Ecole). (Interviewee 22, French)

One engineer (Interviewee 1) illustrated that during his expatriation career field characteristics in France, especially with regard to pertinent aspects for an application, had changed. Therefore, he had to adapt his career habitus, which apparently was no problem for him. Three other French respondents reported that they had no problems to readjust their general habitus to the home country. One engineer (Interviewee 13) was looking forward to the French habitus back home. However, one French manager (Interviewee 4) also stressed his re-entry shock when he moved back to Paris after eight years abroad.

DISCUSSION

The study results demonstrate that expatriation affects the habitus and capital basis. As to the effect on economic capital, we found mixed results. Some earned a higher salary abroad and were able to save money; others reported the contrary. Not surprisingly and confirming e.g. Fink et al.'s (2005) results, we found out that former expatriates had built up incorporated cultural capital. SIRs were especially endowed with additional personal skills, job-related management skills, and market-specific knowledge upon return. From a human capital point of view, this suggests that the SIRs' value for potential employers is enhanced abroad. This would also confirm Begley et al.'s (2008) statement that SIRs are likely to represent a valuable human resource in filling key positions upon return. Our findings concerning the development of institutionalized cultural capital indicate that some received employers' references documenting one's tasks and experiences as is typical in Germany or letters of recommendation, whereas others did not build up any institutionalized cultural capital. It has already been argued that HR-practices vary in different countries (e.g. Larsen & Brewster, 2000), which is confirmed by the results of our study.

We found mixed results regarding the maintenance of social capital abroad, whereas almost all respondents reported to have built up new contacts, particularly outside the employing company. This is in line with already existing research results, e.g. of Antal (2000), Mäkelä (2007), or Jokinen et al. (2008) who found evidence that SIEs also build up social capital but to a lesser extent than AEs. However, more studies are needed to explore in how far expatriation affects the already existing network, since, as our results show, SIRs especially draw on contacts they already had before expatriating when re-entering the native labor market.

Finally, our data indicate that the former expatriates' global and career habitus has been modified abroad. This finding is interesting and adds to the discussion about habitus stability. Bourdieu (1992b) or Iellatchitch et al. (2003) suggest that the career habitus has a dynamic quality and can be modified when changing the career field. This viewpoint is also shared by Mayrhofer et al. (2004a) who further claim that the global, general habitus focuses more on stability as it is developed during life span. In our study, it came up that in some cases, the career habitus had changed abroad, especially with regard to work attitudes, which shows that expatriates apparently understand what is at stake abroad (illusio) and behave according to the rules of the respective career field. The fact that the modified career habitus was not reported to represent a problem for re-entering the native career field is a sign that at the same time SIRs do not unlearn the rules of the game of the native career field. Apparently, agents can adapt their career habitus abroad (modus operandi) but do not lose the ability to invest the right combination of career capital on the native career field and re-adapt easily upon return. In some cases, our results also show that the global habitus had been modified, which would indicate that the global habitus is not as stable as assumed (Mayrhofer et al., 2004a).

Our results give reason to believe that SIRs to Denmark, France, and Germany face different re-entry conditions and that the SIRs' modified habitus and capital portfolio is valued differently with respect to the country of re-entry. Hence, national borders seem to represent virtual boundaries where rules of career fields lose their impact. By showing that self-initiated repatriation can be seen as a move between career fields, we contribute to the request that boundaries of career fields have to be investigated empirically. SIRs to Denmark faced important re-entry problems into their native career field. Especially the 'Janteloven,' an implicit law rooted in the Danish global habitus, appears to be well-suited to explain SIRs' difficulties to re-enter the Danish labor market. Quitting the country can somehow be interpreted as treason, and having worked abroad is apparently seen very negatively. Especially the fact of having expatriated on their own initiative rather than having been sent by a company apparently represents a knock-out criterion for re-entering the Danish career field, which might lead to brain-waste upon return. Acquired cultural or social capital seems not even to be considered any more as one's own decision to expatriate represents an important criterion for exclusion within itself. It appears that the Danish flexicurity labor market, which highlights the importance of external labor markets within the country, is difficult to re-enter once a Dane has expatriated on his own behest. Boundaries of the Danish labor market may very well be open within national frontiers but appear to be more closed from an external perspective, especially for potential re-entering former SIEs. A lateral (re-)entry into the Danish career field appears to be difficult for this group of internationally mobile workers.

For SIRs returning to Germany, international experience seems to be valued positively. In their "Germanic Model" Evans et al. (2002) suggested that recruitment is not elitist and functional expertise is highly valued. Our results confirm the quintessence of this model and provide potential for enlargement. We found no evidence for an elitist recruitment of SIRs. The fact that the German initiative of excellence (2004) might lead to a more elitist recruitment in the future (Hartmann, 2007) seems not (yet) to be to the point. Incorporated cultural capital appeared to be highly important for the re-entry into the German career field. Not only job-related management skills, e.g. functional competences as suggested by Evans et al. (2002), were highly valued, but also personal skills and market-specific knowledge, e.g. language skills, played an important role for a successful re-entry. Moreover, institutionalized cultural capital, especially in the form of employers' references, were crucial in order to underline the international activity. Social capital issues, particularly existing contacts before expatriation, were also pertinent, whereas habitus was not found to affect the re-entry. At least no habitus-related problems could be identified. It rather represented a pull-factor to return home as respondents somehow missed the German global habitus. Having been out of the German career system, a lateral (re-)entry seems possible, and its success depends on the right capital fractions in one's capital portfolio. Especially incorporated and institutionalized cultural capital and, although to a lesser extent, social capital issues play an important role and have to be strongly represented, whereas we found no evidence for economic capital issues being especially pertinent.

Institutionalized capital issues seem to be of special importance for SIRs re-entering the French career field. Our study confirms that recruitment in France is highly elitist (e.g. Hartmann, 1997). It was found to be important at which Grande Ecole one had studied. If the diploma was not prestigious enough, re-entry appeared to be difficult. Only with a sufficiently valued diploma, incorporated cultural capital was taken into consideration at all and represented a pertinent evaluation criterion. The academic literature has already shown the importance of the diploma for careers within the French career field (e.g. Alexandre-Bailly et al., 2007). In our study, we were able to demonstrate that institutionalized cultural capital is also of high importance for successfully moving back into the French career field. Hence, the value of the diploma does not lose its pertinence and institutionalized cultural capital represents a necessary condition for the re-entry into the French labor market. Social capital in the form of external strong ties (Mäkelä & Suutari, 2009), especially former fellow students (Burt et al., 2000), were also found to strongly affect the re-entry. There appears to be a link between institutionalized cultural capital and social capital on the French career field. This leads to a social reproduction effect (Hartmann, 1997) and shows the dependence of the value of one's network from the educational institution where one has studied. Contrary to Evans et al.'s (2002) assumption that recruitment in the Latin Career Model only takes place at entry, in our study, SIRs were also found able to return back into the French career field. Hence, a lateral (re-)entry into the French career system seems possible. This would indicate that boundaries in French careers are not as closed (any more) as indicated in the academic literature (e.g. Dany, 2003; Stahl & Cerdin, 2004), which would be in line with assumptions made by the new career literature (e.g. Sullivan, 1999; Sullivan & Baruch, 2009). In summary, French returnees apparently have to be endowed with institutionalized cultural capital and social capital, whereas incorporated cultural capital and economic capital only played a minor or no role for SIRs' re-entry.

IMPLICATIONS FOR THEORY AND PRACTICE

From a theoretical perspective the study aimed at an enlargement of our understanding about the heretofore neglected topic of self-initiated repatriation. We provide insights about career fields in Europe and showed that to a large extent, the rules of the game in France, Germany, and Denmark differ. Therefore, national frontiers are likely to represent boundaries where rules of the game of career fields lose their impact. Our results confirm in large parts Evans et al.'s (1989) international career model but challenge the fact that a lateral re-entry into the French career system is not possible.

From an organizational point of view, we provide information for potential employing companies about the career capital of SIRs. Companies should consider highly skilled SIRs as a valuable human resource, which, due to the acquired cultural capital, has the potential to contribute to the company success. From an individual perspective, SIRs have to be aware of the rules on their respective native career fields. Although expatriates may a priori not be sure about their return, they are well-advised to watch that the modification of their capital portfolio abroad has no detrimental effect upon return and still fits to the rules of the native career field. French returnees have to be aware of the fact that expatriation may be a risky undertaking if one does not possess sufficiently valued institutionalized cultural capital. Acquired skills and competences are not valued upon return if one does not possess the right diploma. They should stay in contact with former fellow students during their time abroad as these were found to represent valuable social capital when returning into the French career field. German expatriates should especially try to improve their incorporated cultural capital basis. They should also mind to ask for an employers' reference in order to be able to testify their activities abroad as a lack of institutionalized cultural capital can cause problems, also certainly to a lesser extent than for French SIRs. Danes certainly face the most difficult re-entry conditions. Since their international experience, especially self-initiated expatriation is seen very negatively per se, they should particularly highlight the fact of having repatriated on their own behest as this shows the SIRs' commitment to Denmark.

We see the limitations of our study. We investigated self-initiated repatriation collecting information exclusively from SIRs. In further research, HR experts' appraisal about the value of the modified set of career capital should be gathered as they represent the decision-makers vis-à-vis the re-entry into the native labor market. Further, the amount of our respondents is limited, which is why generalization appears to be difficult. Having only a very few Danes in our sample, especially the results about repatriation to Denmark need to be interpreted with the appropriate caution. A further confirmative quantitative study is of interest in order to achieve a statistical generalization of our results.

CONCLUSIONS

Our study was exploratory in nature and aimed at investigating self-initiated repatriation to Denmark, France, and Germany. Applying Bourdieu's Theory of Practice (1972), we took a multi-level perspective and analyzed self-initiated repatriation at the interplay between field, capital, and habitus. We found that expatriates' habitus and career capital had been modified abroad. In line with our expectations, SIRs faced differing re-entry conditions depending on the country of return, which shows that national boundaries represent virtual borders of career fields. Economic capital and habitus issues did not play a major role for the re-entry into the native career field. Agents were found able to adapt their career habitus abroad and at the same time not to lose the ability to invest the right combination of career capital on the native career field. For returnees to the Danish career field, having self-initiated expatriated represented negative symbolic capital within itself as it was interpreted as treason to the home country. Especially the modified set of cultural and social capital was pertinent for re-entering the French and German career field. While in France, having a prestigious diploma, which generally goes hand in hand with a valuable network, was found to be a necessary criterion for successfully re-entering the French career field, German SIRs especially drew on incorporated cultural capital in the form of professional skills and competences. This clearly shows differing rules of the game between national career fields and resulting differences in the composition of symbolic career capital fractions.

NOTES

1. The literature provides many definitions for 'highly-skilled' professionals. We refer to the common definition given by Iredale (2001) who defines them as "having a university degree or extensive/equivalent experience in a given field" (p. 8).

REFERENCES

Al Ariss, A., & Syed, J. (2011). Capital mobilization of skilled migrants: A relational perspective. *British Journal of Management*, 22(2), 286–304.

Alexandre-Bailly, F., Festing, M., & Jonczyk, C. (2007). Choix et formation des dirigeants en France et en Allemagne. In F. Bournois, J. Duval-Hamel, S. Roussillon and J.-L. Scaringella (Eds.), *Comités Exécutifs. Voyage au Cœur de la dirigeance* (pp. 245–250). Paris: Eyrolles.

Andersen, T., Haahr, J. H., Hansen, M. E., & Holm-Pedersen, M. (2008). *Job mobility in the European Union: Optimising its social and economic benefits—Final report*. Retrieved from http://ec.europa.eu/social/main.jsp?langId=en&catId=89&newsId=386.

Andersen, T. & Svarer, M. (2007). Flexicurity—Labour market performance in Denmark. *CESifo Economic Studies*, 53(3), 389–429.

Antal, B. A. (2000). Types of knowledge gained by expatriate managers. *Journal of General Management*, 26(2), 32–51.

Barmeyer, C., & Mayrhofer, U. (2007). Culture et relations de pouvoir: Une analyse longitudinale du groupe EADS. *Gérer et comprendre*, 88, 4–20.

Begley, A., Collings, D. G., & Scullion, H. (2008). The cross-cultural adjustment experiences of self-initiated repatriates to the Republic of Ireland labour market. *Employee Relations*, 30(3), 264–282.

Berthier, P., & Roger, A. (2011). La mobilité internationale des cadres, une occasion de développer et de transférer de nouvelles compétences. In U. Mayrhofer (Ed.), *Le management des firmes multinationales* (pp. 163–180). Paris: Vuibert.

Bourdieu, P. (1972). *Esquisse d'une théorie de la pratique.* Genève: Droz.

Bourdieu, P. (1986). The forms of capital. In J. G. Richardson (Ed.), *Handbook of theory and research for the sociology of education* (pp. 241–258). New York: Greenwood.

Bourdieu, P. (1992a). *Distinction: A social critique of the judgement.* Cambridge: Harvard University Press.

Bourdieu, P. (1992b). *Rede und Antwort.* Frankfurt: Suhrkamp.

Bourdieu, P., & Wacquant, L. (1992). *Réponses.* Paris: Editions du Soleil.

Burt, R. S., Hogarth, R. M., & Michaud, C. (2000). The social capital of French and American managers. *Organization Science,* 11(2), 123–147.

Crossley, N. (2001). The phenomenological habitus and its construction. *Theory and Society,* 30(1), 81–120.

Dany, F. (2003). 'Free actors' and organizations: Critical remarks about the new career literature, based on French insights. *International Journal of Human Resource Management,* 14(5), 821–838.

Dany, F., Mallon, M., & Arthur, M. B. (2003). The odyssey of career and the opportunity for international comparison. *International Journal of Human Resource Management,* 14(5), 705–712.

Datta Gupta, N., & Smith, N. (2002). Children and career interruptions: The family gap in Denmark. *Economica,* 69(276), 609–629.

Denzin, N. K., & Lincoln, Y. S. (2008). *Strategies of qualitative inquiry* (3rd ed.). Thousand Oaks, CA: Sage.

Derr, C. B., & Laurent, A. (1989). The internal and external career: A theoretical and cross-cultural perspective. In M. B. Arthur, D. T. Hall and B. S. Lawrence (Eds.), *Handbook of career theory* (pp. 454–471). Cambridge: University Press.

Doherty, N., & Dickmann, M. (2009). Exposing the symbolic capital of international assignments. *International Journal of Human Resource Management,* 20(2), 301–320.

Evans, P., Lank, E., & Farquhar, A. (1989). Managing human resources in the international firm: Lessons from practice. In P. Evans, Y. Doz and A. Laurent (Eds.), *Human resource management in international firms* (pp. 113–143). London: Macmillan.

Evans, P., Pucik, V., & Barsoux, J.-L. (2002). *The global challenge: Frameworks for international human resource management.* Boston: McGraw-Hill.

Fink, G., Meierewert, S., & Rohr, U. (2005). The use of repatriate knowledge in organizations. *Human Resource Planning,* 28(4), 30–36.

Forstenlechner, I. (2010). Brain drain in developed countries. Can governments do anything to bring expatriates back? *Public Policy and Administration,* 25(1), 156–174.

Hartmann, M. (1997). Soziale Öffnung oder soziale Schließung. Die deutsche und die französische Wirtschaftselite zwischen 1970 und 1995. *Zeitschrift für Soziologie,* 26(4), 296–311.

Hartmann, M. (2007). *Eliten und Macht in Europa. Ein internationaler Vergleich.* Frankfurt am Main: Campus Verlag.

Howe-Walsh, L., & Schyns, B. (2010). Self-initiated expatriation: Implications for HRM. *International Journal of Human Resource Management,* 21(2), 260–273.

Iellatchitch, A., Mayrhofer, W., & Meyer, M. (2003). Career fields: A small step towards a grand career theory? *International Journal of Human Resource Management,* 14(5), 728–750.

Iredale, R. (2001). The migration of professionals: Theories and typologies. *International Migration,* 39(5), 7–24.

Jokinen, T., Suutari, V., & Brewster, C. (2008). Career capital during international work experiences: Contrasting self-initiated expatriate experiences and assigned expatriation. *International Journal of Human Resource Management*, 19(6), 979–998.

King, N. (2004). Using interviews in qualitative research. In C. Casell and G. Symon (Eds.), *Essential guide to qualitative methods in organizational research* (pp. 11–22). London: Sage.

Krais, B. (1988). Der Begriff des Habitus bei Bourdieu und seine Bedeutung für die Bildungstheorie. In B. Dewe, G. Frank and W. Huge, (Eds), *Theorien der Erwachsenenbildung* (pp. 199–213). München: Hueber.

Kruse, J. (2010). *Reader 'Einführung in die Qualitative Interviewforschung'.* Retrieved from http://www.soziologie.uni-freiburg.de/kruse.

Kuckartz, U. (2009). *Computergestützte Analyse qualitativer Daten. Eine Einführung in Methoden und Arbeitstechniken* (3rd ed.). Opladen: Westdeutscher Verlag.

Larsen, H. H., & Brewster, C. (2000). Human resource management in Northern Europe: Trends, dilemmas and strategies. In C. Brewster and H. H. Larsen (Eds.), *Human resource management in Northern Europe* (pp. 1–23). Oxford: Blackwell Business.

Laurent, A. (1986). The cross-cultural puzzle of international human resource management. *Human Resource Management*, 25(19), 91–102.

Lindh, G., & Dahlin, E. (2000). A Swedish perspective on the importance of Bourdieu's theories for career counseling. *Journal of Employment Counseling*, 37(4), 194–203.

Mäkelä, K. (2007). Knowledge sharing through expatriate relationships: A social capital perspective. *International Studies of Management and Organization*, 37(3), 108–125.

Mäkelä, K., & Suutari, V. (2009). Global careers: A social capital paradox. *International Journal of Human Resource Management*, 20(5), 992–1008.

Mayrhofer, W., Iellatchitch, A., Meyer, A., Steyrer, J., Schiffinger, M., & Strunk, G. (2004a). Going beyond the individual. Some potential contributions from a career field and habitus perspective for global career research and practice. *Journal of Management Development*, 23(9), 870–884.

Mayrhofer, W., Meyer, M., Iellatchitch, A., & Schiffinger, M. (2004b). Careers and human resource management: A European perspective. *Human Resource Management Review*, 14(4), 473–498.

Mayrhofer, W., Meyer, M., Steyrer, J., & Langer, K. (2007). Can expatriation research learn from other disciplines? The case of international career habitus. *International Studies of Management and Organization*, 37(3), 89–107.

Mayrhofer, W., Meyer, M., Steyrer, J., Maier, J., Langer, K., & Hermann, A. (2004c, August). *International career habitus—Thick descriptions and theoretical reflections.* Paper presented at the Academy of Management Annual Meeting, Symposium, New Orleans.

Mayrhofer, W., & Schneidhofer, T. (2009). The lay of the land: European career research and its future. *Journal of Occupational and Organizational Psychology*, 82(4), 721–737.

Mayring, P. (2003). *Qualitative Inhaltsanalyse. Grundlagen und Techniken.* Weinheim: Beltz.

McKenna, S., & Richardson, J. (2007). The increasing complexity of the internationally mobile professional. Issues for research and practice. *Cross Cultural Management: An International Journal*, 14(4), 307–320.

Myers, B., & Pringle, J. (2005). Self-initiated foreign experience as accelerated development: Influences of gender. *Journal of World Business*, 40(4), 421–31.

Ng, T. W. H., Sorensen, K. L., Eby, L. T., & Feldmann, D. C. (2007). Determinants of job mobility: A theoretical integration and extension. *Journal of Occupational and Organizational Psychology*, 80(3), 363–386.

Postone, M., LiPuma, E., & Calhoun, C. (1993). Introduction: Bourdieu and social theory. In C. Calhoun, E. LiPuma and M. Postone (Eds), *Bourdieu: Critical perspectives* (pp. 1–13). Chicago: University of Chicago Press.

Ramirez, M., & Mabey, C. (2005). A labour market perspective on management training and development in Europe. *International Journal of Human Resource Management*, 16(3), 291–310.

Richardson, J., & Mallon, M. (2005). Career interrupted? The case of the self-directed expatriate. *Journal of World Business*, 40(4), 409–420.

Rosenbaum, J. E. (1979). Tournament mobility: Career patterns in a corporation. *Administrative Science Quarterly*, 24(2), 220–241.

Schneidhofer, T. M., Schiffinger, M., & Mayrhofer, W. (2010). Mind the (gender) gap. Gender, gender role types, and their effects on objective career success over time. *Management Review*, 21(4), 437–457.

Schreier, M. (2012). *Qualitative content analysis in practice*. London: Sage.

Stahl, G. K., & Cerdin, J.-L. (2004). Global careers in French and German multinational corporations. *Journal of Management Development*, 23(9), 885–902.

Sullivan, S. E. (1999). The changing nature of careers: A review and research agenda. *Journal of Management*, 25(3), 457–484.

Sullivan, S. E., & Baruch, Y. (2009). Advances in career theory and research: A critical review and agenda for future exploration. *Journal of Management*, 35(6), 1542–1571.

Suutari, V., & Brewster, C. (2000). Making their own way: International experience through self-initiated foreign assignments. *Journal of World Business*, 35(4), 417–436.

Tharenou, P., & Caulfield, N. (2010). Will I stay or will I go? Explaining repatriation by self-initiated expatriates. *Academy of Management Journal*, 53(5), 1009–1028.

Thomas, D. (2002). *Essentials of international management: A cross-cultural perspective*. Thousand Oaks, CA: Sage.

Thomas, D., & Inkson, K. (2007). *Careers across cultures*. In H. Gunz and M. Periperl (Eds), Handbook of Career Studies (pp. 451–470). London: Sage Publications.

Understanding the Groups Undertaking Self-Initiated Foreign Experiences

Part III

11 Volunteering Abroad
A Career-Related Analysis of International Development Aid Workers

Maike Andresen and Tanja Gustschin

While employees who are sent abroad by their international companies have been the focus of scholars researching expatriation for several decades, more empirical evidence about the group of those who gather international work experience under their own initiative as well as theoretical substantiation is still needed. The group of Self-Initiated Expatriates (SIEs) is comparably much more diverse as compared with assigned expatriates (AEs) in terms of demographic background and motivation to work abroad (Inkson & Myers, 2003; Richardson & McKenna, 2002) and employing organizations so that several subgroups of SIEs need to be formed (Suutari & Brewster, 2000). However, the vast majority of existing studies about SIEs as well as AEs concerns employees in the private sector with a lack of studies in non-profit organizations. In general, the literature on global mobility outside multinational companies (MNCs) is relatively sparse (Toomey & Brewster, 2008), although bodies such as the United Nations (UN) or Organisation for Economic Co-operation and Development (OECD) as well as a number of non-governmental organizations (NGOs), charities, and religious organizations employ people on a global scale (Brewster, Dickmann, & Sparrow, 2008).

The focus of this study is on volunteer international development workers. International development workers can be seen to constitute one of the subgroups of SIEs. Nevertheless, there are also substantial differences between international volunteers and other expatriates, thus limiting the significance of existing expatriate literature for the context of development assistance. To sum up, development workers are an under-researched group (Hudson & Inkson, 2006), and it is difficult to make assumptions about them based on studies exploring expatriation and volunteerism separately.

Volunteering is defined in sociology as "any activity in which time is given freely to benefit another person, group or cause" (Wilson, 2000, p. 215). According to the German Volunteer Law, a development worker is an individual working in a developing country for a state-approved provider of development assistance. The development worker's service is provided without any prospect of monetary gain (AKLHUE, 2003). As in practice, international volunteers usually receive some remuneration for their work;

however, it is considerably below the market value of their services. Thus, they are also referred to as "quasi-volunteers" (Smith, 1981).

Most of the literature concerning international development assistance focuses on the issues of purpose, form, and effectiveness of development aid, while the people working in this area often remain overlooked. However, the ability to identify and recruit the right people for the task and place them in the right projects is crucial for the success of international development aid (MacLachlan & Carr, 1999). Thus, knowledge about international volunteers is much needed, not only for development aid agencies. More insight into the profile of a development worker would also benefit potential future employers back in the home country since they would be enabled to get a better picture of the job candidate, which, in turn, facilitates the decision how to leverage the special skills in the organizational context.

Therefore, the aim of this study is to contribute empirical data about international volunteers in terms of their demographic characteristics, motivation to go abroad, and a number of career-related issues such as career attitudes and behaviors, learning orientation, and career mobility as well as career success. The construct of the protean career (Hall, 1996; 2002) will be used as theoretical framework for the analysis.

The chapter is organized as follows: review of the issues of international volunteering with a particular focus on motivation and the protean career followed by the presentation of the hypotheses. After an outline of the sample and measures, the findings are presented and discussed. Finally, practical implications of the research and suggestions for further research are given, and conclusions are drawn.

INTERNATIONAL VOLUNTEERING AND EXPATRIATION

International volunteering of development workers involves a kind of expatriation, i.e. a "process of an individual moving to live in a different country" (Brewster, 2002, p. 84). Literature on expatriation distinguishes between assigned expatriates, i.e. employees of an internationally operating enterprise who work and temporarily reside in a foreign country (Dowling, Festing, & Engle, 2008), and SIEs, i.e. individuals who relocate abroad on their own initiative (Hudson & Inkson, 2006; Inkson, Arthur, Pringle, & Barry, 1997) while changing their dominant place of residence, and execute dependent regulary work for a new organization (Andresen, Bergdolt, & Margenfeld, 2012 in this volume). The notion of self-initiated expatriation has also been applied to international volunteers (Fee & Gray, 2011; Hudson & Inkson, 2006).

Although development aid workers most likely are the primary initiators of their international work experience, there is a major involvement of organizational control. Potential international volunteers are "selected, assigned, socialised, supervised and de-briefed" (Hudson & Inkson, 2006, p. 307) by sending organizations and their partner agencies abroad. Although the goals are primarily defined by the organization, it cannot be denied that development workers also have stark personal motives to engage in international development assistance (Rehberg, 2005). In contrast to the majority of SIEs in for-profit organizations (Howe-Walsh & Schyns, 2010), international volunteers usually get cultural adjustment training and some kind of financial support for their relocation expenses by their sending organizations (AGEH, 2011; GIZ, 2011). Additionally, although development workers have only temporary contracts with their sending organizations, major organizations offer assistance upon their return in terms of individual career counseling, occupational orientation seminars, or scholarships for vocational further qualification (AGdD, 2011).

In regard to individual background variables, similarities between international volunteers and SIEs for-profit organizations can be expected. On the one hand, sending organizations require development workers to

Table 11.1   Comparison of Characteristic Features of Different International Employees

Compared areas	AEs	SIEs	International development workers
Initiation	First formalized action is taken by the current organization	First formalized action is taken by the individual	First formalized action is usually taken by the individual
Decision of employment	Decision is made by home / current country organization	Decision is made by host / new country organization	Decision is typically made by new organization
Goals/ motives	Personal and professional motives with a dominance of organization-related goals	Personal and professional motives with a dominance of personal goals	Personal motives as well as sending organization and local partner agency goals
Individual background	Traditionally male, well educated, advanced age, and career stage	Heterogeneous with regard to gender, age, education, and career stage	Heterogeneous with regard to gender, age, education, and career stage
Funding/ compensation	Company salary, overseas allowances	Personal savings, local company salary	Varies depending on organization; personal savings, allowances
Repatriation	Promise of a similar level job	Usually no prearrangement	Repatriation assistance funded by sending organization

have a completed vocational training and several years of work experience (AKLHUE, 2011). On the other hand, there are also volunteer programs especially designed for young people, which enable school leavers to find international volunteer opportunities (BMZ, 2010). Thus, the group of development workers will be heterogeneous in nature as related to age, gender, education, and career stage (Inkson & Myers, 2003; Suutari & Brewster, 2000) as opposed to expatriates assigned by their companies, which usually turn to male, older, and more experienced employees (Brookfield, 2010; Suutari & Brewster, 2000). Unlike AEs and more compatible with SIEs, development workers do not work for financial gain. Moreover, as they change from first-world to third-world and often also from urban to rural areas, they also experience greater cross-cultural transitions (Hudson, 2004; Hudson & Inkson, 2006). Their willingness to relocate to an underdeveloped country is a significant distinctive feature since assigned expatriate research indicates a clear preference for developed, politically stable, and safe countries (Thorn, 2009). Table 11.1 summarizes and contrasts the key features.

MOTIVATION FOR VOLUNTEERING

When people are asked to give reasons for their volunteer activity a number of studies show that altruistic motives, such as the desire to help others, concern for the less fortunate, and compassion toward people in need, predominate (Clary, Snyder, & Stukas, 1996; Independent Sector, 2001; Payne, 2001; Pearce, 1993). These findings suggest that altruism is the essence of volunteering. However, tangible or intangible benefits, such as personal growth, prestige, obtaining skills for a desired future job, interpersonal relations, and keeping taxes down also appear to be driving forces behind volunteering (Smith, 1981; see also, Allen & Rushton, 1983; Pearce, 1993). There is also empirical evidence suggesting that while altruism seems to be the initial motivation to enter a volunteer career, volunteers seem to base their decision to continue volunteering on the ratio of costs and benefits involved in their work (Bierhoff, 2002; Pearce, 1993).

A substantial body of literature emphasizes that volunteering is multi-motivational in nature (Bierhoff, 2002; Bussell & Forbes, 2002; Clary et al., 1996; Pearce, 1993). Six functions potentially served by volunteerism are identified, with *values* (express or act on important values like humanitarianism), *understanding* (learn more about the world or exercise skills that are often unused), *enhancement* (grow and develop psychologically) as typically the more dominant ones followed by *career* (gaining career-related experience), *social* (strengthen social relationships), and *protective* (reduce negative feelings, such as guilt, or address personal problems) as less important functions (Clary & Snyder, 1999; Clary, Snyder, Ridge, Copeland, Stukas, Haugen, & Miene, 1998). Additionally, a suggestion is put forward that the 'value' motivation plays a significant role in the decision to volunteer, while other reasons are likely to influence the kind of activity volunteers engage in (Clary et al., 1996).

The few existing studies on motivation of international development workers suggest a combination of motives, which can be attributed to the functions 'values,' 'enhancement,' 'career,' and 'social' (Hudson, 2004; Lough, McBride, & Sherraden, 2009; Rehberg, 2005; Unstead-Joss, 2008).

Other studies on volunteer motivation (e.g. Bierhoff, 2002; Bussell & Forbes, 2002; Independent Sector, 2001; Payne, 2001; Smith, 1994; Wilson, 2000) confirm the findings of Clary et al. (1998) and yield some additional motives. Especially worth mentioning in the context of this study is the fact that religious beliefs of an individual also play a motivational role (Bierhoff, 2002; Bussell & Forbes, 2002; Payne, 2001). This leads to

Hypothesis 1: International development workers have multiple motives for volunteering abroad.

CAREERS OF INTERNATIONAL DEVELOPMENT AID WORKERS AND CAREER MOBILITY

Arthur, Hall, and Lawrence define career as "the evolving sequence of a person's work experience over time" (1989, p. 8). Despite focusing on work experience, it does not limit careers to paid work (Inkson, 2007). Hall (2002) stresses the subjective perspective and claims that career per se does not necessarily implicate vertical advancement, success, or failure and that the latter two are best assessed subjectively by career actors themselves. He assumes that career is constituted of behaviors and attitudes associated with work-related experiences and activities. As a result, in order to gain a comprehensive understanding of careers, not only external, i.e. observable career choices and behavior, but also internal aspects of career, such as values, attitudes, and motives, have to be considered. Very apposite for the study of development workers is Hall's (1996, 2002) concept of the protean career since individuals exhibiting a protean career attitude base their career decisions on personal values, needs, and search for self-fulfillment. Protean career actors also view their work in the context of life as a whole and rely on themselves for professional progression. Based on the line of argumentation, it is assumed that

Hypothesis 2: The majority of international volunteers display a protean career attitude.

As the notion of career includes attitudes and behaviors, the following hypotheses assess whether the protean career attitude results in corresponding action.

Hall (2002) argues that due to increased complexity in the current work environment, instead of a single lifelong career cycle, contemporary careers increasingly resemble a series of many, two- to four-year-lasting learning cycles. Within each learning cycle, the individual passes through "yet smaller cycles of goal setting, effort, psychological success, and identity change" (Hall & Chandler, 2005, p. 158). The protean careerist repackages "his or her knowledge, skills, and abilities to fit the changing work environment in order to remain marketable" (Sullivan & Baruch, 2009, p. 1544). In a study with 528 international volunteers, Koch and Widmaier (2006) found that the participants had an above-average general education and professional qualification. Almost half of the study participants had two occupations. These facts indicate that development workers are perpetual learners who are motivated for further occupational training. This leads to

Hypothesis 3: International volunteers have a high level of formal education and engage frequently in further qualification measures.

Although a new learning cycle does not necessarily bring about a drastic career transformation involving an occupational change or a change of employer, individuals with protean careers are expected to exhibit greater career mobility. The change in values, personal needs as well as the continuous learning orientation and search for challenging job assignments is likely to cause a person to make career changes from time to time. Professionally skilled individuals with a continuous learning attitude know that their knowledge and skills are valued in the external job market, and they will be loyal to an organization only as long as they feel that that particular organization offers them the best opportunity for professional development at that particular point in time (Crowley-Henry, 2007). This fact could lead to higher organizational mobility. However, literature is inconclusive on this issue, and it is suggested that protean career attitude and organizational mobility may correlate, but a protean careerist does not have to be constantly on the move (Briscoe, Hall, & Demuth, 2006).

Feldman and Ng (2007) distinguish three kinds of career mobility: Occupational mobility refers to changes that entail a new work environment and require fundamentally new skills, training and vocational preparation. An occupational change is usually only possible after a period of occupational re-training. Job mobility implies a transition in work responsibilities or change in hierarchical levels, while the career actor remains in his or her original occupational field. Examples for job changes are transfers to other departments or promotions. Job changes can take place within an organization or can also be accompanied by a change of employer, i.e. organizational mobility. Coppin and Vandenbrande (2007) reported a positive relationship between international mobility and voluntary employer change intentions. This leads to the assumption that

Hypothesis 4: International development workers have a high (a) occupational, (b) job, and (c) organizational mobility.

According to the protean career theory, people interpret career success in individual terms of their central values. Therefore, the subjective career success (e.g. satisfaction with overall career achievements, progress of income, career advancement, skill development, and the job, organizational commitment, professional identification; Feldman & Ng, 2007; Greenhaus, Parasuraman, & Wormley, 1990; Steinbereithner, 2006; Valcour & Tolbert, 2003) rather than the objective aspect of career success (e.g. salary [growth], frequency of promotion, occupational status; Heslin, 2005) is the main driving force behind career development of a protean careerist. De Vos and Soens (2008) found a positive relation between protean career attitude and career satisfaction, which leads to the following hypothesis.

Hypothesis 5: International development workers have a high subjective career satisfaction.

METHODS

Sample Characteristics

The target group of the study are development aid workers who are/were employed at different German non-profit organizations that work closely with the federal government or are founded and sponsored by religious organizations. Study participants were either currently on or had recently returned from their international assignments. Some individuals were not compensated at all, while others were reimbursed for their cost of living and premiums for social insurance. We chose an online survey, as they are better suited to be sent to expatriates in various countries (Dillman, 2000). Potential participants were contacted via e-mail or posts in topic-related forums and on sending organizations' walls on online social networks.

One hundred and twenty-three individuals were recruited. There were more women (49 men, 70 women, and four unreported) and singles (49.6% single, 42.3% married /having a partner, and 8.1% divorced /separated). Male development workers were more likely to have children than females. The age on departure ranged from 18 to 56, resulting in a mean age of 30.89 years (SD = 9.14). It was the first position in a foreign country for 27 participants in the sample, and the remaining 94 volunteers showed a median number of foreign positions of four. At the time of the survey in 2011, the international volunteers (107 German, 14 foreign, and two unreported nationality) spent on average three years abroad with the length of assignment ranging from six months to 12 years (M = 2.99; SD = 2.62). The majority of those having a family were accompanied by their spouse (54.2%) and children (76.2%) to the host country. Prior to the foreign assignment, most of the study participants were either pupils/students (31.6%), full-time (38.2%), or self-employed (8.8%), while approximately one in 10 volunteers was without a job (11.8%). The remaining volunteers were either part-time employed, on vocational further training (4.4% each), or housewife/husband (0.7%).

Instruments and Measures

Motives to Volunteer. To assess the volunteer motivation, 12 motives grouped into three categories ("Achieving something positive for others," "Quest for the new," and "Quest for oneself") developed by Rehberg (2005) were adopted. Sample items included "Helping, giving, doing good," "Becoming acquainted with new cultures," and "Professional orientation, clarification, and development." We used a 5-point Likert scale (1 = to no extent, 5 = to a great extent). A factor analysis with varimax rotation carried out with the present study sample identified three factors with eigenvalues higher than one which accounted for 52.7% of the total variance. The produced factors exactly matched the category pattern suggested by Rehberg. Moreover, participants were given opportunity to add own motives to the list.

Protean Career Attitude. Career attitude was measured using the 14-item Protean Career Attitude Scale developed by Briscoe et al. (2006), which consists of the subscales Self-Directed Career Management (e.g. "Overall, I have a very independent, self-directed career"; α = .81) and Values-Driven Scale (e.g. "I'll follow my own conscience if my company asks me to do something that goes against my values"; α = .75). A 5-point Likert scale ranging from 1 "to little or no extent" to 5 "to a great extent" was used.

Career Mobility. To assess career mobility, we used three items to measure occupational, job, and organizational mobility (Feldman & Ng, 2007). Additionally, the reason of career changes (Sullivan & Baruch, 2009; Taris & Feij, 1999) and job tenure were assessed.

Subjective Career Success. Subjective career success was assessed with five items concerning overall career success ("I am satisfied with the success I have achieved in my career") and satisfaction with some selected aspects of career (e.g. "I am satisfied with the progress I have made toward meeting my goals for income"; Greenhaus et al., 1990, p. 86) on a 5-point Likert scale (1 = strongly disagree, 5 = strongly agree). Cronbach's alpha for this scale yields α = 0.80.

Control Variables and Other Information. As control variables, age at the beginning of the assignment, gender, level of education, employment status, and income as an indicator of objective career success were captured.

RESULTS

In Figure 11.1 motives for the volunteer engagement of development aid assignees are summarized. The reasons within the category "Achieving

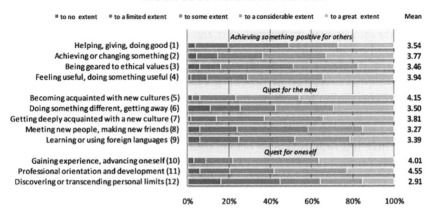

Figure 11.1 Motives to volunteer abroad.

something positive for others" are primarily altruistic in nature. The category "Quest for the new" covers causes that relate to the desire to get to know new cultures and people as well as learn foreign languages. The last motives are connected with issues of personal and career development and belong to the category "Quest for oneself" (Rehberg, 2005).

The majority of respondents report being considerably or greatly motivated by the 'interest in new cultures.' Additionally, almost 80% of development workers expect an opportunity to 'gain experience' and 'advance themselves.' The wish to 'do something useful' and 'achieve or change something' also seems to play a very important role in the decision to volunteer abroad. 'Professional orientation and development' is also among the most common reasons.

In Hypothesis 1 diversity of motives was hypothesized. Only four individuals report altruistic reasons as the primary driving force behind their international volunteering. Surprisingly, there are also nine individuals who do not attach much value to altruistic causes but indicate being rather motivated by 'personal and professional development' issues and motives ascribed to the category "Quest for the new." Additional motives reported were for instance 'seeing for oneself' and 'working towards global justice.' A few respondents got engaged in international volunteering due to lack of employment opportunities in their home country. For one development worker, the foreign assignment was associated with a high-level job, which he could not get in Germany given his low work experience. Similar to that, another participant states that foreigners from developed countries are closer to national decision and opinion makers, which makes them more important than they would have been in their home country. A number of foreign assignees report being motivated by their religious conviction. In general, the great majority of participants indicate varied motivation. Thus, Hypothesis 1 is fully supported.

The Hypotheses 2–4 aim at examining the protean career attitude and some selected aspects of career behavior of international volunteers. In Hypothesis 2 it was postulated that the majority of development workers would exhibit a protean career attitude. Figure 11.2 shows the scatter plot of scale means and the allocation to the corresponding career attitude group, as developed by Briscoe & Hall (2006). A small but significant positive correlation (r = .409; p < .000) between the scales was observed. It emerges that 76.7% of international volunteers are values driven and self-directed in their career decisions and thus have a protean career attitude. Only three individuals (2.6%) belong to the group of dependent careerists who rely on their employer for career progression and do not set own priorities for their career, and 7.8% can be regarded as 'rigid,' i.e. being very values-driven in their career but lacking adaptability skills, which results in inability to fully shape one's career. Also, 12.9% show a reactive career orientation, i.e. they adapt well to new working environments in terms of performance and learning demands but are not guided by personal values in their career decisions. Nevertheless, the majority of those with a rigid, dependent, and reactive career attitude show a tendency toward the protean orientation. Therefore, Hypothesis 2 is supported.

In Hypothesis 3 it was predicted that international volunteers have a high level of formal education and frequently engage in further professional qualification measures. Figure 11.3 features information on general education and vocational training of volunteers as well as their further professional training patterns. Compared to Germany's general population, the proportion of formally highly educated people among development workers

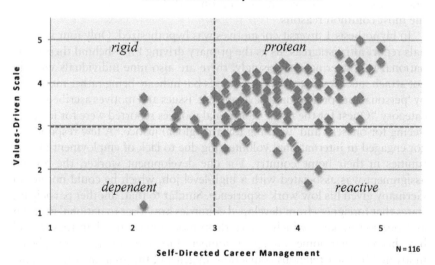

Figure 11.2   Career attitudes of international volunteers.

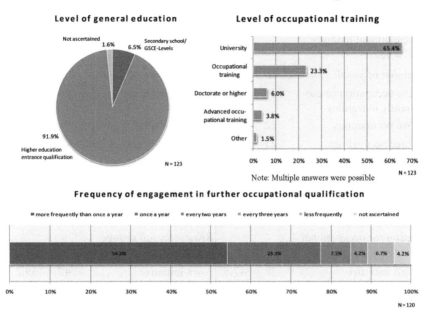

Figure 11.3 General education, vocational training, and frequency of engagement in further qualification.

is very high (Autorengruppe Bildungsberichterstattung, 2010). Additionally, almost 80% of international volunteers take measures to advance their professional qualification at least once a year; a behavior that is in line with the protean career attitude. In this context, measures were defined as both formal learning, such as taking part in seminars, and independent learning of new skills, such as e-learning, reading journals relevant for one's profession etc. As a result, Hypothesis 3 is fully supported.

Hypothesis 4 postulated high career mobility levels of international volunteers. Table 11.2 summarizes relevant information regarding the issue.

Occupational mobility obviously involves the highest degree of change since this kind of shift requires fundamentally new skills. According to the job mobility indices developed by the Danish Technological Institute, Germany's occupational mobility index is .06 (ranging from 0 to 1 with 1 indicating the highest mobility rate) and ranks among the last three European countries (Andersen, Haahr, Hansen, & Holm-Pedersen, 2008), suggesting that occupational changes are not very common. In the current sample, more than half of development aid workers have three or more different occupations (M = 2.84; SD = 1.52). This indicates an above-average occupational mobility as well as willingness and ability to invest in further vocational training. The finding supports Hypothesis 4a.

With respect to job mobility, the study participants have been on average 11.9 years in the labor force, and over 65% of them report at least three

Table 11.2   Career Mobility of International Volunteers

Occupational mobility (N = 122)			Job mobility (N = 120)		
Number of people with	n	%	*Number of people with*	n	%
one occupation or currently in training	34	27.9	no job changes	24	20.0
two occupations	22	18.0	one job change	6	5.0
three occupations	21	17.2	two job changes	11	9.2
more	45	36.9	three job changes	24	20.0
			four job changes	13	10.8
			five job changes	15	12.5
			more	27	22.5
Reason for occupational change			*Reason for job change*		
own initiative	58	47.5	own initiative	47	39.2
external influence	3	1.5	external influence	5	4.2
both	32	26.2	both	46	38.3
not reported	29	23.8	not reported	22	18.3
Organizational mobility (N = 122)			Number of years in labor force	M	SD
Number of organizations worked for	n	%		11.9	10.5
one	19	16.1	Average job tenure in years		
two	14	11.9	current sample	3.09	2.20
three	24	20.3	general population[1]	10.8	
four	19	16.1			
five	21	17.8	*Divided by gender**		
more	21	17.8	male	3.51	2.25
			female	2.63	1.97
			*Divided by age****		
			<20	1.02	0.53
Number of organizational changes as a result of			20–29	2.42	2.32
own initiative	272	66.7	30–39	3.61	1.85
termination of contract by employer	48	11.8	40–49	4.49	1.70
mutual agreement	88	21.5	≥50	5.51	2.21

Note: Asterisks refer to the level of significance: * p < .05; ** p < .01; *** p < .001; [1](IAB, 2010: 4)

job changes (M = 4.24; SD = 2.17). As job changes not necessarily do but can entail organizational changes, a high organizational mobility would provide additional support for Hypothesis 4b.

The study participants have worked for a mean of four different employers (M = 4; SD = 2.5), which results in average tenure of approximately three years, whereas the organizational tenure of Germany's general population is at an average of 10.8 years (IAB, 2010). Female respondents report significantly ($p < .05$) shorter working spells with one employer than their male counterparts. There is a medium and extremely significant positive correlation (r = .60; $p < .000$) between age and organizational tenure in that higher age is associated with longer employment periods with the same employer. Figure 11.4 depicts the kind of work or activity volunteers engaged in after their international development work assignment. From that information assumptions about possible effects of the volunteering experience on volunteers and their career can be made. The data indicates similarities to the findings of Hudson (2004), who identified three major effects. A total of 27.3% stayed in the field of development assistance or intend to do so. This percentage covers individuals who accepted a new foreign volunteer or paid assignment as well as those who work in or are currently looking for employment in the area of development aid in their home country. For all these people the foreign experience "provided a career vehicle" (Hudson, 2004: 253) giving them the chance to explore the

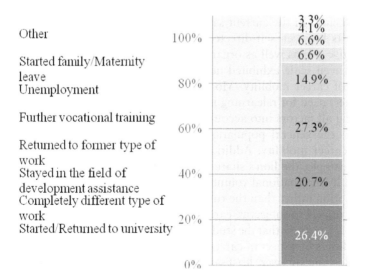

Figure 11.4   Activity after the international development aid project.

new field of work and gain experiences that could have been helpful in finding follow-up jobs in the same or similar working area. Over a quarter of development aid assignees report that they started studying or returned to their university studies. A few of them comment that their choice of course of studies changed after their foreign assignment. This fact again suggests that the volunteer experience influenced an individual's choice of potential occupation or provided an opportunity for career clarification. The second effect refers to development workers who—once back in their home country—started a completely different type of work, which is the case for 20.7% of the respondents of this study. Hudson (2004, p. 253) argues that for this group the development work assignment served as a "'time out' to reflect on possible new career directions". In fact, 72% of the individuals in this group report having been motivated to 'do something different' and to 'get away' to a considerable or great extent. Finally, 14.9% of participants returned to their former type of work. According to Hudson (2004), the driving force behind the decision to volunteer abroad of these individuals is the wish to experience a challenging life or career period and to do something good. This line of argumentation also receives support by the current findings. Compared to the groups considered before, volunteers in this group tended to score slightly higher on altruistic motives and motives that were associated with the 'quest for the new'.

To sum up, the study results provide evidence supporting Hypothesis 4c and, following the previous line of argumentation, potentially also Hypothesis 4b.

Although some scholars regarded organizational mobility to be a proxy for the protean career, Briscoe et al. (2006, p. 34–35, 44) demonstrated that a protean career orientation does not necessarily correlate with mobility preference. In the current sample, a small, significant positive correlation exists between self-directed career management and job mobility ($r = .261$; $p < .01$) as well as organizational mobility ($r = .211$; $p < .05$). The values-driven scale exhibited no significant correlation with either of the aspects of career mobility. Moreover, occupational mobility that implies the highest need for relearning is not related to the protean career.

Taking all factors into account, it should be safe to assume that—compared to the general population—the study participants exhibit a high overall career mobility. Additionally, it is important to note that in the current sample, the lion's share of career transitions was at least partially initiated by international volunteers themselves, while forced mobility was the exception rather than the rule (see Table 11.2).

With respect to subjective career satisfaction, the overall mean scores (see Figure 11.5) suggest that the study participants are reasonably satisfied; however, it differs by aspect of career being considered and current employment status. Respondents were least satisfied with 'income.' The overall expectancy value of monthly income, which is also a measure of objective career success, is €1,825. If the groups of self-, full-, and part-time employed are taken together and analyzed separately from other employment status groups, the

Subjective career satisfaction

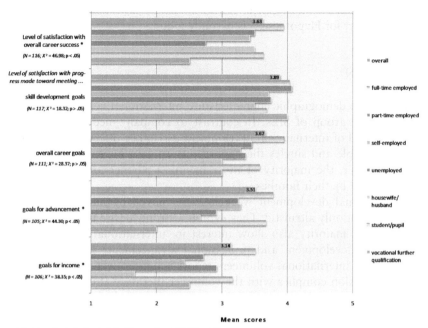

e: Asterisks refer to the level of significance: * p < .05; ** p < .01; *** p < .001

Figure 11.5   Level of satisfaction with selected aspects of career by employment status.

value rises to €2,417. The average income per month in Germany was €3,074 in 2009 (Statistisches Bundesamt, 2010). Volunteers are most satisfied with their 'skill development progress.' This finding supports the assumption that study participants would exhibit a continuous learning orientation.

Worthy of notice is the fact that research participants regard their income level to be an inherent part of career success. In light of the fact that international volunteers engage in development work without any prospect of monetary gain, one could be inclined to assume that to these individuals the income component is rather secondary when it comes to career satisfaction. In fact, international volunteers who were content with the achievement of their goals for 'income' tended also to report higher satisfaction levels with their 'overall career success' (r = .431; *p* < .001) and with the extent to which they felt their 'overall career goals' (r = .475; *p* < .001) were met.

If current employment status is controlled for, a cross-tabulation analysis with Pearson's Chi-square test for significance (see Figure 11.5) showed that full-time employed and students are the most satisfied with 'overall career success' and with the degree of progress made toward meeting personal 'goals for advancement' and 'income' while those in vocational further qualification are comparably discontent with all of the three areas. Unemployed are rather dissatisfied with their 'overall career success' and people currently managing households as their main occupation indicate little satisfaction with the progress made toward achieving their 'goals for advancement' and 'income.' As a result, support for Hypothesis 5 is partially found.

DISCUSSION

In relation to demographic characteristics, international volunteers closely resemble the group of SIEs. In contrast to company-mediated expatriation, the field of international development assistance offers more women, younger people and singles the opportunity to gain international experience; however, the majority of those having a partner and children are accompanied by their families.

International development workers were moved by multiple motives, which are not only altruistic. They exhibit a strong 'desire to serve others,' and the vast majority also show interest in 'internationalism' as well as 'personality development' and 'professional advancement.' The finding that a number of international volunteers report being motivated by their religious conviction complies with the volunteer literature (Lukka & Locke, 2000) and fits into the concept of the protean career, which postulates that career decisions will be values driven.

The majority of international volunteers exhibited a protean career attitude that resulted in corresponding career behavior. First, development assistance usually entails time-limited project work in an international context, which resembles the contemporary notion of work (Hudson, 2004) in international corporations. Second, international volunteers of the current study have a high level of formal education and over three fourths of them engage in further vocational qualification at least once a year in order to adapt to new working conditions and remain marketable in a competitive environment. International volunteers can be seen to be self-directed in career management and are likely to seek out organizations where they can perform personally meaningful work and have an opportunity for continuous learning and skill development.

Accordingly, the study participants displayed high career mobility, and most of career transitions were fully or partially initiated by international volunteers themselves. These findings indicate an autonomous and proactive attitude toward one's career which is reflected in a relationship between mobility and self-directedness in career management but interestingly not with values as the second subscale of the protean career orientation. Moreover, international assignees' willingness to cross not only organizational but also national boundaries is a sign of ability to adjust to unfamiliar settings. The significantly longer organizational tenure of older development aid workers may be due to the fact that they have been longer on the labor market, which increases the probability of finding a good employee-employer match (Groot & Verberne, 1997).

Although a high level of subjective career satisfaction was postulated based on the presumption that discontentment with current working conditions would be addressed with adequate career transitions, the overall level of career satisfaction was not high, and it varied by aspect of career under consideration and especially by the current employment status with those currently unemployed or in full-time further vocational training reporting lower levels of satisfaction. These outcomes reflect Hall and Chandler's (2005) reasoning that over the course of one's working life a career actor's self-confidence can fluctuate. A protean career is seen as a series of learning cycles, and, particularly at the beginning of a new career cycle, individuals face temporary setbacks and failures, which can lead to temporary lower levels of career satisfaction.

In light of the fact that international volunteers engage in development work without any prospect of monetary gain, one could be inclined to think that to these individuals the income component is rather secondary when it comes to career satisfaction. Yet, respondents regard their income level to be an inherent part of their overall career success and income is the aspect of career they are least satisfied with. International volunteers who were content with the achievement of their 'goals for income' tended also to report higher satisfaction levels with their 'overall career success' ($r = .431$; $p < .001$) and with the extent to which they felt their 'overall career goals' ($r = .475$; $p < .001$) were met. Considering the fact that the selected group is very well educated, an above-average income could be expected. However, compared to the population's average, the study participants are an under-paid group. Hence, from an objective point of view on career success, international volunteers have not been very successful. Possible explanations for this fact are that, first, non-profit organizations often pay less than profit-oriented organizations (Warren, 2008), and, second, the higher share of women in the study sample combined with a potentially lower pay level (Statistisches Bundesamt, 2010) is likely to result in a lower average income.

IMPLICATIONS FOR PRACTICE

The results of the motivation analysis allow a number of practice implications for development aid agencies and other non-profit organizations. In order to have a competitive advantage in a situation of "increased competition between these organizations for the limited resources available" (Dolnicar & Randle, 2007, p. 350), organizations need to provide opportunities for personal growth and professional development so that international volunteers are enabled to balance altruistic service to others with self-oriented interests and motives such as self-development goals (Lips-Wiersma, 2002).

Implications for potential employers of former international volunteers are threefold. First, international volunteers can be described as very well-educated and adaptable individuals who can be expected to have a set of transferable skills due to their organizational and international mobility. The vast majority of them fit the description of a protean career actor. For organizations that are looking for independent, competent, and proficient employees as temporary resources for projects of limited duration returned volunteers might be a good option to consider. Second, the study participants exhibited a high and in most cases self-initiated job and organizational mobility, which indicates that they are more loyal to their personal needs and development goals than to their employing organization. Corporations that strive to retain this kind of employees need to emphasize individual career planning (Briscoe, Hoobler, & Byle, 2010) and will have to support them (Biemann & Andresen, 2010) by offering opportunities for continuous personal growth and enhancement of work-related knowledge and skills. Third, since international volunteers are value oriented in their career decisions and most of them demonstrated a desire to serve others it is to be expected that they tend to "asses how the organization as a whole is serving others" (Lips-Wiersma, 2002, p. 394) and will be more likely to work for socially responsible businesses.

Finally, despite the fact that international volunteers worked in the non-profit sector, they regard their income to be an inherent part of career and it is also the aspect where they see the most room for improvement if compared to other components of career satisfaction. Therefore, organizations should also consider financial incentives as part of the package offered to their employees.

LIMITATIONS

Most of the study participants are German, which limits the cross-national generalizability of the results. Additionally, given the self-report nature of the data, social desirability bias may compromise the accuracy of responses. Moreover, the results could also be distorted by selection effects. More than half of the participants were recruited via Foerderungswerk, an organization that is concerned with professional reintegration of former development workers and offers help with vocational orientation and further development upon return. Not all returned international volunteers use the services of the organization so that there is a possibility that a disproportionate number of individuals specifically interested in further vocational training were contacted. Finally, self-selection bias may also jeopardize the generalizability of results. The group of international development aid workers in the sample showed to be very homogeneous so that additional statistical analyses (regression, PLS, intergroup comparisons) did not lead to any significant result or model. This fact limits the interpretation of the data reported.

IMPLICATIONS FOR FUTURE RESEARCH

As empirical evidence on international volunteers is lacking, a number of directions for future research can be suggested. First, further studies across nationally diverse samples are needed in order to establish generalizability of the results. Second, the field would benefit if a more comprehensive international volunteering motivation inventory was developed. For example, religious conviction has been shown to play a motivational role and Hudson stresses the importance of the right timing in terms of the "assignment fitting a particular career and life stage" (2004, p. 172). Little is known about the adjustment process of development workers in the host country. This issue is of particular interest since they experience a higher degree of change as compared to other expatriates. Moreover, more longitudinal analysis is needed to explore the long-term impact of the foreign experience on volunteers with regard to personality growth, skill development, and career.

CONCLUSION

The present study aimed at providing an insight into the profile of an international development aid worker, thus attempting to add to fill a gap in the literature on expatriation. Particular emphasis was placed on demographic characteristics, motivation to volunteer in the international context as well as a number of career-related factors. As expected based on the results of other studies (Lough et al., 2009; Rehberg, 2005), the percentage of female expatriates in development assistance is much higher than in traditional organizational foreign assignments. Over two thirds of the study population were aged between 20 and 40. In line with expectations, the overall gender and age structure resembles that of SIEs. A number of altruistic motives coupled with more self-centered goals such as desire for personal growth and professional advancement as well as interest in new cultures appeared to be the driving force behind the decision to engage in voluntary work abroad. The majority of study participants exhibited a protean career attitude. A high degree of fit between the protean career ideal and development workers' career behavior was revealed. The majority of international assignees were very learning-oriented individuals who are in charge of their own career. The fact that respondents were organizationally and internationally mobile is a sign of willingness and ability to adapt to unfamiliar settings. Not all of them are satisfied with all aspects of their career; however, the findings on subjective career satisfaction show parallels to issues discussed in the protean career literature. Thus, it can be concluded that the research participants fit the description of a protean careerist.

REFERENCES

AGdD (2011). *Förderungswerk für rückkehrende Fachkräfte der Entwicklungsdienste.* Retrieved from http://www.foerderungswerk.de/UNIQ130164308305014/doc2A.html.

AGEH (2011). *What we offer applicants.* Retrieved from http://www.ageh.de/english/what-we-offer/for-applicants.html.

AKLHUE (2003). *Entwicklungshelfer-Gesetz (EhfG).* Bonn.

AKLHUE (2011). *What requirements do I have to satisfy to work as a technical adviser?* Retrieved from http://www.entwicklungsdienst.de/mitarbeit.html?&L=1.

Allen, N. J., & Rushton, P. J. (1983). Personality characteristics of community mental health volunteers: A review. *Journal of Voluntary Action Research*, 12(1), 36–49.

Andersen, T., Haahr, J. H., Hansen, M. E., & Holm-Pedersen, M. (2008). *Job mobility in the European Union: Optimising its social and economic benefits.* Retrieved from http://ec.europa.eu/social/main.jsp?langId=en&catId=89&new sId=386.

Arthur, M. B., Hall, D. T., & Lawrence, B. S. (1989). Generating new directions in career theory: The case for a transdisciplinary approach. In M. B. Arthur, D. T. Hall and B. S. Lawrence (Eds.), *Handbook of Career theory* (pp. 7–25). Cambridge: Cambridge University Press.

Autorengruppe Bildungsberichterstattung (2010). *Bildung in Deutschland 2010: Ein indikatorengestützter Bericht mit einer Analyse zu Perspektiven des Bildungswesens im demografischen Wandel.* Bielefeld: Bertelsmann.

Biemann, T., & Andresen, M. (2010). Self-initiated foreign expatriates versus assigned expatriates: Two distinct types of international careers? *Journal of Managerial Psychology*, 25(4), 430–448.

Bierhoff, H.-W. (2002). *Prosocial behaviour.* Hove: Psychology Press.

BMZ (2010). *Weltwärts—The BMZ's development volunteers service.* Retrieved from http://www.bmz.de/en/what_we_do/approaches/bilateral_development_cooperation/approaches/freiwilligendienst/index.html.

Brewster, C. (2002). Expatriation. In T. Redman and A. Wilkinson (Eds.), *The informed student guide to human resource management* (pp. 84–85). London: Thomson Learning.

Brewster, C., Dickmann, M., & Sparrow, P. (2008). A European perspective on IHRM. In M. Dickmann, C. Brewster and P. Sparrow (Eds.), *International human resource management. A European perspective* (2nd ed.) (pp. 3–18). London, New York: Routledge.

Briscoe, J. P., & Hall, D. T. (2006). The interplay of boundaryless and protean careers: Combinations and implications. *Journal of Vocational Behavior*, 69(1), 4–18.

Briscoe, J. P., Hall, D. T., & DeMuth, R. L. (2006). Protean and boundaryless careers: An empirical exploration. *Journal of Vocational Behavior*, 69(1), 30–47.

Briscoe, J. P., Hoobler, J. M., & Byle, K. A. (2010). Do 'protean' employees make better leaders? The answer is in the eye of the beholder. *Leadership Quarterly*, 21(5), 783–795.

Brookfield Global Relocation Services (2010). *Global relocation trends survey report 2010.* Retrieved from http://www.brookfieldgrs.com.

Bussell, H., & Forbes, D. (2002). Understanding the volunteer market: The what, where, who and why of volunteering. *International Journal of Nonprofit and Voluntary Sector Marketing*, 7(3), 244–257.

Clary, E. G., & Snyder, M. (1999). The motivations to volunteer: Theoretical and practical considerations. *Current Directions in Psychological Science: A Journal of the American Psychological Society*, 8(5), 156–159.

Clary, E. G., Snyder, M., Ridge, R. D., Copeland, J., Stukas, A. A., Haugen, J., & Miene, P. (1998). Understanding and assessing the motivations of volunteers: A functional approach. *Journal of Personality and Social Psychology*, 74(6), 1516–1530.

Clary, E. G., Snyder, M., & Stukas, A. A. (1996). Volunteers' motivations: Findings from a national survey. *Nonprofit and Voluntary Sector Quarterly*, 25(4), 485–505.

Coppin, L., & Vandenbrande, T. (2007). *Voluntary and forced job mobility in Europe.* Retrieved from http://www.eurofound.europa.eu/pubdocs/2007/12/en/1/ef0712en.pdf.

Crowley-Henry, M. (2007). The protean career: Exemplified by first world foreign residents in Western Europe? *International Studies of Management and Organization*, 37(3), 44–64.

De Vos, A., & Soens, N. (2008). Protean attitude and career success: The mediating role of self-management. *Journal of Vocational Behavior*, 73(3), 449–456.

Dillman, D. A. (2000). *Mail and internet surveys: The tailored design method* (2nd ed.). New York: Wiley.

Dolnicar, S., & Randle, M. (2007). The international volunteering market: Market segments and competitive relations. *International Journal of Nonprofit and Voluntary Sector Marketing*, 12(4), 350–370.

Dowling, P. J., Festing, M., & Engle, A. D. (2008). *International human resource management: Managing people in a multinational context* (5th ed.). Andover: Cengage Learning.

Fee, A., & Gray, S. J. (2011). Fast-tracking expatriate development: The unique learning environments of international volunteer placements. *International Journal of Human Resource Management*, 22(3), 530–552.

Feldman, D. C., & Ng, T. W. H. (2007). Careers: Mobility, embeddedness, and success. *Journal of Management*, 33(3), 350–377.

GIZ (2011). *Entwicklungshelfer.* Retrieved from http://www.ded.de/de/stellen-markt/arbeiten-fuer-den-ded-weltweit/entwicklungshelfer.html.

Greenhaus, J. H., Parasuraman, S., & Wormley, W. M. (1990). Effects of race on organizational experience, job performance evaluations, and career outcomes. *Academy of Management Journal*, 33(1), 64–86.

Groot, W., & Verberne, M. (1997). Aging, job mobility, and compensation. *Oxford Economic Papers*, 49(3), 380–403.

Hall, D. T. (1996). Protean careers of the 21st century. *Academy of Management Executive*, 10(4), 8–16.

Hall, D. T. (Ed.) (2002). Careers in and out of organizations. *Foundations for organizational science.* Thousand Oaks, CA: Sage.

Hall, D. T., & Chandler, D. E. (2005). Psychological success: When the career is a calling. *Journal of Organizational Behavior*, 26(2), 155–176.

Heslin, P. A. (2005). Conceptualizing and evaluating career success. *Journal of Organizational Behavior*, 26(2), 113–136.

Howe-Walsh, L., & Schyns, B. (2010). Self-initiated expatriation: Implications for HRM. *International Journal of Human Resource Management*, 21(2), 260–273.

Hudson, S. H. (2004). Volunteering overseas: Motivation, experiences and perceived career effects. A thesis presented in partial fulfillment of the requirements for the degree of Doctor of Philosophy. Wellington: Massey University.

Hudson, S. H., & Inkson, K. (2006). *Volunteer overseas development workers: The hero's adventure and personal transformation. Career Development International*, 11(4), 304–320.

IAB (2010). *IAB-Kurzbericht: Aktuelle Analysen und Kommentare aus dem Institut für Arbeitsmarkt- und Berufsforschung.* Retrieved from http://doku.iab.de/kurzber/2010/kb1310.pdf.

Independent Sector (2001). *Giving and volunteering in the United States: Findings from a national survey.* Washington, DC: Independent Sector Publications Center.

Inkson, K. (2007). *Understanding careers: The metaphors of working lives.* Thousand Oaks, CA: Sage.

Inkson, K., Arthur, M. B., Pringle, J., & Barry, S. (1997). Expatriate assignment versus overseas experience: Contrasting models of international human resource development. *Journal of World Business*, 32(4), 351–368.

Inkson, K., & Myers, B. A. (2003). 'The big OE': Self-directed travel and career development. *Career Development International*, 8(4), 170–181.

Koch, J., & Widmaier, C. (2006). *Untersuchung zur beruflichen und sozialen Reintegration ehemaliger Entwicklungshelfer und Entwicklungshelferinnen.* Retrieved from http://www.oneworld-jobs.org/fileadmin/Redaktion/Publikationen_AK/AGdD_Rk Studie_06.pdf.

204   *Maike Andresen and Tanja Gustschin*

Lips-Wiersma, M. (2002). Analysing the career concerns of spiritually oriented people: Lessons for contemporary organizations. *Career Development International*, 7(7), 385–397.

Lough, B. J., McBride, A. M., & Sherraden, M. S. (2009). *Measuring volunteer outcomes: Development of the international volunteer impacts survey*. St. Louis: Center for Social Development.

Lukka, P., & Locke, M. (2000). Faith, voluntary action and social policy: A review of research. *Voluntary Action: The Journal of the Institute for Volunteering Research*, 3(1), 25–41.

MacLachlan, M., & Carr, S. C. (1999). The selection of international assignees for development work. *The Irish Journal of Psychology*, 20(1), 39–57.

Payne, S. (2001). The role of volunteers in hospice bereavement support in New Zealand. *Palliative Medicine*, 15(2), 107–116.

Pearce, J. L. (1993). *Volunteers: The organizational behavior of unpaid workers. People and organizations*. London: Routledge.

Rehberg, W. (2005). Altruistic individualists: Motivations for international volunteering among young adults in Switzerland. *Voluntas: International Journal of Voluntary and Nonprofit Organizations*, 16(2), 109–122.

Richardson, J., & McKenna, S. (2002). Leaving and experiencing: Why academics expatriate and how they experience expatriation? *Career Development International*, 7(2), 67–78.

Smith, D. H. (1981). Altruism, volunteers, and volunteerism. *Journal of Voluntary Action Research*, 10(1), 21–36.

Smith, D. H. (1994). Determinants of voluntary association participation and volunteering: A literature review. *Nonprofit and Voluntary Sector Quarterly*, 23(3), 243–263.

Statistisches Bundesamt (2010). *Statistisches Jahrbuch 2010 für die Bundesrepublik Deutschland mit ‚Internationalen Übersichten'*. Wiesbaden: Statistisches Bundesamt.

Steinbereithner, M. A. (2006). *Career success in not for profit organizations. Personalwirtschaftliche Schriften: Vol. 24*. Munich: Hampp.

Sullivan, S. E., & Baruch, Y. (2009). Advances in career theory and research: A critical review and agenda for future exploration. *Journal of Management*, 35(6), 1542–1571.

Suutari, V., & Brewster, C. (2000). Making their own way: International experience through self-initiated foreign assignments. *Journal of World Business*, 35(4), 417–436.

Taris, T. W., & Feij, J. A. (1999). Measuring career mobility: An empirical comparison of six mobility indexes. *Quality and Quantity*, 33(2), 157–168.

Thorn, K. (2009). Influences on self-initiated mobility across national boundaries. *Research Working Paper Series*, 2, 1–30.

Toomey, E., & Brewster, C. (2008). International HRM in international organisations. In C. Brewster, P. Sparrow and M. Dickmann (Eds.), *International human resource management: Contemporary issues in Europe* (2nd ed.). (pp. 289–306). London: Routledge.

Unstead-Joss, R. (2008). An analysis of volunteer motivation: Implications for international development. *Voluntary Action: The Journal of the Institute for Volunteering Research*, 9(1), 3–20.

Valcour, P. M., & Tolbert, P. (2003). Gender, family and career in the era of boundarylessness: Determinants and effects of intra- and inter-organizational mobility. *International Journal of Human Resource Management*, 14(5), 768–787.

Warren, Z. (2008). Occupational employment in the not-for-profit sector. *Monthly Labor Review*, 131(11), 11–43.

Wilson, J. (2000). Volunteering. *Annual Review of Sociology*, 26(1), 215–240.

12 Self-Initiated Expatriation in Academia
A Bounded and Boundaryless Career?

Julia Richardson

Academia offers a potentially rich source of information about international mobility. Where self-initiated expatriation is concerned, it may be especially fruitful because according to Ackers (2005a) international mobility among academics is "not so much driven by industrial recruitment companies but rather takes place through networks, individual motivation, and risk" (p. 103). Echoing the theme of individual initiative further, Baruch and Hall (2004) describe academics as 'free agents' who can move their career and research agendas "fairly easily from one university to another" (p. 249). We might safely assume, therefore, that most academics taking a position outside of their 'home' country—be it on a temporary or permanent basis—are doing so out of their own volition and are thus 'self-initiated.' Moreover, given the push toward internationalization of higher education, some academics may well be feeling a greater need to engage in some form of international mobility in order to enhance their marketability (Ackers, 2004; 2005a; 2005b; Ackers & Gill, 2008; Gill, 2005; Selmer & Lauring, 2010). Indeed, according to some researchers "[c]areer progression in scientific research *demands* a very high level of mobility in order to achieve the level of international experience necessary for progression" (Ackers, 2005a, p. 104).

Drawing on published work from four different studies, this chapter will explore the career experiences of Self-Initiated Expatriate (SIE) academics. Its specific focus will be the extent to which their careers reflect the six dimensions of the 'boundaryless career,' a concept that has dominated contemporary career studies for a number of years. A key concern here will be to examine the kinds of boundaries that SIE academics may encounter and specifically the impact of those boundaries on their career opportunities and experiences. In this respect the chapter is an important resource for institutions and particularly chairs and directors seeking to attract and retain faculty with international experience. It will also be an important resource for internationally mobile faculty themselves and/or those considering an international move. As far as current career scholarship is concerned, the chapter has two objectives. First, it extends Dowd and Kaplan's (2005) study of tenure-track faculty in the US to evaluate the boundaryless career framework for understanding the careers of SIE academics. Second, it addresses recent calls for more critical analysis of the boundaryless career concept and suggestions that career boundaries (whether subjective or objective) are, in fact, ubiquitous (Roper, Ganesh, & Inkson, 2010).

In order to ensure that the chapter is appropriately contextualized, we will begin by introducing the 'boundaryless career' as a dominant framework in contemporary career theory. We will also consider its putative synergy with SIE academics' careers and self-initiated expatriation more generally. After introducing each of the four studies, we will then explore the extent to which SIE academic careers are, indeed, 'boundaryless.'

THE BOUNDARYLESS CAREER

The concept of the boundaryless career derives from the seminal work of Arthur and Rousseau (1996) who suggested that such careers are characterized by six 'specific meanings or emphases':

1. Moving across the boundaries of separate employers
2. Drawing validation—and marketability—from outside the present employer
3. Being sustained by external networks or information
4. Breaking traditional organizational boundaries, notably those involving hierarchical reporting and advancement principles
5. Rejecting existing career opportunities for personal or family reasons
6. Perceiving a boundaryless future regardless of structural constraints

There is little doubt that the idea of 'boundarylessness' has had a strong influence on career scholarship (Roper et al., 2010; Sullivan & Arthur, 2006; Sullivan & Baruch, 2009). So much so, in fact, that according to Briscoe and Hall, it "frames" the thinking of academics and practitioners alike (2006, p. 5). With this level of influence, it may well be that the boundaryless career is, indeed, "an idea whose time has come" (Pringle & Mallon, 2003, p. 839). Yet, some scholars have challenged the idea of boundarylessness and its underlying assumption of individuals taking charge of their own careers and moving 'seamlessly' across organizational and perhaps even national boundaries (see, for example, Dowd & Kaplan, 2005; King, Burke, & Pemberton, 2005; Roper et al., 2010; Zikic & Richardson, 2011). Adding another dimension to this challenge, this chapter will suggest that rather than being boundaryless some careers, such as SIE academics careers, are both bounded *and* boundaryless.

Several scholars have pointed to the potential synergy between the boundaryless career and academic careers (e.g. Arthur & Rousseau,

1996; Baruch & Hall, 2004; Dowd & Kaplan, 2005). Indeed, according to Baruch and Hall (2004), the academic career model has a "strong fit" with the boundaryless career model. In a more recent study, however, Dowd and Kaplan (2005) have argued that academic careers "can be characterized as *either* bounded *or* boundaryless, depending on the individual" (p. 2005). Drawing on interviews with 35 tenure-track faculty in the US, they developed a typology of four academic career types, two of which were examples of academic careers as 'boundaried' (the Probationer and the Conservationist) and two of which were boundaryless (the Maverick and the Connector). Each type, they suggested, can be distinguished according to five distinct factors: role/identity, motivation factors, tenure concerns, other concerns, and approach to career management. As an example of someone leading a bounded academic career, a 'Probationer' is a 'traditional teacher/researcher' who is more connected to their institution than their discipline. By comparison, as an example of someone leading a boundaryless academic career, a 'Connector' has a 'multi-faceted' identity with greater allegiance to their discipline. A Probationer is motivated by intellectual challenge and prefers a structured environment, whereas a Connector is more interested in career autonomy. Probationers have little knowledge of the tenure system in their institution and thus of their ability to achieve tenure. Connectors, on the other hand, are less concerned with achieving tenure, believing that they could find a position elsewhere relatively easily if necessary. Probationers are concerned with basic teaching skills and personal issues whereas Connectors show less concern with such matters. Finally, Probationers are more likely to rely on their employer to manage their careers, whereas Connectors are more likely to engage in career self-management. Although this study focused solely on academics who were either from the US or Canada and were not considered SIEs, it offers a useful starting point for this chapter by presenting empirical evidence that while some academic careers may be boundaryless (the Maverick and the Connector) others are bounded (the Probationer and the Conservationist). [1]

In addition to its putative synergy with academic careers, the boundaryless career framework has also been identified as a potentially useful framework to understand international and specifically, expatriate and SIE careers (e.g. Inkson, Arthur, Pringle, & Barry, 1997; Richardson & Zikic, 2007; Stahl & Cerdin, 2004). Thus, for example, several researchers in the field have described SIEs as taking responsibility for their own careers, explicitly crossing both organizational *and* national boundaries, engaging in expatriation for family/personal reasons and drawing heavily on external networks and connections (see, for example, Bozionelos, 2009; Doherty, 2010; Doherty, Dickmann, & Mills, 2011; Thorn, 2009).

Having introduced the boundaryless career framework and its potential synergy with academic and SIE careers more generally, we will now focus specifically on the careers of SIE academics.

SIE ACADEMICS

International mobility in academia is attracting particular interest among migration scholars and management/careers scholars. Why so? Migration scholars are interested in the topic because of its connection to economic and social policy concerns about 'brain drain' and knowledge transfer within regions such as the European Union (see, for example, Ackers, 2005a; Ackers & Gill, 2008; Carr, Inkson, & Thorn, 2005). Management/careers scholars' interest in the topic is a reflection of academia's importance as a continuously evolving, global employment sector (Baruch & Hall, 2004).

As noted above, drawing on publications from four recent studies, this chapter will explore the potential synergy between the boundaryless career framework and the careers of SIE academics. While this is clearly a limited sample, the studies address the experiences of a relatively broad range of SIE academics (i.e. different nationalities, different countries, different disciplines, tenured, and tenure track etc.) and offer a useful starting point for further research and conversations in the field. Brief outlines of each of the studies (The International Study; The Canadian Study; the European Study, and the Italian Study) are provided below. The International Study and the Canadian Study were both conducted by the author of the chapter with colleagues (Mallon, McBey, McKenna, and Zikic), the European Study was conducted by Lauring and Selmer, and the Italian Study was conducted by Ackers and Gill.

THE INTERNATIONAL STUDY

This qualitative study, conducted in 2000, comprised in-depth interviews with 30 British SIE academics in universities in Turkey, Singapore, the United Arab Emirates (UAE), and New Zealand (for a detailed overview, see Richardson, 2008). The sample of host countries offers a useful insight into SIE academics' experiences in different cultural contexts—particularly regarding 'cultural distance' from their home country, in this case Britain. A wide range of disciplines were represented such as the humanities, business, ESL, math, engineering, technology, and the natural sciences. All interviewees in Singapore, Turkey, and the UAE were on contractually limited appointments, which came with various titles, i.e. professor, associate professor, assistant professor. In this respect for them 'tenure' was not an option. All interviewees in New Zealand were either on 'confirmation track' (the equivalent of tenure track) or 'confirmed'—i.e. tenured. Seventeen interviewees were female, and 13 were male. Fourteen interviewees were married or living with a partner, whereas 16 were single. Most had been living in their host country for between one and two years though three had been there for 9–10 years. The semi-structured interviews explored a broad range of themes, including the 'drivers' to expatriation, interviewees' experiences of expatriation and their reflections of that experience in terms of its contribution to professional development and impact on family/personal relationships.

THE CANADIAN STUDY

This qualitative study, conducted in 2003, comprised interviews with 44 academics who had moved to Canada to take an academic position in one of six Canadian universities (two small universities located in small communities and four large universities (i.e. 40,000+ students) in or near to large cities). These institutions were strategically targeted based on information in studies indicating that geographic location, particularly proximity to large cities, may influence academics' experiences of relocation and willingness to relocate (e.g. Ambrose, Huston, & Norman, 2005). Just under three quarters of interviewees were male, and though several disciplines were represented, over half were from either the natural or medical sciences. The age distribution was reasonably well balanced—between 24 and 56 years old—as were the number of years participants had been in Canada. Sixty-six percent of interviewees were tenured, and the remainder was on tenure track (i.e. assistant professors). This study also comprised semi-structured interviews exploring the 'drivers' to expatriation, interviewees' experiences of expatriation, and its perceived contribution to professional development and impact on family/personal relationships. In this study, however, more focus was given to the professional/career implications of self-initiated expatriation, and particularly recognition of internationally gained experience. There was also a greater focus on interviewees' perceptions of the impact of internationalization of higher education on their career aspirations and experiences.

THE EUROPEAN STUDY

This large quantitative study was based on data drawn from a web survey conducted in 2008 of 428 SIE academics from 60 countries working in 35 universities in Northern Europe (see Lauring & Selmer, 2011; Selmer & Lauring, 2010). The majority of universities in the sample were in Sweden (10), while Denmark was least represented (three). The study targeted primarily science faculty departments. The researchers divided the sample into two groups—'younger' and 'older' SIE academics. The average age of the younger participants was 32.19 (SD 2.96). They had, on average, spent 2.14 years in their respective host country and had, on average, worked abroad as an SIE academic for 4.42 years, including their current position. Among this younger grouping, 67.5% was male, 50.8% were married, and the majority held relatively lower ranks as Research/Teaching Assistants.

The older grouping had an average age of 47.98, had spent 8.11 years in their current host country (SD 7.41), and had worked overseas as an SIE for 14.92 years (SD 8.89). Most of this cohort were married and had achieved a relatively senior rank i.e. full professor. Various approaches to analysis were used using SPSS, e.g. Pearson Correlation, one-way Anova, and multivariate analysis of covariance (MANCOVA). Thus far, publications based on this study have focused on drivers to expatriation and the impact of demographic variables on the experience of self-initiated expatriation (see Lauring & Selmer, 2011; Selmer & Lauring, 2010)

THE ITALIAN STUDY

This year-long study conducted from 2007–2008 comprised 141 short questionnaires conducted to collect demographic data and 52 semi-structured interviews with Italian academics who were working or had previously worked in the UK (43 were based in the UK at the time of the study and nine had returned to Italy). Of the 43 interviewees in the UK, four had already arranged their return to Italy, 19 were uncertain as to whether they would return, and 20 indicated that they would be unlikely to return. Six of the interviewees had returned to Italy at some point but had left again to return to the UK. The aim of the study was to examine 'scientific mobility' within the European Research Area (ERA) in the context of political concern about knowledge transfer within the European Union, with a specific focus on Italian academics' experiences and views of returning to Italy (Ackers & Gill, 2008; Gill, 2005).

SIE ACADEMICS' CAREERS AND THE BOUNDARYLESS CAREER

We turn now to the six meanings or emphases of the boundaryless career and consider them in light of published work based on the findings of these four studies.

MOVING ACROSS THE BOUNDARIES OF SEPARATE EMPLOYERS

On the face of it, all four studies provide clear evidence that SIE academics reflect this theme—indeed they would have to have done so to be included in the respective studies. We can extend the idea of crossing boundaries even further because SIE academics move not just across 'the boundaries of separate employers' but also across the boundaries of separate *countries*. They are 'taking charge' of their own careers by independently moving to another country in addition to another organization, which suggests a high level of proactivity, a key component of the boundaryless career concept.

Exploring this concept further, the International Study and the Canadian Study found that most interviewees felt that academia allows for, and in some cases actively encourages, international mobility (see Richardson, 2009; Richardson & Mallon, 2005). The Italian Study also reported that not only was international mobility 'expected,' but it was also a 'requirement' given the paucity of research opportunities in Italy: "owing to a lack of positions at home, some Italian scientists simply had to go abroad if they wanted to work in research" (Gill, 2005, p. 330). These findings suggest that not only does an academic career offer opportunities for boundary crossing, but it is also, as Ackers (2005a) has suggested, an *expected* and perhaps even *necessary* part of contemporary academia. On this dimension, then, it seems that SIE academic careers are indeed boundaryless. However, all four studies also reported fairly widespread experiences of individuals encountering certain 'boundaries' either when they engaged in international mobility or when they attempted to do so. The Italian Study, for example, noted that "pathways between positions in different countries are not always straightforward" (Gill, 2005, p. 330) and that "the Italian domestic system was relatively impenetrable to foreign workers (Gill, 2005, p. 326). The Canadian and International Study also reported that although they had secured positions in their host countries, some academics faced challenges getting their overseas experience 'recognized and rewarded' during applications for tenure and promotion or, if already tenured, during applications for full professorship and/or for internal and external research funding (see Richardson, 2009; Richardson & Mallon, 2005; Richardson, McBey, & McKenna, 2006; 2008; Richardson & Zikic, 2007). Interviewees in these two studies identified 'disciplinary boundaries' as having the greatest impact on their ability to transfer their knowledge and skills from one institution/country to another. SIE academics in the sciences, engineering, and ESL reported that because there were fewer boundaries in their disciplines they could engage in international mobility fairly easily (see Richardson et al., 2008). This also meant, they said, that they had more opportunities to engage in self-initiated expatriation than academics in the arts and humanities. SIE academics in the arts and humanities voiced similar opinions suggesting that whether they could engage in self-initiated expatriation was directly impacted by their disciplinary field. The demographic data and professional histories of SIE academics in both of these studies supported this idea since those in ESL, science and engineering were more likely to have worked in two or more countries than those in the arts and humanities.

Based on the findings reported here then, it seems that SIE academics' careers do reflect the first theme in terms of crossing both organizational *and* national boundaries. Yet, the findings also suggest that SIE academics' ability to cross those boundaries and their subsequent experiences of having done so are impacted by disciplinary boundaries and boundaries in their host institution's tenure, promotion, and funding practices such as circumscribed recognition of international experience/achievements.

DRAWING VALIDATION—AND MARKETABILITY—
FROM OUTSIDE THE PRESENT EMPLOYER

Arthur and Rousseau (1996) explicitly identify academics as reflecting this second theme: "A second meaning occurs when a career, like that of an academic or a carpenter, draws validation—and marketability—from outside the present employer" (p. 6). Though the International, the Canadian, and the Italian Study provided general support for this argument, there were some notable contradictions and inconsistencies.

First, all SIE academics in the Canadian and International Study felt that gaining international experience had added to their overall marketability regardless of the institution they were working in (see Richardson, 2009; Richardson & Mallon, 2005; Richardson & Zikic, 2007). Moreover, though some said that they had not specifically expatriated in order to enhance their career prospects, they believed that the international experience they had acquired had given them considerable advantage in the academic marketplace (see Richardson & Mallon, 2005; Richardson et al., 2006; 2008). All interviewees in these two studies connected this advantage with what was invariably described as the 'internationalization' of higher education (particularly research and teaching responsibilities). Second, however, as noted earlier, the majority also reported that although their international experience was an advantage during recruitment, it received varying levels of recognition and/ or reward during subsequent tenure and promotion and/or research funding applications (see Richardson, 2009; Richardson & Mallon, 2005; Richardson et al., 2006; 2008; Richardson & Zikic, 2007). By comparison, SIE academics in the Italian study said that their international experience was a significant barrier to their being recruited to work in an Italian university. Taken together, these findings seem to suggest that some SIE academics' marketability may be *connected to,* rather than *disconnected from,* their employer.

Beyond institutional concerns, the International, the Canadian, and the Italian Study all seem to suggest that SIE academics' marketability is also connected to the country or countries in which they had gained their experience. The Italian study, for example, reported that gaining experience outside of Italy may be a liability where "(m)oving abroad can impede the ability to re-enter the 'home' system" (Gill, 2005, p. 330). Indeed, one interviewee in that study commented that "It's important to be there, and in Italy being there and being seen is quite crucial if you want to get a permanent position" (p. 327). Some interviewees in the Canadian and in the International Study also said that marketability (and hence transferability of one's skills across national boundaries) is impacted by the *country* in which that experience has been gained (see Richardson et al., 2006; 2008). Thus, for example, there was fairly widespread agreement that experience gained in the US and some parts of Europe bestows more marketability than experience gained in other countries. This finding echoes Altbach's (2004) concern that some developing countries may be less able to attract and retain 'top' academics precisely because of the detrimental impact that working in them is perceived to have on a scholarly career. It also suggests that SIE academics' careers (and perhaps even academic careers more generally) draw validation and marketability not only from their employer but also from the employer's national context.

BEING SUSTAINED BY EXTERNAL NETWORKS OR INFORMATION

There is fairly widespread agreement that establishing networks with colleagues both inside and outside one's host institution is essential in academia (Amabile, Patterson, Mueller, Wojcik, Odomoriok, Marsh, & Kramer, 2001; De Janasz & Sullivan, 2004). The International Study (see Richardson & Mallon, 2005), the Canadian Study (see Richardson et al., 2006), and the Italian Study (see Gill, 2005) clearly reflected the influence of external networks on academics' experiences of self-initiated expatriation. The data supporting this finding could be divided into two sub-themes: first, the extent to which external networks had impacted on interviewees' ability to engage in self-initiated expatriation (i.e. to get jobs in other countries); second that they developed and maintained networks external to both their current host institution and host country. Focusing on the first theme, connections developed through international research collaborations, meetings, and conferences were regularly cited as impacting on decisions and/or opportunities to expatriate/repatriate (see Gill, 2005; Richardson & Mallon, 2005; Richardson et al., 2008). Moreover, while their international experience received varying levels of recognition, most participants continued to develop and maintain networks with academics outside their host institution *and* country. In fact, many SIE academics in all three studies said they were *specifically and deliberately* developing networks with academics in certain institutions or countries in order to support their career advancement (see Gill, 2005; Richardson & Mallon, 2005; Richardson et al., 2008). This finding adds further to the theme introduced above: that validation and marketability are *connected to* rather than *disconnected from* institutional and national contexts. Furthermore, most SIE academics in the Canadian and International Study also attached considerable importance to developing strong networks within their *host* institution. The main issue, in this respect, was a concern about the need for 'local' (mostly institutional) networks to facilitate their career advancement.

BREAKING TRADITIONAL ORGANIZATIONAL BOUNDARIES, NOTABLY THOSE INVOLVING HIERARCHICAL REPORTING AND ADVANCEMENT PRINCIPLES

According to Baruch and Hall (2004), "The academic career model is based on very few hierarchical levels" and "even within this structure, the stages do not necessarily mean a supervisor-subordinate relationship" (p. 248). Yet, they also acknowledge that the rank and tenure system is underpinned by principles of hierarchy and rule-based advancement. The findings of the International and the Canadian Study indicated that the strength of hierarchical reporting and advancement principles existed more in some countries than others. In Canada and New Zealand, for example, they were as Baruch and Hall (2004) suggest experienced more as part of the 'background' of their professional lives. In these countries there was also fairly widespread agreement that their professional lives were characterized by dyadic relationships with colleagues and fairly egalitarian relationships with institutional managers such as deans and school directors. They did not experience any distinction between their positions as SIEs and their local counterparts. On the other hand, interviewees in Turkey, the UAE, and Singapore said that there were very clear and oftentimes multiple hierarchies and strict reporting systems in their institutions, particularly regarding communications with deans and school directors (see Richardson, 2008). Yet, there was widespread agreement that these systems applied to all academics not just SIEs. To that extent the synergy between this theme and SIE academics seems to be more a reflection of national culture than expatriate status.

REJECTING EXISTING CAREER OPPORTUNITIES FOR PERSONAL OR FAMILY REASONS

In what they refer to as the 'two-body problem' and echoing the work of other scholars (e.g. Forster, 2001), Wolf-Wendel, Twombly, and Rice (2003) draw our attention to the impact of family on academic careers. Themes relating to family permeated all four studies: The International Study, the Canadian Study, the European Study, and the Italian Study. Some SIE academics, for example, reported rejecting job offers or not pursing careers in certain countries and pursuing careers in others specifically because of the potential impact on their family (see Richardson, 2007; Selmer & Lauring, 2010). Others spoke of returning to their home country in order to be nearer to family, particularly aging parents and/ or to maintain closer relationships with extended family members (see Gill, 2005; Richardson, 2007). There was also some talk of electing to expatriate to countries nearer to the home country so that they could "go home" more easily—again in order to maintain close relationships with family (see Gill, 2005; Richardson & McKenna, 2005).

In addition to family reasons, all four studies identified other personal drivers to self-initiated expatriation. A particularly common personal reason was a 'search for adventure' or simply to experience a new or different culture. This was an especially dominant driver for SIE academics in the International Study (see Richardson & Mallon, 2005) and the European Study (see Selmer & Lauring, 2010). Indeed it was the most influential driver in the International Study, where 29 of the 30 participants said that it had impacted on their decision to expatriate. The Canadian Study also identified a search for adventure or at least the desire to experience a new culture as a dominant driver (see Richardson et al., 2006). The European Study reported that younger SIE academics showed more of a tendency to be motivated by the search for adventure than older academics (see Selmer & Lauring, 2010). Another personal reason that emerged in the International, Canadian, and European Study was the desire for 'life change' where some SIE academics had wanted to leave difficult circumstances in their home country such as economic hardship or concerns about personal safety etc. Interestingly, the European Study reported that male SIE academics were more likely to be motivated by the need for 'life change' as a personal driver to SIE (Selmer & Lauring, 2010).

PERCEIVING A BOUNDARYLESS FUTURE REGARDLESS OF STRUCTURAL CONSTRAINTS

Discussions of the previous five themes have addressed some of the constraints that SIE academics experience. These constraints, or what we have called 'boundaries,' can be understood as structural in the sense that they related to SIE academics' experiences of the science context or institutional context within which academic careers evolve (Kaulisch & Enders, 2005). SIE academics in the International and the Canadian Study, for example, said that institutional processes and policies impacted directly on their experience of SIE such as whether research conducted outside of their host country was recognized in tenure and promotion or research funding decisions (see Richardson, 2009; Richardson & Zikic, 2007). Turning to the 'science context,' SIE academics in the arts and humanities recognized that their opportunities for international mobility might be more limited than their counterparts in the sciences. Yet, they still felt that they could continue to expatriate (see Richardson, 2008). Conversely, however, the Italian Study suggested that institutional practices in Italian universities and the broader science context of academia in Italy created barriers to repatriation, which for some were deemed unassailable (see Gill, 2005). Therefore, SIE academics in that study challenge this last dimension because they felt that, while they could pursue their careers outside of Italy, for some, it would be virtually impossible to return.

DISCUSSION

Drawing on recently published work from four studies of SIE academics, this chapter has explored whether each of the six specific emphases or meanings of the boundaryless career can be applied to SIE academics' careers. In this respect it extends Dowd and Kaplan's (2005) exploration of academic careers as bounded or boundaryless and answers Pringle and Mallon's (2003) call to evaluate boundaryless career theory's potential contribution to our understanding of diverse rather than narrow populations. The chapter has

suggested that while there are strong synergies between each of the six emphases and SIE academic careers, they are not a direct fit. Rather, the connection between them is more nuanced where, for example, although Dowd and
Kaplan (2005) identified academic careers as either bounded or boundaryless
(i.e. Probationers and Conservationists versus Mavericks and Connectors),
this chapter has suggested that SIE academic careers can be *both* bounded *and*
boundaryless. Introducing further complexity, the chapter has also suggested
that in addition to reflecting some boundaryless career themes and not others,
some SIE academic careers may reflect and challenge the same theme. Thus,
for example, in as much as they might be able to cross organizational and
national boundaries, once having done so encounter certain boundaries when
their international experience receives only limited recognition in institutional
processes such as tenure and promotion and/or researching funding.

Addressing the first theme, then, the chapter has suggested that SIE
academics are indeed taking charge of their careers and moving across
the boundaries of separate employers. Yet, it has also suggested that such
movement is often impacted by disciplinary boundaries where some disciplines are more transferable than others. The relationship between ability to engage in self-initiated expatriation and one's academic discipline or
field of study reflects Mayrhofer, Meyer, and Steyrer's (2007) conception of
'career capital,' where certain disciplines seem to have 'career capital' that is
more transferable than others. This finding also reflects Leong and Leung's
(2004) argument that 'traditional scientific disciplines' such as engineering
and medicine have more value—or at least more transferability—because
of their "social relevance and their previous success in improving human
life" (p. 351). This, it seems, gives them a more universal appeal and thus
allows academics operating within those fields to move across organizational and national boundaries more easily. Indeed, it is notable that in the
European Study, Selmer and Lauring (2010) focused solely on academics in
science faculty departments because of their assumption that "science as an
academic discipline may be less constrained by cultural, social and institutional factors than, for example, humanities and social sciences" (p. 172).

In a related point and turning to the second theme, the chapter has suggested that although SIE academics draw some validation and marketability
from outside their employer/institution, their marketability is still impacted
by the employer's/institution's reputation or standing in the academic marketplace. Echoing Marafioti and Perretti's (2006) contention that European and other non-US scholars experience 'a liability of foreignness' when
working in the US, there was also some evidence that the country in which
they had gained their experience impacts on SIE academics' marketability.

The chapter has provided very clear evidence that external networking,
theme three of the boundaryless career, is an important activity for SIE
academics, particularly regarding career development and opportunities
for research collaborations and future opportunities to expatriate. In fact
the International Study and the Canadian Study both provided widespread

evidence that SIE academics actively engage in networking with colleagues within and outside their host institution and country. It was suggested, however, that while external networks were important, *internal* networks (i.e. within both their own institutions and host countries) were also important in order to avoid what Inkson et al. (2004) describe as the problem of 'not knowing whom.' This finding clearly suggests that SIE academic careers are sustained by *both* internal and external networks.

Turning now to theme four, the extent to which SIE academic careers break 'traditional organizational boundaries' is less clear and seems to be related to the national context and most likely the culture of academia within a given country or institution. Thus, for example, drawing on the findings from the International and the Canadian Study, individuals in institutions in Singapore, Turkey, and the UAE spoke of clear and fairly rigid reporting and hierarchical systems,whereas those in Canada and New Zealand acknowledged the existence of such systems but characterized them as being more 'in the background.'

Moving on to theme five, all four studies provided evidence that SIE academics appear to both reject *and* embrace existing career opportunities for personal or family reasons. Indeed, it was quite clear that family and personal preferences play a key role in how their careers have evolved. In some instances, for example, parents had specifically expatriated in order to give their children a chance to experience a different culture. Many of those without children had expatriated in order to experience living in a different culture themselves. On the other hand, there were some accounts of *not* expatriating to a specific location because of limited educational facilities for children or employment opportunities for spouses. Either way, the main point here is that family and personal issues impacted directly on SIE academics' decisions to expatriate and on their careers more broadly.

For the final theme, theme six, there was widespread evidence that whereas some SIE academics saw themselves as having a 'boundaryless future' (but only because they felt that the existent boundaries could be overcome), others believed that structural constraints such as those in the Italian academic system meant that their careers were, in fact, bounded. This finding echoes Marafioti and Perretti's (2006) assertion that, in management scholarship at least, disciplinary and national boundaries "have remained largely intact, isolating scholars into relatively autonomous communities" (p. 2006).

PRACTICAL IMPLICATIONS

This chapter provides important information for recruiters and managers such as departmental chairs and deans seeking to internationalize their institutions by attracting and retaining international faculty. It also speaks to the concerns of government policy makers about 'brain drain' and 'brain gain' by demonstrating the need to ensure that international experience is consistently recognized and rewarded, not just at the recruitment stage but also during subsequent decisions about tenure and promotion and/or distribution of research opportunities and funding. Where individual academics are concerned, the chapter has suggested that despite the rhetoric of the need for international mobility/experience for career progression, some caution is necessary. Those considering such a move would be well-advised to 'do their homework' (or as Richardson et al. [2008] suggest—get a Realistic Job Preview) starting with how much value their international experience will be accorded by their host institution, not only during the recruitment process but also in later decisions about tenure and promotion and research funding. Those expecting to repatriate at some later point would also be well-advised to find out how much value international experience is accorded in their home country. Above all else, the chapter has suggested that although SIE academic careers may have some elements of boundarylessness, they are also characterized by certain boundaries. In other words, SIE academic careers are *both* bounded *and* boundaryless.

Although the chapter has drawn on a fairly wide body of empirical data more research is needed to develop this exploration further. A larger quantitative study, perhaps along similar lines to Selmer and Lauring's (2010; 2011) work, that operationalizes each of the themes as part of a larger survey would be especially useful. To be sure, given the trend toward increasing international mobility among academics, much work is yet to be done in order to expand our understanding of them and of self-initiated expatriation more generally. Moreover, given the importance of the boundaryless career model in contemporary career theory, testing its application to other groups of SIEs may also be a potentially rich avenue of research.

NOTES

1. This information is not included in their 2005 paper but was confirmed through personal correspondence with the authors.

REFERENCES

Ackers, H. L. (2004). Managing relationships in peripatetic careers: Scientific mobility in the European Union. *Women's Studies International Forum, 27,* 189–201.

Ackers, H. L. (2005a). Moving people and knowledge: Scientific mobility in the European Union. *International Migration, 43*(5), 99–129.

Ackers, H. L. (2005b). Promoting scientific mobility and balanced growth in the European research area. *Innovation, 18*(3), 301–317.

Ackers, H. L., & Gill, B. (2008). *Moving people and knowledge: Scientific mobility in an enlarging Europe.* Cheltenham, UK: Edward Elgar.

Altbach, P. G. (2004). Globalization and the university: Myths and realities in an unequal world. *Tertiary Education and Management, 10*(1), 3–25.

Amabile, T. M., Patterson, C., Mueller, J., Wojcik, T., Odomoriok, P. W., Marsh, M., & Kramer, S. J. (2001). Academic-practitioner collaboration in management research: A case of cross-profession collaboration. *Academy of Management Journal, 44,* 418–431.

Ambrose, S., Huston, T., & Norman, M. (2005). A qualitative method for assessing faculty satisfaction. *Research in Higher Education, 46,* 803–830.

Arthur, M. B., & Rousseau, D. M. (1996). Introduction: The boundaryless career as a new employment principle. In M. B. Arthur and D. M. Rousseau (Eds.), *The Boundaryless Career: A New Employment Principle for a New Organisational Era* (pp. 3–20). Oxford: Oxford University Press.

Baruch, Y., & Hall, D. T. (2004). The academic career: A model for future careers in other sectors? *Journal of Vocational Behavior, 64,* 241–262.

Bozionelos, N. (2009). Expatriation outside the boundaries of the multinational corporation: A study with expatriate nurses in Saudi Arabia. *Human Resource Management, 48*(1), 111–134.

Briscoe, J. P., & Hall, D. T. (2006). The interplay of boundaryless and protean careers: Combinations and implications. *Journal of Vocational Behavior, 69*(1), 4–18.

Carr, S. C., Inkson, K., & Thorn, K. (2005). From global careers to talent flow: Reinterpreting "brain drain." *Journal of World Business, 40*(4), 386–398.

De Janasz, S. C., & Sullivan, S. E. (2004). Multiple mentoring in academia: Developing the professorial network. *Journal of Vocational Behavior, 64,* 263–283.

Doherty, N. (2010, August). *Self-initiated expatriates—Mavericks of the global milieu.* Paper presented at The Academy of Management, Montreal, Canada.

Doherty, N., Dickmann, M., & Mills, T. (2011). Exploring the motives of company-backed and self-initiated expatriates. *International Journal of Human Resource Management, 22*(3), 595–611.

Dowd, K. O., & Kaplan, D. M. (2005). The career life of academics: Boundaried or boundaryless? *Human Relations, 58*(6), 699–721.

Forster, N. (2001). A case study of women academics' views on equal opportunities, career prospects and work-family conflicts in a UK university. *Career Development International, 6*(1), 28–38.

Gill, B. (2005). Homeward bound? The experience of return mobility for Italian scientists. *Innovation, 18*(3), 319–341.

Inkson, K., Arthur, M. B., Pringle, J., & Barry, S. (1997). Expatriate assignment versus overseas experience: International human resource development. *Journal of World Business, 32*(4), 351–368.

Inkson, K., Carr, S. C., Edwards, M., Hooks, J., Jackson, D., Thorn, K., & Allfree, N. (2004). From brain drain to talent flow: Views of expatriate Kiwis. *University of Auckland Business Review, 6,* 7–26.

Kaulisch, M., & Enders, J. (2005). Careers in overlapping institutional contexts. *Career Development International, 10,* 130–144.

King, Z., Burke, S., & Pemberton, J. (2005). The bounded career: An empirical study of human capital, career mobility, and employment outcomes in a mediated labour market. *Human Relations, 58,* 981–1007.

Lauring, J., & Selmer, J. (2011). Marital status and work outcomes of self-initiated expatriates—Is there a moderating effect of gender? *Cross Cultural Management: An International Journal, 18*(2), 198–213.

Leong, F. T. L., & Leung, K. (2004). Academic careers in Asia: A cross-cultural analysis. *Journal of Vocational Behavior, 64,* 346–357.

Marafiotti, E., & Perretti, F. (2006). International competition in academia: The European challenge. *Journal of Management Inquiry, 15*(3), 318–326.

Mayrhofer, W., Meyer, M., & Steyrer, J. (2007). Going beyond the individual: Some potential contributions from a career field and habitus perspective for global career research and practice. In H. P. Gunz and M. Peiperl (Eds.), *Handbook of Career Studies* (pp. 215–240). Thousand Oaks, CA: Sage.

Pringle, J., & Mallon, M. (2003). Challenges for the boundaryless career odyssey. *International Journal of Human Resource Management, 14*(5), 839–853.

Richardson, J. (2007). Family matters. *Personnel Review, 35*(4), 469–486.

Richardson, J. (2008). *The independent expatriate: Academics abroad.* Saarbrucken, Germany: VDM Publishers.

Richardson, J. (2009). Geographical flexibility—A cautionary note. *British Journal of Management, 20*, 160–170.

Richardson, J., & Mallon, M. (2005). Career interrupted? The case of the self-directed expatriate. *Journal of World Business, 40*, 409–420.

Richardson, J., McBey, K., & McKenna, S. D. (2006). *International faculty in Canada: An exploratory study.* Working Paper Series IC60046 (2006-D-22). Ottawa, Canada: HRSDC & SSHRC.

Richardson, J., McBey, K., & McKenna, S. D. (2008). Integrating realistic job previews and realistic living conditions previews: Realistic recruitment for internationally mobile knowledge workers. *Personnel Review, 37*(5), 490–508.

Richardson, J., & McKenna, S. D. (2005). Exploring relationships with home and host countries: A study of self-directed expatriates. *Cross Cultural Management: An International Journal, 12*(5), 4–23.

Richardson, J., & Zikic, J. (2007). The darker side of an international academic career. *Career Development International, 2*, 164–186.

Roper, J., Ganesh, S., & Inkson, K. (2010). Neoliberalism and knowledge interests in boundaryless careers discourse. *Work, Employment and Society, 24*(4), 661–679.

Selmer, J., & Lauring, J. (2010). Self-initiated academic expatriates: Inherent demographics and reasons to expatriate. *European Management Review, 7*, 169–179.

Stahl, G. K., & Cerdin, J. L. (2004). Global careers in French and German multinational corporations. *Journal of Management Development, 23*(9), 885–902.

Sullivan, S. E., & Arthur, M. B. (2006). The evolution of the boundaryless career concept: Examining physical and psychological mobility. *Journal of Vocational Behavior, 69*(1), 19–29.

Sullivan, S. E., & Baruch, Y. (2009). Advances in careers research and theory. *Journal of Management, 35*(6), 1542–1571.

Thorn, K. (2009). The relative importance of motives for international self-initiated mobility. *Career Development International, 14*(5), 441–464.

Wolf-Wendel, L., Twombly, S. B., & Rice, S. (2003). *The two-body problem.* Baltimore: Johns Hopkins University Press.

Zikic, J., & Richardson, J. (2011, August). *No country for old men? Exploring the careers of international medical graduates in Canada.* Paper presented at the Academy of Management Conference, San Antonio.

13 Self-Initiated Career Characteristics of Danish Expatriated Engineers

Torben Andersen and Erling Rasmussen

The fluctuations in world economy during the last two decades have presented us with several interesting challenges, when it comes to the movement of labor. First and foremost the increasing economic globalization (Edwards & Rees, 2006) has led to unseen growth figures for more than a decade, up to the crisis in the world economy in autumn 2008, and then afterwards the major recession, characterizing specific sectors as well as countries. We have, in other words, experienced a phase where globalization was making the world supposedly flatter (Friedman, 2005) and much more potentially mobile for managers and employees and with the arrival of the recession, a contraction of the different national economies, leading to major restriction and obstacles in this area within companies, i.e. the world is curved and mobility patterns are highly unpredictable (Smick, 2008). It is in many respects a time period of many—and perhaps profound—changes and this also goes for mobility patterns among employees and managers.

One of the often discussed topics in the area of international mobility of labor is, what some have called the end of the classical (gold card) expatriate, and perhaps also of the expatriate in general. The claim has been presented during the last couple of decades, and in particular supported by the empirical mapping of new, and more flexible, employment models, where the old, and supposedly inflexible model, is succeeded by a variety of modern approaches e.g. short-term assignments based on employees acting as frequent flyers, flexi workers etc. (Mayerhofer, Hartmann, & Herbert, 2004). The more flexible employment models vary not only in form and time, but also in contents, i.e. pay level, fringe benefits, extras etc. are reduced to a much lower level if not removed (some companies are removing benefits for employees working in another country with the EU). And this has—since the arrival of the economic crisis—been even more relevant for many companies. This is, indeed very much in contrast to the pre-2008 crisis large focus on the contents of the employment model, in order to convince the expat to take the assignment (Suutari & Brewster, 2001). We have, on the one hand, seen companies during the growth period having focused increasingly on benefit and support services as a key element in recruitment, selection, retention (Caligiuri, Joshi, & Lazarova, 1999), and on the other hand, many of the modern employment models have not included these extras, both because of the general trend toward fewer gold card expats and because of the economic recession. The question is therefore whether it is possible to see the end of the classical expat or perhaps a sort of a split up, a polarization, in the topic covered in the different employment models?

The continuation of the classical expatriate in some form is supported by the argument that there seems to be a need for a certain pool of internationally competent managers and executives, in order to manage the economic globalization process (recession or not). In addition Benson, Pérez-Nordtvedt, and Datta claimed in 2009 that the number of first time expats was increasing (Benson et al., 2009), and that this type of employees was still occupying a very important role in the running of the multinational companies (MNCs), both in relation to control (Edström & Galbraith, 1977; Martinez & Jarillo, 1989; Scullion, 1994) and in relation to management development (Black, Gregersen, Mendenhall, & Stroh, 1999; Carpenter, Sanders, & Gregersen. 2000; Evans, Pucik, & Barsoux, 2002; Spreitzer, McCall, & Mahoney, 1997). In particular Evans and colleagues argue that the expatriates still are powerful vehicles for global coordination and that this type of employment is maintained and developed by much more open intra-company networks of career opportunities (Evans et al., 2002). This could mean that we in future will see that foreign assignments take several new forms—in larger companies being based on an infrastructure as mentioned or in small and medium-sized companies being based on external providers like e.g. the recruitment company Stepstone (being present in 11 countries) advertising for engineers working abroad, e.g. Siemens Denmark looking for an employee for their Munich branch or Vestas headquarters in Denmark searching for a person to a job in Malmö and one in Dortmund.

The claim of the continuous need for expats in MNCs is also based on the perspective that the global economy is being highly knowledge intensive, and this seems to challenge organizations and companies continuously— i.e. they have to rely on knowledge-based control forms, where the use of foreign assignments is one out of several different. In particular the transfer of technical and managerial skills, through the use of expatriates, has been one of the key elements in the research carried out (Morley & Heraty, 2004). In addition, with the frequently occurrence of international reorganizing, downsizing, outsourcing, and offshoring, the demand for skilled employees could be rather stable, and thereby not removing an employment model often characterizing managers and specialists like engineers.

Finally the pressure on the classical expat has come from a somehow new direction, and perhaps in a much more profound manner—the increasing number of people going abroad to live and work, doing it without any prior company attachment (see initially Inkson, Arthur, Pringle, & Barry, 1997; Suutari & Brewster, 2000; Vance, 2005) for empirical studies rooted in New Zealand, Finland, and the US. The question is whether the group of self-initiated behaviors (overseas experiences, foreign assignments, and career strategies) studied here, could mean a breakup of older employment patterns and leaving the classical model. Will it be possible to detect more profound changes characterizing longer-term foreign stays, perhaps individuals moving toward immigration patterns?

It is, however empirically difficult to precisely determine the phenomena self-initiated, i.e. 'not being sent abroad by employer but on own initiative,' without asking directly and perhaps checking this with the company they are working for. And how do we interpret the behavior of a young engineer, first being sent out on an assignment and then looking for a next job out there—is this self-initiated career behavior? We will return to this in the concluding section. But here has been an increasing interest in differentiating the characteristics of self-initiated career from those of the more standardized expatriate contracts, and in particular the individual background, motivation, and compensation principle and development (Sparrow, 2009).

THE DATA

The study is founded on data from four surveys carried out by the Danish Society of Engineers (IDA)—a professional body and trade union for technical and scientific professionals. IDA has about 85,700 members (by July 2012). The engineers (together with economists) in Denmark have a relatively long tradition for working abroad (e.g. one out of five of all the members of the one economists' association had been working abroad, see Andersen and Scheuer [2004]). In this respect, we have a rather interesting population with many experiences in this domain, and they tend to be rather well organized in a limited number of organization. Union density is among university graduate associations; like economists and engineers estimated to be about 76% (Due, Madsen, & Pihl, 2010). IDA estimates density to be 60% for private sector employed and 71% for public sector employed.

Every second year IDA conducts a survey among its members staying and living abroad (during the last decade in 2003, 2005, 2007, and 2009). The survey has been developed over time, and starting with a few questions in 2003 to a much broader frame today. Thereby only a limited number of data exist across all four surveys. The present chapter is therefore highly data driven and findings based on our access ability to data. The study is based on descriptive statistics, illustrating a development over time in fixed categories, but it also triggers a lot of qualitative questions concerning new developments in direction of more self-initiated career behavior, i.e. we are relying on standardized data on employment conditions and combining them with attitudinal data concerning the job.

It is however also, rather seldom one find these types of aggregate profession data. Even though engineers as mentioned above probably are one of the groups most sent out on foreign assignments, there is surprisingly little focus on professions. Only Suutari and Brewster (2003) carried out a major study of Finnish engineers. In addition there are a few cross-sector studies, with a focus on professions (Anderson, 2001). This is rather limited compared to the numerous studies of expatriation and foreign assignment in MNC. In addition many of the smaller quantitative studies have been mapping relative recent developments, and this combined with the often myriad of factors, which are influencing the international assignments (Yan, Guorong, & Hall, 2002), have made many of the conclusions in this filed relatively weak (Sparrow, 2009).

RESULTS

The selection of themes from the surveys carried out by IDA is based on pragmatism, i.e. themes that are often bargaining issues between IDA and the employers and at the same time reasons of some centrality in the scientific debate concerning expatriation. This is in particular: type of employment and (direct and indirect) costs associated with the international assignments. How many and what kind of jobs do the engineers occupy, when living and working abroad, and are there developments in certain directions, e.g. toward more specialist types or other forms characterizing demands from local context to people going by their own initiative? Concerning the themes, data has been collected on

- Formal job title
- Pay level
- Benefits

Besides direct contents measure, the surveys also included data on outcomes over time and attitudes toward foreign assignments; they are presented below:

- Seniority
- Type of employer
- Reasons for working abroad
- Career implications
- Considerations on repatriation

FORMAL JOB TITLE

Formal job title is an important measure of the status of the expatriate, and it can show to which degree the distribution of expats on generalists and specialists—i.e. is it managerial (economic and behavioral) control and coordination or management development the company is pursuing through the assignments? A relatively large proportion of the Danish engineers living abroad are placed in upper management positions: One out of seven hold executive positions, and a similar size group is placed in other management positions, i.e. almost one third are managers. If one also includes project managers (15% in 2007 and 18% in 2009), the management group covers about half of the respondents. Only around one fifth are employees, with no management responsibility, and the figure is decreasing from 21% in 2007 to 16% in 2009. We interpret this as a reaction to the economic crisis hitting the world (and the Danish) economy autumn 2008, i.e. the number of employed engineers (in non-managerial jobs) has probably been reduced in the cost cutting exercise many Danish companies had to go through. Eighteen percent in 2007 and 16% in 2009 are considering themselves senior specialist. Here it could be argued that almost one fifth being specialists is a rather high number, especially when much of the literature explains how specialists tend to be employed on much shorter terms, travelling around fixing problems perhaps all over the corporation. But the high level of senior specialists could also, as it is shown in the later section on seniority, be caused by the fact that quite a large proportion of the engineers have been abroad several years, leading us to the following question: Do many of these managers and specialists initiate their own career in the host country or region, after the first or second assignment, and if the many top management jobs in the subsidiaries are still occupied by Danes, parent country nationals (PNCs), and only to a lesser extent of host country national or third country nationals, could this be an indicator of people being promoted or creating their own career out there?

PAY LEVEL

Looking at pay level among the engineers, who are comparatively highly remunerated, we see a similar tendency, as in the case of formal job title. Pay before tax, including pension, was in 2007 for more than half of all the engineers above €6000 per month. In 2009 about every third was paid more than €8000 per month, and according to the statistical census of IDA, 19% (101 expats) earned more than €10,000 per month in 2009. These figures have to be interpreted with care, because of the many factors influencing pay (composition of the remuneration package, local pay levels in the different countries, local level of taxation, the Danish traditions of rather egalitarian pay structures etc.). In addition one of the highly influential factors on pay level is the local level of taxation on pension (e.g. locally paid pension in Malaysia is tax free compared to the +40% tax in Denmark, providing a high incentive to place a large proportion of the pay as pension). Taking into consideration that world crisis has hit many sectors and professions, the pay level of the engineers seems to be continuing at the same level in 2009, and it is rising (partly because of the inflation but also relative, probably because of the increasing level of formal job titles). Pay is still good, and half of the respondents hold management positions; this gives the impression of a group of expatriates with a broader set of competences and skills, rather than narrow functional skills, often provided by lower-level specialists in short spells of time. Work abroad among engineers is not just shorter-term technical assignments but also are the occupation of general managerial positions.

BENEFITS

Pre-economic crisis arguments tend to emphasize a development toward more complex remuneration packages, designed to 'sell' the foreign assignments, to increasingly skeptical—domestic rooted—younger talents and managers (Andersen & Scheuer, 2004). This could first of all increase the number of elements in these packages, showing more 'exotic' services and second the amount and value attached to old and new benefits. Pulling in the opposite direction is the post-crisis rationalizations and the general development in the last decade away from the classical 'gold card expatriation' (Selmer, 2001).

The most often provided benefits to the Danish engineers abroad is pension and health insurance, and second is free IT (telephone, labtop and internet connection) and home trip (and transportation). It is, in other words, rather classical and modest benefits (similar to what many domestic employees receive today and taking into consideration that pension and health insurance is not relevant in many of the European countries). The services provided are what would normally be considered an element of a mid-level management package, even though many of the respondents are in top management positions. It is, of course, limited how many new initiatives can be identified in a study like this, but there seems to be neither an end of the gold card expat nor a change toward totally new services and no development toward phasing out benefits, e.g. moving toward local terms. The interesting question is whether this is illustrating that many engineers are still sent out and employed by a Danish company, or how a large a degree of self-initiated careerists receive the same benefits as the classical expiates? We will return to this question when the reasons for going abroad are discussed.

SENIORITY

Departing from the classical employment themes and moving toward the more outcome-oriented aspects of the employment conditions, seniority has, for a long time, been one of the most indirectly discussed themes

Table 13.1 Danish Engineers, Being Members of IDA, Working and Living Abroad, Number of Years Abroad, 2003–2009, (%)

Time	2003	2005	2007	2009
<1 year	7	13	14	14
1–2 years	17	13	18	16
3–5 years	24	21	18	20
6–10 years	16	20	16	15
10>	35	34	34	35
Total	100	100	100	100
N	894	664	598	563

Source: IDA, International Member Survey, 2003–2009.

concerning a successful expatriation. How long of a time people stayed abroad was an indicator of the effectiveness of how well they adapted and, more recently, in addition to whether they tended to build up an international career. Looking at seniority, we perhaps find the most challenging data, in as much as the relative proportion of engineers living and working abroad for longer spells of time is quite high.

Almost 200 of the participating respondents, who are living and working abroad have been doing this for more than 10 years, and this figure has been extremely stable during the whole period. More than one out of three of the respondents have been out 6–10 years, i.e. half of the engineers have been out at least for two 'so called' standard periods (normally contracts run for two or three years in Danish MNCs). A very high seniority, many holding management position, with high pay, is indeed pointing toward a group of engineers making career moves in a certain direction. Are these people showing an extremely high loyalty to their Danish employer, or are they shifting employer creating a career out there?

TYPE OF EMPLOYER

The Danish engineers working and living abroad are mainly employed by a local company—48% in 2007 and 36% in 2009. It would be rather straightforward to claim that this is the proof of self-initiated career behavior. But the large number is probably caused by several different reasons: First locally owned companies are hiring Danish engineers; no doubt, case studies show this. Second, Danish MNCs do open subsidiaries as a local company and being 'locally' employed can be out of legal, tax, and cost-saving reasons and not necessarily because of the expatriates being localized. Some engineers are still employed in the headquarters (in the Danish company), and this we choose to call the classical expat. However, today this is a minority—less than one fourth are employed this way.

However we do also see changes occurring in relation to 'local employer'—twelve percentage points down from 2007 to 2009. This could be caused by some of the respondents being self-employed (not measured in 2007). It could, however, signal a move toward a more localized group of people creating a permanent life abroad, furthermore taking into consideration that about 40% of the participating engineers had their spouses with them and that the spouses similarly were working mainly for a local employer. It is also a situation in which the ties to the mother company become looser, thereby supporting the supposed emerging trends toward more independent global careerists (Suutari & Brewster, 2000).

REASONS FOR WORKING ABROAD

The +500 engineers participating in the IDA surveys have been presented with a relatively large variety of options for replying why they were working abroad. Many of them could be categorized as rather traditional, see Table 13.2 below.

The data points in the direction of primary emphasis on personal developmental reasons (first and third upper scores are personal ambition and career; professional development ranging from 40% to 57% during the whole period). Second, the engineers leave for social reasons (learn about other cultures and family reasons). '*Demand* from company' is the lowest score for all years! It is only in 2% of the cases (still *wish* from company is somewhat higher—between 11 and 17% of the cases). But the engineers who

Table 13.2   Danish Engineers, Being Members of the Danish Engineering Association, and Living Abroad, Reasons for Taking the Job, 2003–2009, (%)

Reasons	2003	2005	2007	2009
Personal ambitions and career	57	46	51	55
Learn about other cultures	–	47	43	41
Professional development	44	40	40	44
Family reasons	23	20	22	22
Higher pay and better living conditions	–	17	19	18
Lower tax	–	14	12	16
Wish from the company	17	14	11	14
Others	20	12	12	9
Unemployed	9	12	11	9
Demand from company	2	2	1	2
N	766	684	554	548

Source: IDA, International Member Survey, 2003–2009.

work abroad do it for several—positive—reasons and not mainly because of pressure from their employer. The surveys by IDA are not composed into a panel data study, and interpretation has to be carried out with caution, i.e. people who have declined foreign assignments do not participate in the survey as well as engineers living and working in Denmark. Finally the figures are open for interpretation, and we do believe that engineers increasingly look for jobs abroad themselves, from home, perhaps in existing jobs, carrying out what Harris and Brewster (1999) called coffee machine selection, not necessarily within the company but also out of the company. Earlier studies by IDA show that about one third of all foreign assignments are arranged though web-based job portals and personal networks, somewhat anecdotal evidence but still pointing in the same direction. Foreign assignments are increasingly an individual, developmental, and positive choice by knowledge workers like engineers.

CAREER IMPLICATIONS

Finally the engineers' perceptions on career matters were collected in the last two surveys (2007 and 2009), and their answers were similarly positive, i.e. the majority of them consider the foreign assignment as a career-enhancing thing, and one fourth indicate that it had no effect. In other words, the rather negative career implications argument seen in earlier expatriate literature is not mirrored in this set of data.

There is, of course, a bias in this type of study, asking those who have taken the assignment (and not those who have not or have gone home before time) and asking about how they feel about it. Still it is only one out of every 10, who think the effect will be negative, and these answers include the many having been out there +10 years. One also has to take into consideration that career implications can be interpreted in at least two different frames of reference: domesticcareer or global career, i.e. the rather

Table 13.3 Danish Engineers, Being Members of IDA, Working and Living Abroad, Perception of Expatriation as a Career Influencing Factor, 2003–2009, (%)

Time	2003	2005	2007	2009
Better	48	51	54	51
Unchanged	19	20	19	27
Worse	11	10	11	8
No idea	21	19	16	14
N	777	645	578	556

Source: IDA, International Member Survey, 2003–2009.

general question posed can be interpreted either in relation to chances of reaching higher position in the headquarters, in the parent country, or top-positions abroad. The latter option seems particularly relevant, taking into consideration that many of the engineers have been out there for +10 years. In the last survey carried out by IDA (in 2009), the respondents were asked abroad about how they viewed repatriation-relevant topics like (1) date of returning to job in Denmark; (2) certainty for job when repatriating, and (3) expecting to go back to Denmark. Many of the engineers are tied rather loosely to their organizations, in 2007 two out of three had no date of return, and in 2009 it was 49% (of the engineers with a Danish employer). In this way repatriation considerations seem to be rather distant and not to a very large extent linked to the present employer. In addition taking into consideration that 27% expect *not* to go back and 35% don't know if they will, this leaves us with only little more than one third of the respondents expecting to go back to Denmark after ending the contract. A certain level of uncertainty is quite normal when we look at foreign assignments, the ending dates, and future jobs within the same company. However, to a much lesser extent than we can see here. Perhaps, this is our most impor-tant indicator of future self- initiated career behavior.

In the technical commercial domain, where engineers are by far are the most dominant type of personnel, there has, in the Danish case during the last couple of decades, developed a stepwise career model: The large major-ity of mainly younger engineers start as employees, moving to become proj-ect managers rather quickly and end up as unit or department managers, when performing well, before turning into directors, the most skillful of them. This could also be the case when it comes to international aspects, taking into consideration that the majority of Danish companies already have been, or are in the process of, outsourcing and offshoring functions.

SUMMARY

Summing up the development of the three aspects of the Danish engineers' employment conditions abroad, we see signs of managerial professionals (Peiperl & Johnsen, 2007). Many of them are placed in executive positions, they are well paid, and they receive standard expat benefits. In addition the majority of them are locally employed, they have been abroad for a long time, and they do this voluntarily out of professional developmental and, to some extent, for social reasons. The majority of the participating engineers undoubtedly feel pulled more by these career and social factors than pushed by their employers at that time, i.e. they have chosen to look for a job abroad, either through a web-based search, personal networks (IDA has established networks of members abroad, sometimes on a Scandi-navian basis) inside or outside their organizations, or they have developed their career out there.

Many of these people have probably, before the first survey was carried out by IDA, been sent overseas on a temporary basis to complete a more time-based task or accomplish an organizational goal, i.e. the classical definition of an expatriate on a foreign assignment. However, time based here frequently means longer spells of time, and it seems to be the case that many—after their first foreign assignment—stay out there and exploit the acquired global management skills. Since Denmark does not allow dual citizenship, they stay Danish and perhaps keep their membership of the engineers association—IDA.

This way, we do see elements of more self-initiated expatriation among the engineers, where they fulfill the required competences of today, exceeding the pure functional and technical skills and solving the immediate production problem. Of much more importance are international and intercultural skills as engineering projects increasingly represent cross-border co-operations as a result of the large majority of Danish companies having outsourced and offshored.

Working and living in a foreign country substantially change a managers' view on international work (Benson et al., 2009; Tung, 1987), and international experiences are multifaceted. They consist of many different jobs and job experiences, and they—not to forget—add up (Takeuchi, Tesluk, Yun, & Lepak, 2005). Our claim is that many Danish engineers do go through these processes during their foreign assignments and that they acquire the necessary management knowledge and skills for the development and running of globally distributed work.

Much of the self-initiated career literature is assuming a high degree of voluntariness as a basis for individual choice, but it is (as we have implied above) indeed debatable to how large a degree it is based on a rational calculus, one's own initiative. Studying this profession for some years now, we tend to believe that several of the participating engineers have been very uncertain about the first foreign assignment before accepting it, and then after having been out there for a period, accepted the second with greater joy or left for another job locally (seeking a promotion). Furthermore, some of them are perhaps making a virtue out of a necessity, meaning their first career choice has made it rather difficult for them to return.

LIMITATIONS

The study is based on aggregate descriptive statistics, and assumptions are made concerning the individual level logics behind and among the majority of respondents. Further qualitative studies are necessary in order to find how models work within companies abroad, and, in particular, how individuals move and for what reasons. In addition the IDA surveys used here do not clearly stipulate, what constitutes as expatriate assignment (like it is often similarly different what is included in other studies—some talk about more than one year, while others use two or three (Konopaske & Werner, 2005).

The respondent's criteria for participating in the IDA surveys are 'Living and working abroad' and being members of IDA. This excludes Danish engineers living in the southern part of Sweden but working in Denmark (commuting daily) and Danish engineers living in northern Germany, crossing the southern Danish border. In other words local cross-border commuters—mainly people doing it for tax reasons—are not included in this study. Similarly, foreign engineers working for a Danish company, in Denmark, and perhaps being sent out on a foreign assignment, are only included if they are members of IDA. This is probably very few people, i.e. one third of the country nationals' mobility and career behavior is not included in the study.

The international IDA data presented here has a bias towards more experienced managers. It is directed toward people who are already out there; several of them are in continuously high positions (senior management with perhaps high potential) relying on their social-professional networks, which greatly influence the success or failure of the foreign assignment, as an important element in the continuous career development carried out (Benson et al., 2009). However, IDA also organizes many younger engineers, and it is not to the same extent that their attitudes toward foreign assignments and potential reasons for—in the future—take the first steps toward a self-initiated career, which has already been mapped.

REFERENCES

Anderson, B. A. (2001). Expatriate management: An Australian tri-sector comparative study. *Thunderbird International Business Review, 43*(1), 33–51.

Andersen, T., & Scheuer, S. (2004). Attitudes to foreign assignments among Danish economists. *Thunderbird International Business Review, 46*(6), 725–742.

Benson, G. S., Pérez-Nordtvedt, L., & Datta, D. K. (2009). Managerial characteristics and willingness to send employees on expatriate assignments. *Human Resource Management, 48*(6), 849–869.

Black, J. S., Gregersen, M. E., Mendenhall, M. E., & Stroh, L. K. (1999). *Globalizing people through international assignments.* New York: Addison-Wesley.

Caligiuri, P. M., Joshi, A., & Lazarova, M. (1999). Factors influencing the adjustment of women on global assignments. *International Journal of Human Resource Management, 10*(2), 163–179.

Carpenter, M. A., Sanders, W. G., & Gregersen, H. B. (2000). International assignment experience at the top can make a bottom-line difference. *Human Resource Management, 39*(2/3), 277–285.

Due, J., Madsen, J. S., & Pihl, M. D. (2010). *LO-dokumentation 1/2010. Udviklingen I den faglige organisering: årsager og konsekvenser for den danske model.* København: LO.

Edström, A., & Galbraith, J. R. (1977). Transfer of managers as a coordination and control strategy in multinational organizations. *Administrative Science Quarterly, 22*(2), 248–263.

Edwards, T., & Rees, C. (2006). *International human resource management*. Harlow: FT/Prentice Hall.

Evans, P., Pucik, V., & Barsoux, J. L. (2002). *The global challenge. Frameworks for international human resource management*. New York: McGraw-Hill.

Friedman, T. L. (2005). *The world is flat. The globalized world in the twenty-first century*. London: Penguin.

Harris, H., & Brewster, C. (1999). The coffee machine system: How international selection really works. *International Journal of Human Resource Management*, *10*(3), 488–504.

IDA (2003–2009). *International membership survey*. Copenhagen: The Danish Engineering Association.

Inkson, K., Arthur, M. B., Pringle, J., & Barry, S. (1997). Expatriate assignment versus overseas experience: Contrasting models of international human resource development. *Journal of World Business, 32*(4), 351–368.

Konopaske, R., & Werner, S. (2005). US managers' willingness to accept a global assignment: Do expatriate benefits and assignment length make a difference. *International Journal of Human Resource Management, 16*(7), 1159–1175.

Martinez, J. I., & Jarillo, J. C. (1989). The evolution of research on coordination mechanisms in multinational corporations. *Journal of International Business Studies, 20*(3), 489–514.

Mayerhofer, H., Hartmann, L. C., & Herbert, A. (2004). Career management issues for flexpatriate international staff. *Thunderbird International Business Review, 46*(6), 647–666.

Morley, M., & Heraty, N. (2004). International assignments and global careers. *Thunderbird International Business Review, 46*(6), 633–646.

Peiperl, M., & Johnsen, K. (2007). Global careers. In H. Gunz and M. Peiperl (Eds.), *Handbook of Career Studies* (pp. 350–372). Thousand Oaks, CA: Sage.

Scullion, H. (1994). Creating international managers: Recruitment and development issues. In P. Kirkbride (Ed.), *Human Resource Management in Europe* (pp. 197–212). London: Routledge.

Selmer, J. (2001, June). *(S)he'll do! Expatriate selection when people are not exactly queuing-up for the job*. Paper presented at Human Resource Global Management Conference, Barcelona, Spain.

Smick, D. (2008). *The world is curved. Hidden dangers to the global economy*. New York: Penguin.

Sparrow, P. (2009). *Handbook of international human resource management. Integrating people, processes, and contexts*. Chichester, UK: John Wiley & Sons.

Spreitzer, G. M., McCall, M. W., & Mahoney, J. D. (1997). Early identification of international executive potential. *Journal of Applied Psychology, 82*(1), 6–29.

Suutari, V., & Brewster, C. (2000). Making your own way: Self-initiated foreign assignments in contrast to organisational expatriation. *Journal of World Business, 35*(4), 417–436.

Suutari, V., & Brewster, C. (2001). Expatriate management practices and perceived relevance. Evidence from Finnish expatriates. *Personnel Review, 30*(5), 554–577.

Suutari, V., & Brewster, C. (2003). Repatriation: Empirical evidence from a longitudinal study of careers and expectations among Finnish expatriates. *International Journal of Human Resource Management, 14*(7), 1132–1151.

Takeuchi, R., Tesluk, P. E., Yun, S., & Lepak, D. P. (2005). An integrative view of international experience. *Academy of Management Journal, 48*(1), 85–100.

Tung, R. L. (1987). Expatriate assignments: Enhancing success and minimizing failure. *Academy of Management Executive, 1*(2), 117–126.

Vance, C. (2005). The personal quest for building global competence. A taxonomy of self-initiating career path strategies for gaining business experience abroad. *Journal of World Business, 40*(4), 374–385.

Yan, A., Guorong, Z., & Hall, D. T. (2002). International assignments for career building: A model of agency relationships and psychological contracts. *Academy of Management Review, 27*(3), 373–391.

14 Ethnic Minority Migrants or Self-Initiated Expatriates?

Questioning Assumptions in International Management Studies

Akram Al Ariss[1]

The experiences of Europeans, Americans, Australians, and New Zealanders undertaking international mobility, frequently denoted by 'expatriates,' are extensively discussed in the literature on self-initiated expatriation. However, experiences of individuals coming from less developed countries, often referred to as 'migrants,' remain under-theorized. Instead, studies of migrants focus on individuals with lower levels of skills or on skilled individuals who are underemployed or even unemployed. In order to address this knowledge gap, this chapter has two goals: First, to review and question the terminology used in the international management literature regarding migration and expatriation; second, to propose an alternative approach for future research in this area. By doing so, the chapter seeks to provide a theoretical contribution to this field. The chapter is structured in this order.

A REVIEW OF THE LITERATURE ON INTERNATIONAL MOBILITY

Work and life experiences of persons working outside their countries of origin are extensively discussed in the literature on self-initiated expatriation. Self-Initiated Expatriates (SIEs) are described as remaining abroad on a permanent or temporary basis (Al Ariss, 2010; Cao, Hirschi, & Deller, 2012). This literature, however, suffers from three inadequacies in accounting for international work-life experiences. First, the international experiences of skilled people moving from developing to developed countries are under-researched. Instead, research considers SIE as a relatively homogenous group (Howe-Walsh & Schyns, 2010). Second, this literature pays no regard to the intersectional significance of ethnicity and gender as conditional factors in the career experiences of the internationally mobile workforce. Third, this literature does not sufficiently explore the work challenges and opportunities available for ethnic minorities in Western countries. Ethnicity is understood as socially constructed and includes language, history, religion, and styles of dress among other characteristics (Giddens, 2001). The following section exposes these three gaps in further detail.

A great deal of important research focuses on the experiences of persons from developed countries undertaking an international experience (Dickmann & Baruch, 2011). For example, Inkson and Myers (2003) focus on the 'Big OE,' that is to say overseas experiences undertaken mainly by young people from New Zealand. Jokinen, Brewster, and Suutari (2008) discuss the work experiences of professionals from Finland. Using a sample of 563 expatriates (almost half of them SIEs, the others corporate expatriates), Cieri, Sheehan, Costa, Fenwick, and Cooper (2009) studied the intention of Australian professionals to repatriate. Their findings show that SIEs are likely to be more open to the prospect of remaining overseas than corporate expatriates. Compared to European and American expatriates, there is research evidence that ethnic minority migrants in Western contexts are likely to be subject to more discrimination in organizations (Jehn & Bezrukova, 2004). To address this first gap, Al Ariss (2010) and Siljanen and Lamsa (2009) along with other researchers such as Berry (2009) and Berry and Bell (2012) suggest that further research in international management studies is required in order to expose the diversity of international experiences. For instance, studying the experiences of skilled migrants from less developed countries would be one possible direction for theoretical expansion (Al Ariss & Syed, 2011; Ramboarison-Lalao, Al Ariss, & Barth, 2012).

Research on the international careers of women is gaining an increasing interest. In reviewing the literature on expatriation, Hutchings, Metcalfe, and Cooper (2010) find four key barriers to women undertaking international assignments: corporate resistance; foreigner prejudice; women's own disinterest; and lack of family and other support mechanisms. In the context of self-initiated expatriation, Myers and Pringle (2005) investigate the influence of gender. They conducted qualitative interviews with 26 women and 24 men from New Zealand and found that SIE women accrued more benefits from their international experience than men in terms of accelerated career development, more interesting job opportunities, and an increase in capital accumulation. More recently, Tharenou (2010) found that women initiate their own expatriation more often than they are assigned abroad by their company, and usually as often as men. The same author explains that women self-initiate their expatriation in part as an attempt to redress the disadvantage they face in managerial career advancement. Nevertheless, while such key research investigates the existence of barriers to international careers for Western women (Hutchings et al., 2010), little is known about the international career experiences of ethnic minority migrant women in Western contexts (Al Ariss, 2010). There is therefore a need to better understand the intersectional influence of ethnicity and gender on the career experiences of migrants.

Career barriers and opportunities available for ethnic minority migrants are under-researched. Frequently, people undertaking an international experience are conceptualized as free agents who can cross organizational and national borders (Cerdin & Le Pargneux, 2010). While such studies are key in acknowledging and portraying the power of expatriate agency, less focus is placed on the barriers that constrain their career choices and their capital mobilization strategies in developing their careers (Al Ariss, 2010; Bozionelos, 2009; Richardson, 2009;). For example, Zikic, Bonache, and Cerdin (2010) examine the boundary crossing experiences and adaptation of 45 migrant professionals in Canada, Spain, and France. These authors indicate the problem, in Canada, of migrants' credentials remaining unrecognized. In New Zealand, by interviewing 80 recruitment specialists, Coates and Carr (2005) found that while migrants are granted entry depending on their knowledge of the English language and based on their qualifications, they are often offered jobs that are incompatible with these qualifications. Migrants can also face discrimination in accessing jobs and advancing careers. Legal barriers and discrimination can lead to migrants' underemployment (Tatli, 2011). Drawing on the themes above, I now move on to questioning the terminological use of the terms 'expatriate' and 'migrant' in the literature.

MIGRANT OR SIE? A TERMINOLOGICAL DILEMMA

The distinction between migrants and SIEs is not very clear in the literature on international mobility. Al Ariss, Koall, Özbilgin, & Suutari (2012) point out however that there are implicit differences in the way the terms 'migrant' and 'SIE' are constructed and used. I intend to explore these constructed differences in more depth in order to uncover the implications for international management research. Al Ariss et al. (2012) argue that the term 'migrant' often denotes a distinction based on ethnicity and that it is frequently used to refer to individuals from developing countries. Berry and Bell (2012) and Berry (2009) suggest that such a use leads to ethnic stereotypes. SIEs, on the other hand, are referred to in more positive terms. Unlike in the studies

Table 14.1 Stereotypes Constructed in Describing Migrants and SIEs

Migrants	SIEs
Coming from developing countries	Coming from developed countries
Without agency and unable to act and advance their careers	Capable of strategically advancing their careers
Lack of integration and assimilation in the host country	Successful in becoming accustomed to and integrating in the host country
Lack of skills and qualifications that are transportable across countries	Possessing skills and qualifications that are transportable across countries
International mobility conceived as a necessity rather than a choice	International mobility conceived as a choice rather than a necessity

on migrants, terms such as 'integration' or 'assimilation' or even 'discrimination' are rarely used in the context of academic papers on SIEs. Racial construction of who can and cannot be considered as an SIE seems to be of importance here. Table 14.1 outlines the stereotypes that are constructed in the international management literature. These stereotypes, while implicitly, contribute to creating a disparity between the status of a migrant and that of a SIE. They encompass country of origin, individual agency, the ability to integrate in a host country, available and recognized skills and qualifications, and choice/necessity leading to international mobility.

Thus there is a tendency in the literature on international management to overlook the agency of ethnic minority migrants, while focusing on more on groups under the label of SIE. In order to combat such tendencies, Al Ariss et al. (2012) propose strategies for pursuing constructive research on this topic. In the next sections, I build on these proposals, discussing how these strategies could be used to expand our field and make it more inclusive.

TOWARD MORE INCLUSIVE AND REFLEXIVE RESEARCH IN INTERNATIONAL MANAGEMENT

Rather than reinforcing the differences constructed between migrants and SIEs, I explain how the field can become more reflexive and inclusive. This line of research follows the suggestions by Al Ariss and Crowley-Henry (forthcoming). The idea behind reflexivity in international management research is to reflect on the way in which research is carried out (Hardy, Phillips, & Clegg, 2001) by explaining "that research comes from a particular standpoint" (Swan, 2008, p. 395). Social facts are socially constructed and every agent, including the researcher, imposes a vision of reality that corresponds to his/her point of view (Bourdieu, 2001). There are two main elements in reflexivity: one is related to the researcher and the other to participants. First, reflexivity requires that social researchers show awareness throughout the research process of their own personal experiences and preconceptions that influence the phenomenon under investigation (Bourdieu & Wacqant, 1992; Easterby-Smith, Golden-Biddle, & Locke, 2008). For example, researchers should recognize that the terminology they use has certain implicit meanings within the context of the topic, international mobility. Second, reflexivity, specifically in qualitative research, also entails recognizing the subjectivist nature of research participants' accounts rather than taking these as an absolute objective truth. This requires questioning participants' as well as one's own presuppositions and attitudes, and the way these might influence research design, findings, analysis, and writing. Being reflexive acknowledges that full objectivity remains unattainable as hidden motives and values, for both the researcher and the research participants, will always be present to influence the research process. My point here is that reflexivity leads to a greater understanding of the role and impact of the researcher upon the research process through "engaging about our own thinking" (Johnson & Duberley, 2003, p. 1279) and to an increased trustworthiness of collected data (Cassel, 2005) by voicing the unspoken through critical data analysis (Finlay, 2002). Adopting a reflexive approach could be done by maintaining a research diary of the researcher's own impact upon research (from choice of topic through to the end of the writing process) and documenting observations during data collection. Researching international mobility is not a process free of value judgment and politics (Al Ariss et al., 2012). On the contrary, while many of the research choices (including those made during the writing process) remain hidden, they occur in a context shaped by the standpoint of the researchers. Further theoretical and methodological expansions are discussed by Al Ariss et al. (2012). These are summarized in Table 14.2.

Table 14.2   Methodological Approaches in International Mobility

Over-hierarchical themes	Specific themes
Cross-disciplinary	Migration, sociology, psychology, management and organization studies, geography, medicine, among others
Reflexivity	Position of the researcher regarding his/her research topic, researcher's history, and background and how this influences research, researcher's rationale in choice of research questions/methods/theories/concepts
Objective measures	Duration of stay, purpose of international mobility, country of origin/destination, type of contract
Subjective measures	Work-life experiences of the international mobile workers as perceived by them, self-identification in terms of status (e.g. migrant vs. expatriate), intentions to remain in/leave a country
Data sources	Interviews conducted with participants/focus groups, case studies, surveys, datasets, policy documents, grey literature, organizational guidelines, photographs and images, videos, national/regional/international press, observation

Source: Al Ariss et al., 2012.

CONCLUSION

This chapter explained some of the key gaps in the literature on international mobility. It also questioned some of the hidden assumptions regarding terminology in this literature. I demonstrated how researchers, consciously or unconsciously, can contribute to constructing exclusion of ethnic minority migrants. In order to deal with this issue, the chapter explained how reflexivity can help to expand the field of international mobility by making it more transparent and inclusive. As a final call, I urge the community of international scholars to move from the narrow direction of study that focuses on the differences and similarities between SIEs and migrants, to offering a better understanding of the dynamics of international mobility in an inclusive and comprehensive way.

NOTES

1. Université de Toulouse, Toulouse Business School.

REFERENCES

Al Ariss, A. (2010). Modes of engagement: Migration, self-initiated expatriation, and career development. *Career Development International, 15*(4), 338–358.

Al Ariss, A., Koall, I., Özbilgin, M., & Suutari, V. (2012). Careers of skilled migrants: Towards a theoretical and methodological expansion. *Journal of Management Development, 31*(2), 92–101.

Al Ariss, A., & Syed, J. (2011). Capital mobilization of skilled migrants: A relational perspective. *British Journal of Management, 22*(2), 286–304.

Berry, D. P., & Bell, M. P. (2012). "Expatriates": Gender, race and class distinctions in international management. *Gender, Work & Organization, 19* (1), 10–28.

Bourdieu, P. (2001). *Science de la science et réflexivité*. Paris: Editions Raisons d'Agir.

Bourdieu, P., & Wacquant, L. J. D. (1992). *An invitation to reflexive sociology*. Chicago: The University of Chicago Press.

Bozionelos, N. (2009). Expatriation outside the boundaries of the multinational corporation: A study with expatriate nurses in Saudi Arabia. *Human Resource Management, 48*(1), 111–134.

Cao, L., Hirschi, A., & Deller, J. (2012). Self-initiated expatriates and their career success. *Journal of Management Development, 31*(2), 159–172.

Cassell, C. M. (2005). Creating the role of the researcher: Identity work in the management research process. *Qualitative Research, 5*(2), 167–179.

Cerdin, J.-L., & Le Pargneux, M. L. (2010). Career anchors: A comparison between organization-assigned and self-initiated expatriates. *Thunderbird International Business Review, 52*(4), 287–299.

Cieri, H. D., Sheehan, C., Costa, C., Fenwick, M., & Cooper, B. K. (2009). International talent flow and intention to repatriate: An identity explanation. *Human Resource Development International, 12*(3), 243–261.

Coates, K., & Carr, S. C. (2005). Skilled immigrants and selection bias: A theory-based field study from New Zealand. *International Journal of Intercultural Relations, 29*(5), 577–599.

Dickmann, M., & Baruch, Y. (2011). *Global careers.* New York: Routledge.

Easterby-Smith, M., Golden-Biddle, K., & Locke, K. (2008). Working with pluralism. Determining quality in qualitative research. *Organizational Research Methods, 11*(3), 419–429.

Finlay, L. (2002). Negotiating the swamp: The opportunity and challenge of reflexivity in research practice. *Qualitative Research, 2*(2), 209–230.

Giddens, A. (2001). *Sociology,* 4th ed. Cambridge: Polity Press.

Hardy, C., Phillips, N., & Clegg, S. R. (2001). Reflexivity in organization and management theory: A study of the production of the research "subject." *Human Relations, 54*(5), 531–560.

Howe-Walsh, L., & Schyns, B. (2010). Self-initiated expatriation: Implications for HRM. *International Journal of Human Resource Management, 21*(2), 260–273.

Hutchings, K., Metcalfe, B. D., & Cooper, B. K. (2010). Exploring Arab Middle Eastern women's perceptions of barriers to, and facilitators of, international management opportunities. *International Journal of Human Resource Management, 21*(1), 61–83.

Inkson, K., & Myers, B. A. (2003). "The big OE": Self-directed travel and career development. *Career Development International, 8*(4), 170–181.

Jehn, K. A., & Bezrukova, K. (2004). A field study of group diversity, workgroup context, and performance. *Journal of Organizational Behavior, 25*(6), 703–729.

Johnson, P., & Duberley, J. (2003). Reflexivity in management research. *Journal of Management Studies, 40*(5), 1279–1303.

Jokinen, T., Brewster, C., & Suutari, V. (2008). Career capital during international work experiences: Contrasting self-initiated expatriate experiences and assigned expatriation. *International Journal of Human Resource Management, 19*(6), 979–998.

Myers, B., & Pringle, J. (2005). Self-initiated foreign experience as accelerated development: Influences of gender. *Journal of World Business, 40*(4), 421–431.

Ramboarison-Lalao, L., Al Ariss, A., & Barth, I. (2012). Careers of skilled migrants: Understanding the experiences of Malagasy physicians in France. *Journal of Management Development, 31*(2), 116–129.

Richardson, J. (2009). Geographic flexibility in academia: A cautionary note. *British Journal of Management, 20*(S1), S160–S170.

Siljanen, T., & Lamsa, A. M. (2009). The changing nature of expatriation: exploring cross-cultural adaptation through narrativity. *International Journal of Human Resource Management, 20*(7), 1468–1486.

Swan, E. (2008). Let's not get too personal: Critical reflection, reflexivity and the confessional turn. *Journal of European Industrial Training, 32*(5), 385–399.

Tatli, A. (2011). A Multi-layered Exploration of the Diversity Management Field: Diversity Discourses, Practices and Practitioners in the UK. *British Journal of Management, 22*(2), 238–253.

Tharenou, P. (2010). Women's self-initiated expatriation as a career option and its ethical issues. *Journal of Business Ethics, 95*(1), 73–88.

Zikic, J., Bonache, J., & Cerdin, J.-L. (2010). Crossing national boundaries: A typology of qualified immigrants' career orientations. *Journal of Organizational Behavior, 31*(5), 667–686.

Contributors

Akram Al Ariss, ESC Toulouse, France

Torben Andersen, University of Southern Denmark, Denmark

Maike Andresen, University of Bamberg, Germany

Franziska Bergdolt, University of Bamberg, Germany

Torsten Biemann, University of Cologne, Germany

Chris Brewster, University of Reading, Henley Business School, United Kingdom

Jean-Luc Cerdin, ESSEC Business School, France

Michael Dickmann, Cranfield University, United Kingdom

Noeleen Doherty, Cranfield University, United Kingdom

Michael Dorsch, University of Vaasa, Finland

Thomas Egner, University of Bamberg, Germany

Fabian J. Froese, Korea University Business School, Korea

Tanja Gustschin, Accenture Services GmbH, Germany

Kerr Inkson, The University of Waikato, New Zealand

Jil Margenfeld, University of Bamberg, Germany

Vesa Peltokorpi, Japan Advanced Institute of Science and Technology, Japan

Erling Rasmussen, Auckland University of Technology, New Zealand

Julia Richardson, York University, Canada

Vesa Suutari, University of Vaasa, Finland

Kaye Thorn, Massey University, New Zealand

Matthias Walther, University of Bamberg, Germany

Index